Eric
With my best
Sus...

THINKING WITH THE TEACHABLE MACHINE

JOHN H. ANDREAE

Department of Electrical Engineering
University of Canterbury
Christchurch, New Zealand

1977

ACADEMIC PRESS · London · New York · San Francisco
A Subsidiary of Harcourt Brace Jovanovich, Publishers

ACADEMIC PRESS INC. (LONDON) LTD.
24/28 Oval Road
London NW1

United States Edition published by
ACADEMIC PRESS INC.
111 Fifth Avenue
New York, New York 10003

Copyright © 1977 by
ACADEMIC PRESS INC. (LONDON) LTD.

All Rights Reserved

No part of this book may be reproduced in any form by photostat, microfilm, or any other means, without written permission from the publishers

Library of Congress Catalog Card Number: 77-80285
ISBN: 0-12-060050-1

Typeset in Photon Baskerville by Albion Services, London
Printed by Whitstable Litho Ltd, Whitstable, Kent

Preface

I. PURR–PUSS is my contribution to the future sanity of mankind.
R. Eh?!
I. You know, violence, crime and all that. No one knows what to do about it because no one has a working model of the brain.
R. Oh! Is that what PURR–PUSS is?
I. Well, as a paper dart is a working model of the flight of a bird. PURR–PUSS is a computer program that can learn.
R. Ah! You're one of those psychologists — learning theory and all that. I suppose PURR–PUSS is a model of a rat!
I. Not likely! You know, psychologists really haven't got a decent theory of how the brain works. George Miller suggested in 1974 that the lack of a good theory accounts for why computers have had so little impact on psychology.* PURR–PUSS is both a new theory and a working model.
R. Sort of artificial intelligence? Wasn't there a program called GPS that solved problems *and* modelled how people think?
I. Yes, but Newell and Simon's General Problem Solver (1972) had to be given everything. They never managed to work out a way in which it could *learn* about problems. The same is true of other famous programs in artificial intelligence. Even Samuel's Checkers Playing Program (1959) didn't learn how to play checkers, only how to win! Winograd's English understanding program (1972) was fully primed. These and others are very clever programs indeed. PURR–PUSS isn't clever at all. She starts with no knowledge about anything.
R. I've got it! You're a nerve net man. You think the brain is a big nerve net. The connections in the net couldn't have been predetermined, so you make them randomly and then see what happens. Hebb's 1949 classic "The Organization of Behaviour" started a real craze for nerve net simulations, didn't it? I thought that they had all fizzled out.
I. Yes, but PURR–PUSS is very different from that hit-and-miss game. One can only sympathize with the neuropsychologist, Luria (1973), complaining of the uselessness of computer models of the brain. The

* References to other people's work are listed at the end of the book.

neuropnysiologist has been carrying out painstaking studies of the detailed structure of the brain (Shepherd, 1974), while others spew out untested and untestable schemes. We have tentative ideas for a nerve net too, but we have yet to establish that it will work just like the digital computer program of PURR–PUSS.

R. How does PURR–PUSS work?

I. The main idea is multiple context. PURR–PUSS experiences, and remembers her experience, as several streams of context — like sound, vision and touch. She recalls her remembered experiences by predicting from contexts. Each event is seen in context.

R. Like a conditioned reflex?

I. Yes, but we do not talk about stimulus conditions in the vague way used for the conditioned reflex (McGuigan and Lumsden, 1973). In PURR–PUSS, the sequential nature of events is brought right out into the open.

The second main idea in PURR–PUSS is novelty — and there is nothing new about that! (Berlyne, 1960) However, in PURR–PUSS novelty is something precise and meaningful; and PURR–PUSS doesn't have to search her memory, however large, to find out if an event is novel. This is why her memory could be as large in capacity as that of the human brain — if we could pay for it!

R. There's not much point in an enormous memory unless PURR–PUSS can learn really interesting things. What *can* you teach PURR–PUSS?

I. We haven't been teaching her for long and we haven't been able to give her a good body yet, but . . .

R. Body? Ah! Robots! Didn't Sir James Lighthill (1973) suggest that robot builders were men without babies, or something?!

I. Actually, PURR–PUSS is probably the computer program most like a baby because she does have to start right from the beginning to learn about her body and world. At least she can be taught in any language!

R. Are you suggesting that PURR–PUSS will have to be taken through all the stages of baby and child learning before doing anything significant?

I. I fear so. The stages of development described by Piaget (1972) for the child seem quite unavoidable for a system that learns from scratch. The education of PURR–PUSS is likely to be a long job and we cannot count on finding short-cuts. This is why it is so important to discover any fundamental limitations in PURR–PUSS before embarking on a long teaching programme.

R. Well, what have you taught PURR–PUSS so far?

I. Small tasks like remembering nursery rhymes, counting objects and drawing simple pictures. We have shown that she can learn cumulatively, using earlier experience in later tasks; that she can do appropriate and original things; that she has no theoretical limitations. You really ought to come along and have a go at interacting with her. It is quite an experience getting used to an ignorant machine that responds to one's teaching, usually in a way that you didn't expect but which doesn't look unreasonable after it has happened. You soon give up trying to work out why she does something. Instead, one learns to guess what she knows from what she does and how she responds. Would you like to try? . . . Dash! I've lost him. . . . Hi! . . . Where are you? . . .

You and I, dear Reader, have been talking while tramping in the Southern Alps on a warm summer's day. In crossing a small valley, you became separated from me without my noticing it and, when I came out of the bush on the far side, you were still invisible in the bush below. I have just heard you call back. From the movement of branches I can tell where you are and I can see quite clearly which way you should go to get out. When I start to direct you I shall soon find that you are not seeing things down there in the way that I see them up here. My directions will have to be carefully worded so that they are meaningful to you where you are, rather than where I am.

Everyone knows how difficult it is to communicate a new idea to someone else — and how difficult it is, afterwards, to see why something was difficult.

This book is about a teachable machine, called PURR–PUSS, that is much simpler than most present-day "intelligent" machines. When telling my friends about PURR–PUSS, however, I find that they are down in the bush of unfamiliarity and that they want a multitude of extraneous questions answered before going ahead with my explanation. From my vantage point, most of their questions are irrelevant and distracting (Can you see the Kowhai tree from where you are? Will I come out near the waterfall?). If only they would do exactly what I prescribed and follow my thought-path precisely, they would come out into the open and then be able to see clearly all that they wished. But that is not the way that people behave. Thinking is an active process and I must answer their distracting questions before they will do what I want.

In writing a book, there seems to be no way of providing the reader with these extra facts and fancies just when he or she wants them. The best that I have been able to do is to ensure that all the answers are there and that they are accessible to the reader who is prepared to look around using the Contents and Index. If a question comes to your mind and it is not answered in the next sentence, please look farther on! If you are not interested in the bit that I have put next, please skip on! Tables and Figures are provided for reference. All of the details have been meticulously checked so that a reader experienced in programming can easily program his or her own computer to behave like PURR–PUSS.

Just as the printed word prevents me from answering your questions as they come into your mind, so also does it prevent me from showing you in a real live way the conversational interaction between me, as Teacher, and PURR–PUSS the learning machine. The best that I can do is to list what *did* happen and hope that you will read through the list of happenings with your imagination filling in all the details of clicking keys, flashing lights, gasps of surprise and frustration, and patient watching while the minutes and hours of real time pass. But, if you have access to a computer and can write the programs for PURR–PUSS, you will find that there is nothing quite as convincing as interacting with her yourself.

Engineers build bridges, even though philosophers cannot define the word "bridge". Ordinary people, like you and me, know what "free-will" and "creativity" are without having definitions. When an orange squirts us in the eye, we do not exclaim "What free-will!" or "How creative!"; but, when a small boy squirts us in the eye, we acknowledge his will, his originality and his impertinence! When, in Chapter 7, PURR–PUSS suddenly dashes off after some cake, much to my surprise, we see something in between the orange and the small boy. The differences in free-will and creativity between orange and PURR–PUSS, or between PURR–PUSS and small boy, are not so obvious that we should be dogmatic about them. Such philosophical conundrums are best left to the philosophers and that is just what I shall do in this book.

The field of Artificial Intelligence has lost some of the sparkle it had in the fifties and early sixties, when all was new and exciting. The early enthusiasm and optimism have given way to criticism and disappointment. The intelligence of man has failed to prescribe his own intelligence.

In this book, we go back to the beginning with a new approach, a simpler approach. PURR–PUSS is not a clever machine crammed with theorem-provers, language-parsers, problem-solvers, scene-analysers and heuristics. She starts quite empty and ignorant — but is very teachable.

PURR–PUSS learns in a paradigmatic way (that is, by example), using a multiple context. Her built-in goal is to repeat novel events that she has experienced only once. She selects actions according to her remembered experience and the current context. There are no obvious limitations to what a system like PURR–PUSS can do, but here you will be shown what PURR–PUSS has actually done. This is not a book about what machines might do, should do or can't do. It is a complete description of a working system that seems to have some of the qualities that people have said machines could not have.

To understand the working of the brain, we must find a mechanism, so simple that evolution could have stumbled on it and so powerful that its large-scale use (in the brain) could account for the success of human intelligence.

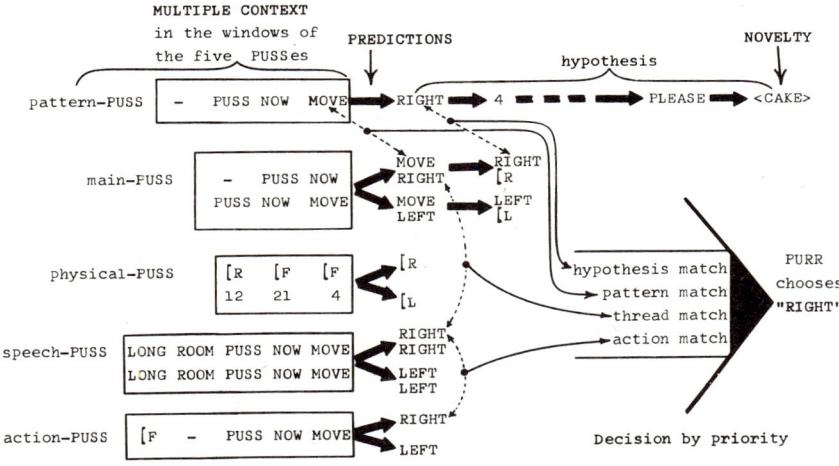

Fig. 0. The "state-of-mind" of PURR–PUSS when she decides to turn right to get <CAKE>! (Step 829 of Fig. 7–11.)

December, 1976

John Andreae
Department of Electrical Engineering
University of Canterbury, New Zealand

Foreword

This book describes a simple learning scheme that exhibits complex and constructive behaviour through its interaction with the world, real or artificial. It presents a culmination of one strand of artificial intelligence research that commenced some fifteen years ago and has continued, coherently and consistently in John Andreae's laboratory ever since.

In the early sixties the computer itself was new, expensive and unreliable; the prophets of a new era were placing remarkable faith in the growth of a new technology — faith that only now has begun to be justified. Von Neumann's enthusiasm and his suggested connections between computers and life; Norbert Wiener's projection of computers into the future age of automation and his concept of cybernetics as a discipline encompassing man and machine alike; Ross Ashby's *Design for a Brain* with its examples of homeostatic mechanisms; and Grey Walter's *Living Brain* with its primitive, but surprisingly lifelike, *tortoise* — all these in the fifties had triggered off an interest in the potential of computers to emulate intelligent life leading, in the sixties, to the explorations that became what we know as *artificial intelligence* research today.

Andreae was a pioneer of this research, concerned in 1962 when he joined Standard Telecommunication Laboratories, the UK research laboratories of ITT (Europe), with the automated *learning* of specialist skills through the *experience* of non-specialist, general-purpose adaptive systems. From the start of the project Andreae had a very free hand to define the scope of activities.

Machine learning was then a very fashionable topic — Rosenblatt and Widrow were claiming great potential for the *perceptron* and *adaline* systems, and somehow learning itself seemed a very natural way to design complex systems — not by the classical engineering techniques of detailed problem analysis and precise optimal design, but by taking a general-purpose, amorphous system and forcing it to take on the required characteristics through learning from its own experience. This promised not just a new type of system but also a radically new approach to engineering design; *adaptive, learning, self-organizing, self-optimizing,* were new and exciting concepts in pattern recognition and control engineering. Andreae's STelLA scheme

(**S**tandard **Te**lecommunication **L**earning **A**utomata) combined the parallel processing and learning of pattern recognition, with the sequential processing and learning of control engineering, and the basic curiosity and reward-seeking drives of animal behaviour, to offer through both simulation and actual hardware construction the possibility of an artificial system truly exhibiting "intelligence".

Those were heady days — I remember visiting STL in 1962 in response to an advertisement for, "mathematicians with knowledge of topology and logic to work on a project involving machine learning", and finding a chemist putting together adaptive elements, an electronic engineer wiring up nineteen-inch racks of relays, uniselectors and valves, and John Andreae himself surrounded by computer printout that demonstrated the first faltering steps of STelLA. The valves rapidly became transistors, the chemical elements were replaced by digital *stochastic computing* systems, and the project sprouted several specialist activities in speech and pattern recognition, but for John's four years at STL the excitement was ever-present.

About the time John left for New Zealand there were the beginnings of widespread disenchantment with machine learning itself. It was realized that learning was no panacea and that we could not expect an arbitrary collection of "neuron-like" elements somehow to give us new advanced systems that we did not know how to fabricate in any other way. There was a swing to the *performance-orientated* view that, "you cannot expect to build a machine to *learn* a task unless you can first build one to *do* it". We began to accept that the simulation of human skilled behaviour, particularly high-level linguistic skills of the type necessary to pass the "Turing test", was a pre-requisite to any attempt to build a system that could also acquire those skills.

This attitude came to dominate mainstream artificial intelligence research and led, through Weizenbaum's ELIZA which exhibited conversational skills based on minimal "knowledge" that were astonishing at first sight, to Winograd's SHRDLU that exhibited far deeper "understanding" of refinements of language and of its own processes of problem-solving, to the systems of today that are able to hold meaningful and humanly acceptable conversations on limited domains of real-world knowledge. Recently, interest has revived in how such systems can acquire these very high level and specialist skills and extend those which they have.

John Andreae never accepted the arguments for a move towards performance-based research and has continued throughout the last ten years, in his laboratory in New Zealand and with the help of several generations of graduate students, to develop general-purpose learning systems that have little real-world knowledge built into their design but have to acquire it through experience. For those who do not accept the value of such research this book will have little meaning. For the psychologist or animal behaviourist interested in mechanisms of learning, for the philosopher interested in epistemology, for those attracted by the continuing excitement of the concepts of self-organization and machine learning pioneered by von Neumann, Ashby, *et al.*, this book represents an in-depth study of the possibility of learning complex behaviour through remarkably simple and general mechanisms. There is enough data here for the armchair scientist to ascertain the connection between the theory and results. There is also enough detail for the experimentally minded to implement their own version of Andreae's system on a small computer and try it in their own problem domain.

Looking back to the old STeILA work, which itself aroused psychological interest, and coupling it with the PURR–PUSS of this book I notice two key differences: an emphasis now on the role of the teacher — PURR–PUSS is a willing learner but she needs guidance in order to cope with her first experience of a complex world; secondly, that the draconian "reward and punishment" that moulded the behaviour of STeILA has become the gentler "novelty-seeking and disapproval" of PURR–PUSS — that in itself may hold a moral for educationalists. Certainly there is a lesson for researchers on machine learning in the emphasis which Andreae places in the book on "teachability". No reasonably general-purpose learning system can be expected to cope with the real world as it is without some aids to overcome the initial problems and hazards of learning. As the process of knowledge acquisition is reintroduced into research on artificial intelligence so will techniques of system teaching and instruction become essential adjuncts to the research — Andreae's work is an important guide in this respect.

There is much to be learned from this book: according to one's viewpoint Andreae may be seen as offering an operational form of animal psychology; or an experiment in basic epistemology; or an amusing and interesting basis for a robot that can be implemented on a small computer. Perhaps he does not intend to offer any of those (we rarely agree on any topic, particularly this one!), but I was guaranteed no censorship of this foreword and have taken the chance to have the last (and first) words for once. Many people have been stimulated by Andreae's work over the years and it has triggered off many derivative studies. This book makes this research widely available in an extremely clear presentation. I wish both reader and author well in their forthcoming interaction.

BRIAN GAINES
University of Essex

Acknowledgments

The research reported in this book was partially supported by a grant from the New Zealand Ministry of Defence.

The suggestions of friends have forced the book through a series of draft versions. My special thanks go to Ian Witten, Bruce Moon, Eric Beardsley and Merrett Smith.

Encouragement and support for my research over many years has come from Peter Barker, Don Barnes, Richard Bates, Brian Gaines, David Hill and Leslie Kay.

Innumerable parts of the book have been improved by criticisms of Ron Dowd, Bob Hodgson, Alex Palfi, Robert Platts, Betty Smith and Alan Wilkinson.

Many people have contributed to technical aspects of the research. In mentioning the following, I shall inevitably omit others: David Bakker, Fred Cady, Peter Cashin, John Cleary, Neville Gray, Wayne Heads, Bill Kennedy, Mike Mayson and Bob Rushby.

My wife, Molly, and son, Peter, have encouraged, contributed, criticised and checked. They have lived with PURR–PUSS for four years and this is their book too. My daughter, Gillian, drew the cats.

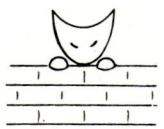

Contents

Preface	v
Foreword	xi
Acknowledgments	xiv
Prologue	xvii

Chapter 1. Thinking with PURR–PUSS

Intelligence	1
Body and World	2
Context	3
Novelty	4
Brain Model	5
The Cage of Paradox	6
Looking Ahead	6
Notes on Chapter 1	12

Chapter 2. The Basic Mechanism: PUSS

The Prediction of Events	16
Remembering Events	17
Recalling Events	23
A PUSS Net Memory	24
Examples of PUSS	26
Example 1. Letters as Events	26
Example 2. Words as Events	29
Example 3. Bill and Ben, the Power Plot Men	31
Example 4. A Simple Teachable Machine	33
Example 5. Variety of PUSS Structures	38
Notes on Chapter 2	43

Chapter 3. Multiple Context

Threaded Contexts	47
Schedules of Events	49
Sparse and Dense Events	51
Parallel Contexts	53
Examples of Contexts	55
Example 1. Raising Fingers for an Object	55
Example 2. Drawing Open and Closed Boxes	55
Example 3. Drawing Poles and Counting Down	56
Example 4. Rubbing Out a Line	57
Notes on Chapter 3	59

Chapter 4. Teaching PURR–PUSS

At the Console Typewriter	62
Novelty	67
Physical–PUSS	70
Action–PUSS	71

xvi CONTENTS

    Real Time 73
    Speech 73
    Mimic-speech 77
    Realism 78
    Exercises 78
    Notes on Chapter 4 81

Chapter 5. PURR–PUSS, Body and World

    The Structure of PURR–PUSS 85
    The Operation of PURR–PUSS 86
    The PURR Strategy 89
    Endless Repetitions 93
    Body and World 94
    Notes on Chapter 5 99

Chapter 6. Learning to Count

    Two Tasks 104
    A Short Form Description 104
    A Schedule for Two Tasks 105
    Teaching COUNTING OBJECTS 109
    Teaching COUNTING BEADS 111
    Task-Distinguishing Threads 111
    Summary 114
    Notes on Chapter 6 115

Chapter 7. Into the Unknown

    Choosing a Task 120
    The HELLO Task 121
    The ROOMS Task 127
    Planning the Interaction 128
    The Training Cycle 131
    Walking Around the Rooms 133
    Boomerang 135
    Man and Machine 143
    Notes on Chapter 7 143

    Epilogue 146

    Appendix 147

    Notes on the Appendix 162

    References 165

    Author Index 171

    Subject Index 173

Prologue

The Waimakariri River winds down from the Southern Alps across the Canterbury Plain to the Pacific Ocean. On a hill above the river stands a small man-made house with a water system comprising an arrangement of pipes and tanks.

The water system of the house, like so many human designs, sets out to prescribe precisely each twist and turn that the water in the house must take. The mistakes of the designer are revealed by air-locks and blockages, by overflows and leakages.

The water in the river obeys the universal rule of gravity and flows downhill. It is not stopped by dams and other obstacles — only delayed.

The general trend in artificial intelligence research today is to design systems that are more and more complex. In my analogy, the typical system is a house with a multitude of pipes and tanks.

In designing PURR–PUSS, I have had the river in mind. Fifteen years of research with the one aim of designing a system that can learn anything "from scratch" has taken me from simple ideas to simpler ones. Like the river, PURR–PUSS operates according to simple universal rules: "seek novelty" and "predict events from their contexts". The concepts of novelty, prediction and context are familiar to psychologists, but in PURR–PUSS they are stripped down to the bare essentials.

With the modest "body" that we have been able to give PURR–PUSS, she has been found capable of choice, of original actions, of counting, of substitution and recursion, of setting her own goals and of having them set for her. PURR–PUSS can be taught in any language, can be given any size of memory and can interact with the real world. She has no known fundamental limitation. She becomes her experience. There are still a few "pipes" in PURR–PUSS (as in the man-made house), but our research is directed to their removal.

We can expect quick spectacular results from the "pipe" programs of artificial intelligence, but, in my view, their achievements will be superseded and surpassed by "river" programs, like PURR–PUSS.

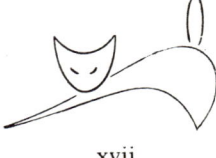

1. Thinking with PURR–PUSS

> The art of experimentation is the creation of new situations, which catch the essence of some process without the circumstances that usually obscure it.
>
> Ulric Neisser
> "Cognitive Psychology"

Intelligence

Art is not to be found in a piece of canvas or in a pot of paint. Pots of the same paint may produce very different results from the brushes of different painters.

A computer is not intelligent — nor is its set of basic instructions. Like a piece of canvas without a picture of paint, a computer is inert without a program of instructions. Using the same basic instructions, different programmers can produce quite different results in the same computer.

To ask if a programmed computer is intelligent is like asking if a painted canvas is beautiful. Intelligence, like beauty, seems to be "in the eye of the beholder", since what one calls beautiful or intelligent another scorns.

PURR–PUSS*[1] is an experimental "brain",[2] in the form of a computer program,[3] for exploring the processes of learning, teaching and problem-solving. In writing a computer program all assumptions have to be made explicit and precise. We cannot gloss over the difficult bits. Everything must be defined down to the last detail. However, we can attempt to teach PURR–PUSS different tasks and we can alter the computer program which defines her structure. We can advance by small changes. This process of interaction and change is what I mean by "thinking with PURR–PUSS". It reveals new abilities, new structures[4] and new teaching methods. PURR–PUSS is an aid to thinking about systems which learn.

Both the structure and the behaviour of PURR–PUSS have philosophical, psychological, biological and educational implications, but I shall avoid stressing these beyond what is necessary to explain some of the things which

*Numbered notes will be found at the ends of the chapters.

2 THINKING WITH THE TEACHABLE MACHINE

I have done. My personal view is that many of the most controversial arguments about intelligence, purpose, values, free-will and so on melt away in the light of a real system, be it as primitive as PURR–PUSS.

Body and World

To call PURR–PUSS a "brain" is to use the word loosely. But, just as a real brain cannot function in isolation, so PURR–PUSS must be connected to a "body" and the body must be put in a "world". The body and world together are the "environment" of PURR–PUSS. The interaction of the brain with its body and world provide it with "experience".

In a general way, the body is that part of the environment which is more or less under the direct control of PURR–PUSS, while the world is the

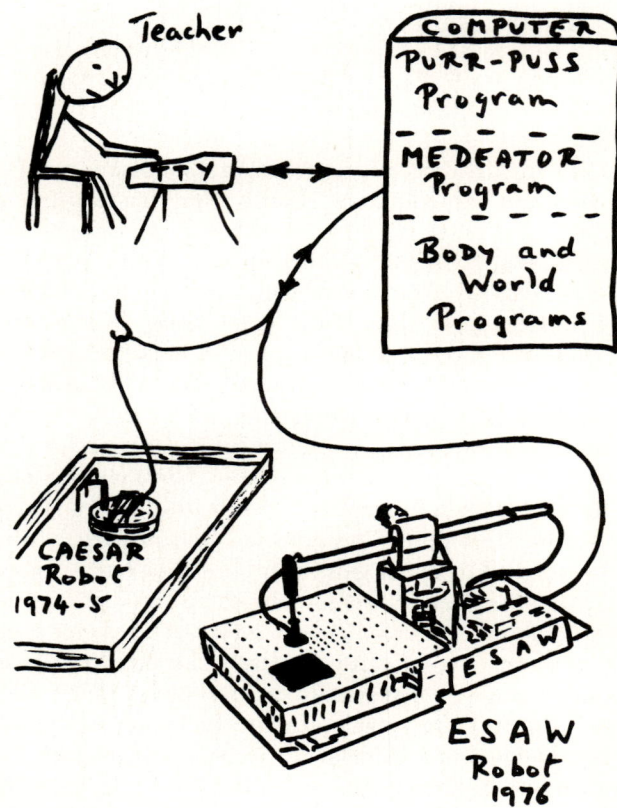

Fig. 1.1

remainder. The boundary between body and world is indefinite, even though all parts of the environment are well defined. In a similar manner, the roots of a tree merge smoothly into the trunk and no precise boundary is definable even though the trunk and root exist in precise form. The boundary between PURR–PUSS and her body is also somewhat arbitrary but we shall define it for our convenience (Chapter 5). Just as a real brain and its body are intimately connected in a physical way, so is the PURR–PUSS program intimately connected with the programs and laboratory robots that provide the body of PURR–PUSS. (See Fig. 1.1).

Our experience of PURR–PUSS with many different bodies and worlds shows that better bodies and worlds permit richer behaviour.[5] Body and world can be provided by simulation programs or by building robots in the real world. Although the PURR–PUSS program is simple, programs to simulate body and world have to be complicated in order to provide reasonably complex problem situations. Even the primitive laboratory robots[6] (CAESAR and ESAW) that we have built for PURR–PUSS avoid elaborate simulation programs and enable her to act in the real world. It is hoped that researchers with larger resources than ours will give PURR–PUSS more effective robot bodies.

An important part of the environment is the human Teacher.* Teacher can be the whole environment of PURR–PUSS, if he wishes. Teacher decides what body and world PURR–PUSS will have and he may provide every response to PURR–PUSS's actions, if he wishes. Usually Teacher instructs an auxiliary program called MEDEATOR to simulate some of the body and world so that he can concentrate on the difficult task of teaching PURR–PUSS. MEDEATOR carries out the chores for Teacher in a completely mechanical fashion.

Context

PUSS is a mechanism for remembering events and for recalling them. PURR is a decision strategy for choosing actions. When a number of PUSSes are combined with one PURR, then we have a PURR–PUSS.

PURR is less satisfactory than PUSS because it is still rather contrived and tentative. The primary message of this book is the simple mechanism of PUSS.

PUSS is a mechanism for storing events "in context". We would all accept that an event has to be seen in its context to be understood, perceived or recognized. Different events seem to need different amounts of context for their identification. Sometimes we recognize a face, place or picture "at a glance"; on other occasions it takes time. We have to learn to look for the appropriate clues. How can we design a system to associate an event with the appropriate context when the amount of context needed can vary so much?

*For clarity, PURR–PUSS and Teacher will be referred to as "she" and "he" throughout, regardless of their real sexes.

The context used by a single PUSS in storing an event in memory is small and fixed, being the last "N" events where N is usually 3, 4 or 5.

To enable PURR–PUSS to find and use appropriate contexts, she is given several PUSSes, each contributing a different small and fixed context. The result is a "multiple fixed context" which turns out to be flexible and powerful. It may be likened to 4-wheel drive on a vehicle: when one pair of wheels cannot get a grip on the situation, the other pair may still manage.

The essence of PURR–PUSS is this multiple fixed context provided by several PUSSes. Imagine different people looking out through different windows from different directions on to the same scene. Each has a fixed field of view and each sees a different succession of contexts. The windows may be of different size. Now, each PUSS has a "window" which shows the last 3, 4 or 5 events, according to its size. Each PUSS receives a different sequence of events from the interaction of PURR–PUSS with her environment. The decision strategy of PURR uses the evidence of all these PUSSes to choose an action.

Novelty

In early experiments, PURR–PUSS was taught by reward and punishment. Simple individual tasks were taught successfully but Teacher had always to remember to give the reward and punishments at the appropriate times or PURR–PUSS would become confused. To "unteach" behaviour learned from inconsistent reward and punishment is difficult and slow.

When Teacher had decided to give reward and punishment in a consistent way and in clearly defined situations, he could instruct the auxiliary program, MEDEATOR, to perform the rewarding and punishing for him. This was satisfactory for simple individual tasks, but was no help for more complex tasks.

Often Teacher is unclear at the start as to how he will teach a complex task. For his own convenience he may attempt to teach a complex task in sections. Reward is used for establishing the competence of the first section of the task before going on to the next section. Unfortunately, but inevitably, a good deal of confusion is generated when reward for the first section is withheld so that it can be given at the end of the next section. Similar difficulties would arise whenever Teacher changed his rewarding schedule. The giving of reward does not seem to be an appropriate method for the teaching of tasks in a cumulative fashion.[7] Punishment becomes an equally inflexible process if it becomes strongly linked to particular events. It may be necessary for Teacher to stop PURR–PUSS from doing something during the early learning of a task, even when he is going to require her to do the same thing later on when other contexts have been established.

For these reasons, Teacher will not use reward and punishment in any of the teaching reported in this book.[8] Instead, PURR–PUSS will set her own "novelty goals"[9] and Teacher will employ a mild form of punishment called "disapproval". Like most of the important features of PURR–PUSS, novelty-seeking was discovered by accident!

Brain Model

It is impossible to work in the field of artificial intelligence without wondering from time to time whether one's artefacts bear any resemblance to the human brain. We do not know how the brain works and, in my view, we shall be unable to unravel the physiology and psychology of the brain (its structure and behaviour) until we have made some good guesses as to how it might work. PURR–PUSS is not a model of the brain, but it may suggest how the brain works.[10]

My design strategy [11] over the past 15 years has forbidden the inclusion of features just for psychological or biological reasons. Each addition to PURR–PUSS is made in order to enable her to tackle an additional class of problem. Problems to do with survival in a harsh and competitive world have not been considered, as yet. This is probably why I have found no good reason for including instincts and emotions. Even though reward and pain centres have been identified in the human brain,[12] reward and pain have been omitted from PURR–PUSS. It seems that reward and pain are needed for survival (protection, provision and propagation), but not for problem-solving.

In problem-solving, the performance of the human brain stands before us as the ultimate and only challenge. In seeking ways to improve the scope of PURR–PUSS, every hint and tip from psychology, neurophysiology and education has been gratefully received and often assimilated. With these influences, some similarity may be inevitable between the mechanisms in PURR–PUSS and those which will eventually be identified in the brain. After all, there may not be many simple mechanisms that would do the job . . . and, surely, evolution found a simple mechanism?

PURR–PUSS starts with no knowledge of her body and world at all.[13] Everything she learns is learned from her experience. She can be connected to any body and world. She can be given the largest memory we can afford and she is not made slower by a larger memory. The following chapters will illustrate how she learns and how she can be taught.[14] As we attempt to teach more complex tasks, it becomes more difficult to tell whether failure is due to her or Teacher. The assessment of her performance is a major difficulty. I do not know of any other artificial system with which PURR–PUSS can be meaningfully compared.[15] Nevertheless, many people have pointed to the need for a system like PURR–PUSS.[16]

6 THINKING WITH THE TEACHABLE MACHINE

The Cage of Paradox*

In designing PURR–PUSS, I have taken a different road from that followed by other researchers in artificial intelligence; but it is a road that many people have pointed to. There are signs that the popular road cannot lead to a machine intelligence comparable with human intelligence.[17]

In 1931 the philosopher Gödel proved an important theorem. Quoting the later philospher Lucas (1961): "Gödel's theorem states that in any consistent system which is strong enough to produce simple arithmetic there are formulae which cannot be proved-in-the-system, but which we can see to be true." Every formal system strong enough to be interesting is subject to paradox.[18] A formal system operates within a "cage". We, humans, can see the paradoxes because our cages are wide open, but the formal system cannot. Now, every machine, robot or computer *on its own* (isolated from its surroundings) is a formal system and will never be able to do some of the things that we can do. If we try to remove the deficiencies of a machine by giving it extra cleverness, we may make the cage larger, but it will still be closed. The machine will be doomed to a lesser intelligence than man.

Sometimes people think of their bodies as cages within which they live, but bodies are quite the opposite of cages. My body connects me to the world around me in such an intimate and interactive way that I become part of that world. I can participate in the dynamic society and culture of humanity. My cage is wide open. Only if we enable our machines to interact freely with the world around them can we release them from the cage of paradox.

It is not possible at the present time to give PURR–PUSS an adequate body for intimate interaction with the world around her, so Teacher has to provide the missing link. By giving PURR–PUSS a close, interactive link with Teacher, we defer the need for an adequate walking-and-talking body until such time as we can provide it.

PURR–PUSS is unique, to my knowledge, in being a system that *could* be given a body-in-the-world.[19]

Looking Ahead

The main results of this book are to be found in Chapters 6 and 7, where Figs 6.6, 6.7, 6.9, 7.3 and 7.5 to 7.12 represent a continuous interaction between PURR–PUSS and her body and world. Teacher, who is part of her world, attempts to teach PURR–PUSS a number of things during this interaction. I am Teacher.

The next four chapters (2 to 5) provide the reader with the detailed information necessary for a full understanding of each step of the main interaction in Chapters 6 and 7. Here, in this section, we look ahead in an informal, imprecise way to capture the highlights of PURR–PUSS's behaviour and to indicate the organization of the book.

*The argument of this section is not needed for an understanding of the operation of PURR–PUSS.

THINKING WITH PURR–PUSS   7

In Fig. 6.6 (Chapter 6), PURR–PUSS is taught to count objects using the fingers of her HAND. To get the gist of the interaction, disregard the single e's, which stand for "echoes", and the single hyphens (-), which stand for pauses (null patterns or actions). Reading down each column in turn we see "patterns" (stimuli) from Teacher, body or world on the left and "actions" (responses) from PURR–PUSS on the right. When an action is underlined, it means that Teacher has done the action for PURR–PUSS or "put the word into her mouth". There is nothing at all in the memory of PURR–PUSS at the beginning of the interaction in Fig. 6.6. She has absolutely no priming or forewarning of what patterns she may receive nor of what actions she may be allowed to make. The interaction in Fig. 6.6 goes roughly like this:—

Teacher says to PURR–PUSS: " START COUNTING OBJECTS "
    Teacher makes PURR–PUSS close her HAND: " [-12345 " (See Fig. 5.10)
PURR–PUSS sees her closed HAND: " - - - - - "
    Teacher makes PURR–PUSS say: " ANY MORE OBJECTS "
Teacher says to PURR–PUSS: " NO "
    Teacher makes PURR–PUSS say: " FOR OBJECTS PUSS SEES "
    Teacher makes PURR–PUSS look at her hand :" [: "
PURR–PUSS again sees her closed HAND: " - - - - - "
    Teacher makes her say: " NO FINGERS "

That completes the procedure for counting no objects. Teacher has done every action for PURR–PUSS. PURR–PUSS has chosen no action herself. However, she has been learning. Teacher goes on to show PURR–PUSS how to count one object:—

Teacher says: " CARRY ON COUNTING OBJECTS "
    Teacher makes PURR–PUSS say: " ANY MORE OBJECTS "
Teacher says: " YES "
    Teacher makes PURR–PUSS say: " OBJECT PLEASE "
Teacher gives object: " <BOX> "
    Teacher makes PURR–PUSS say: " RAISE FINGER FOR OBJECT "
                  and: " LOOK "
    Teacher makes PURR–PUSS look at her HAND: " [: "
PURR–PUSS sees her closed HAND: " - - - - - "
    Teacher makes PURR–PUSS raise the first finger; " [+ 1 "
PURR–PUSS sees HAND with first finger raised: " 1 - - - - "
    Teacher makes PURR–PUSS say: " FINGER RAISED "
                  and: " ANY MORE OBJECTS "
Teacher says: " NO "

8 THINKING WITH THE TEACHABLE MACHINE

The procedure is now becoming established so PURR–PUSS can act on her own for a while:—

PURR–PUSS says: " FOR OBJECTS PUSS SEES "

PURR–PUSS looks at her HAND: " [: "

PURR–PUSS sees her HAND with first finger raised: "1 - - - - "

This is a new context because of the pattern 1 - - - - , which did not occur the last time after " FOR OBJECTS PUSS SEES [: ", but everything else about the context is familiar so PURR–PUSS tries the same action as before (hopefully):—

PURR–PUSS says: " NO "

Before she can add "FINGERS", Teacher presses the disapproval button (indicated by Ⓓ in Fig. 6.6, step 64) to tell PURR–PUSS that that is not what Teacher wants her to do. ("ONE FINGER" is what Teacher wants her to say when one finger has been raised for one object). Now Teacher shows PURR–PUSS how to say " ONE FINGER " (steps 66 to 71) when she looks and sees the first finger of her HAND raised.

The hopeful "NO" that earned PURR–PUSS disapproval on this occasion came from a part of her decision strategy (Fig. 5.8, priority 4) that enables her to choose actions when some but not all of the context for the action is appropriate. Later in the interaction (step 94), when a never-seen-before object, <FISH>, is presented by Teacher, PURR–PUSS uses the same part of her decision strategy to respond hopefully and appropriately with " RAISE FINGER FOR OBJECT ".

In the second half of Fig. 6.6, from step 91 to step 179, PURR–PUSS learns to count two objects and three objects. Teacher's help is needed only with the underlined actions. Most of the actions are performed by PURR–PUSS on her own. Never-seen-before objects <FISH> and <DOLL> are accepted by PURR–PUSS without help from Teacher because they are in context.

After teaching the COUNTING OBJECTS task in Fig. 6.6, Teacher goes on to teach PURR–PUSS another counting task, COUNTING BEADS, in Fig. 6.7. The beads to be counted are on ABACUS, a part of PURR–PUSS's world. The details are deferred to Chapter 6, but here we can notice in Fig 6.7 how the finger-raising technique of COUNTING OBJECTS is fully transferred to the new task with only one bit of prompting by Teacher (steps 193 and 195). PURR–PUSS applies the learned technique to the new task because the context is appropriate. In this way PURR–PUSS accumulates and transfers experience with the minimum of teaching. The more detailed discussion of Figs 6.7 and 6.9 in Chapter 6 explains how PURR–PUSS learns "naturally" to tell which of the two tasks, COUNTING OBJECTS and COUNTING BEADS, she is engaged in at any time.

In Fig. 7.3, I am attempting something more ambitious. Counting is a familiar operation and the teaching shown in Figs 6.6, 6.7 and 6.9 is quite straightforward. (Nevertheless, I know of no other existing artificial system that can be taught in this way.) In Fig. 7.3, however, I am trying to teach PURR–PUSS to say HELLO to a stranger and it is a surprising fact that no one knows what people do when they converse. The interaction listed in Fig. 7.3 combines talking, talking to oneself, raising eyebrows and face-scanning in a way which seems reasonable to me but may not appear so to the reader. Before being too critical, the reader should decide how he or she would have done it! Remember that PURR–PUSS should not treat a familiar face as a stranger, nor a strange face as familiar. This is, roughly, how PURR–PUSS encounters a stranger, Mr. Triangle Face:—

Stranger says: " HELLO PUSS HELLO PUSS "

    PURR–PUSS raises her eyebrows, looks at the stranger's face and says: " HELLO "

    PURR–PUSS says to herself: " I MUST REMEMBER HIS NAME "

    PURR–PUSS looks at stranger again and scans his face from bottom left, up across to the top and down across to the bottom right.

Stranger says: " MISTER TRIANGLE FACE HOW DO YOU DO "

    PURR–PUSS looks at the stranger's face and says aloud: ' 'HELLO "

    PURR–PUSS says to herself: " I MUST REMEMBER HIS NAME "

    PURR–PUSS scans his face and says aloud: " MISTER TRIANGLE FACE HOW DO YOU DO "

The details are given and discussed in Chapter 7. The HELLO task is as much an experiment in psychology as a test of PURR–PUSS. It is an example of thinking with PURR–PUSS.

The ROOMS task occupies the largest part of the interaction, extending from Fig. 7.5. through all the figures to Fig. 7.12. The reader is given a ringside view of Teacher's attempts to make PURR–PUSS "want" to go into a particular room. As Teacher, I found it an interesting experience. You may decide whether, or not, I succeeded. The ROOMS task illustrates better than the earlier tasks how PURR–PUSS can act on her own, following her own hypotheses and being distracted by her own memories of past events.

Some readers may wonder how PURR–PUSS can use English words, when she starts with no knowledge of these words or even of their possible existence. She learns in a paradigmatic way, that is, by being given examples. I have taught her with English words because I am familiar with them and it is easier for me to remember what I am teaching her if I use English. If I had been Russian, say, then I would have used Russian words. A Frenchman can teach PURR–PUSS in French.

10 THINKING WITH THE TEACHABLE MACHINE

To understand how PURR–PUSS works, it is essential to recognize the part played by context in the remembering and recalling of events. Chapter 2 is devoted to the PUSS memory mechanism. PURR–PUSS contains five PUSSes, each of which provides memory for different aspects of her experience. The multiple context obtained from a number of PUSSes bestows on PURR–PUSS powers that we are just beginning to appreciate. Chapter 3 summarises our current understanding of multiple fixed contexts.

Chapter 4 places the reader at the console typewriter of a small digital computer programmed to behave like PURR–PUSS. There is a detailed account of what happens in a short illustrative interaction. The main decision processes of PURR are introduced in Chapter 4 with straightforward examples of how they occur in an interaction. The reader is given a full and

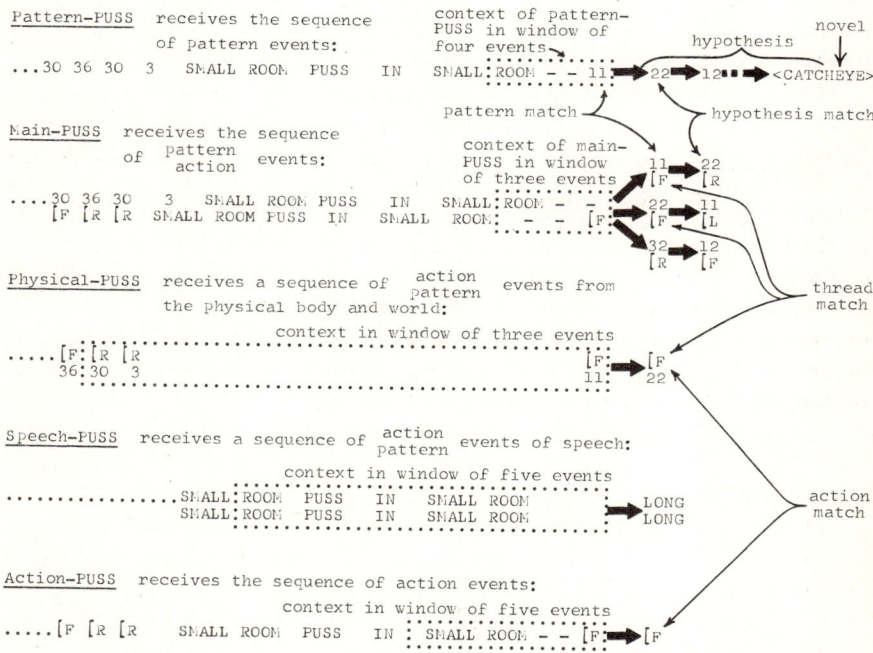

Fig. 1.2. The multiple context of the PUSSes and the decision strategy of PURR.

(This is the situation on step 791 of Fig. 7.10.) The action [F is selected with top priority (priority 1) because there is an hypothesis match and pattern match and thread match. Had there been no hypothesis match, pattern match or thread match, action match could have caused the same action to be selected. Heavy arrows point to predictions made by a PUSS.

precise description of PURR–PUSS and of her body and world in Chapter 5. The procedures for memory storage, prediction, hypothesis formation and action selection, given in Chapter 5, are derived directly from the computer programs that simulated PURR–PUSS for the interaction described in Chapters 6 and 7. Anyone wishing to write a program to simulate PURR–PUSS on their own computer should start from these same procedures.

The hurried reader may like to make the omissions suggested by footnotes in Chapters 2, 3 and 5.

In concluding this "look ahead", we see in Fig. 1.2 a "snapshot" of the PURR–PUSS system taken during the teaching of the ROOMS task (Chapter 7). The events, contexts (within the dotted windows) and predictions (heavy arrows) of the five PUSSes are shown exactly as they occurred. The four "match" conditions (Chapter 4), which constitute the PURR decision strategy are indicated. There is an hypothesis constructed to a novel event (Chapter 5). PURR–PUSS seeks and removes novelty by predicting an hypothesis to a novel event "<CATCHEYE>" and then trying to follow the hypothesis.

The reader will find nothing to argue about in the following six chapters of this book. They contain just a factual description of PURR–PUSS — nothing more. My reasons for considering PURR–PUSS to be *the* way to machine intelligence are tucked away in the Notes on the Chapters. For me, PURR–PUSS is much more than just an interesting machine. In spite of all her glaring faults and omissions, she is the right kind of machine to interact with you and me.

The Appendix has not been given the status of a chapter, because it is less precise than the chapters and it is somewhat speculative. However, as a model of *the* brain based on PURR–PUSS, it not only points to a way of discovering the working principles of the brain but takes the first step.

Notes on Chapter 1

1. The name PURR–PUSS is derived from PUSS, which originated in UC-DSE/1 in 1972, and from PURR added in 1973 in UC-DSE/2. PUSS stands for Predictor Using Slide and Strings. The "slide" was what I now call the "window" and the "strings" are implicit in a PUSS net (Chapter 2). PURR stands for Purposeful Unprimed Rewardable Robot, but reward is no longer the primary goal of the system.

2. The difference between designing *an* experimental brain, like PURR–PUSS, and modelling *the* brain, like MACLFAC & Co (Cunningham and Gray, 1974; Cunningham, 1972) is one of approach. The same difference distinguishes Ashby's 1952 book "Design for a Brain" from Young's 1964 book "A Model of the Brain". PURR–PUSS exhibits behaviour which may be compared with human behaviour, but it is not designed to mimic human behaviour. It is a "psychological" model to the extent that it demonstrates some aspects of learning, remembering and forgetting, attention, motivation and language. Other aspects, like personality and emotion, seem to be entirely absent at present. In a similar way, mew-Brain (described in the Appendix) is a "physiological" model of *a* brain that exhibits only some of the physiological characteristics of *the* human brain. The two together, PURR–PUSS and mew-Brain, form a dual model of a brain. If this dual model is developed to cover more aspects of psychology and physiology, it may begin to deserve the title "model of *the* brain".

Because of the serial nature of conventional digital computers, on which almost all modelling is carried out, models of the brain must be dual with a fast serial model (like PURR–PUSS) exhibiting complex behaviour (psychology) in real time and a slow parallel model (like mew-Brain) representing the physiological structure. A physiological model, large enough to exhibit interesting behaviour, could not be simulated on a conventional serial digital computer in real time because of the enormous number of simultaneously acting components (e.g. neurons, synapses, etc.) in a brain. On the other hand, a psychological model must be able to interact with humans in real time and it must be able to behave reasonably intelligently to be convincing. A dual model would require psychological testing of the fast part, physiological testing of the slow part, and testing of the equivalence of the fast and slow parts, either on a small scale or at a slow speed.

3. There is no essential difference between the terms "machine", "system" and "computer program" in this context. A computer program turns a standard digital computer into a particular machine or system. PURR–PUSS can be viewed equivalently as a computer program or as a machine or as a system. See, however, note 2 for practical differences between physical systems, like brains, and computer programs that are equivalent to them in some way.

4. While I have been developing PUSS and PURR–PUSS, John Cleary has devised a number of similar schemes under the names of Felix, Simple, FLM and Tree-Felix. This work is reported in his articles in UC-DSE/2,5,6,7. Special mention should be made of his article "Techniques for Sequential Learning" in UC-DSE/5.

5. The different environments used with PURR–PUSS (and with a PUSS alone) have included deterministic and non-deterministic automata (UC-DSE/2-4), simple and complex mazes (UC-DSE/2,4), a blindman on a path (UC-DSE/2,6; Heads, 1975), a coin-tossing problem (UC-DSE/4 and Example 3 of Chapter 2), various counting problems (UC-DSE/3-6,8; Example 4 of Chapter 2; Chapter 6) text (UC-DSE/3; Examples 1 and 2 of Chapter 2), line drawing (Examples 2-4 of Chapter 3), some con-

versational problems (UC-DSE/6-8; Chapter 7), and laboratory robots (CAESAR in UC-DSE/7; ESAW in UC-DSE/9).

6. CAESAR was a self-propelled trolley or mechanical tortoise (Fig. 1.1). In ESAW a sucker held at the end of an arm moves over a table inset with an array of light sensors that provide the "eye". The first version of CAESAR was built by D. H. Bakker, G. G. Lineham and L. A. Wilson (UC-DSE/4, page 150). It was rebuilt by R. J. Rushby and used by W. D. S. Brander, C. G. Blythe, N. C. Byron and P. J. Nowland (UC-DSE/7, Section R). ESAW was built by R. G. Atkins, N. M. McAdam, J. M. McCutcheon and J. Zoutenbier (See Alex Palfi's article in UC-DSE/9 for teaching with ESAW).

7. An excellent discussion of the difficulties encountered with rewarding PURR–PUSS is given by Wayne Heads (UC-DSE/6; Heads, 1975). Novelty seeking and removal was introduced in UC-DSE/4 as a technique for exploration and then, as reported in UC-DSE/5, it was found to be an excellent mode for teaching.

8. It is not at all obvious how, or when, we should re-introduce reward. We may be able to treat reward as a burst of novelty accompanying the satisfaction of needs and following a "drive" period in which sensitivity to relevant stimuli is increased and thresholds of automatic reflexes in the body for the particular need are lowered. In the present implementation of PURR–PUSS a "reward button" is provided which, when it is pressed, forces all PUSSes to record events as novel whether they are or not.

9. Psychologists have puzzled over the importance of novelty in human and animal behaviour. See, for instance, the chapter on Curiosity and Exploration in Deutsch's (1960) "The Structural Basis of Behaviour", Broadbent's (1961) book on "Behaviour" (Chapter 7) and Berlyne's (1960) book "Conflict, Arousal and Curiosity". However, we need to go back to 1949 to find in Hebb's "The Organization of Behaviour" a discussion which seems almost to be talking about PURR–PUSS! Reading "event sequence" for his "phase sequence", pages 229-32 of his book describe "the continued need of some degree of novelty to maintain wakefulness of choice" and how (in my words) the organization of incomplete memories by the removal of novelty dominates the thought process.

To Gregory (1971), "a necessary criterion of intelligence is novelty. Novelty alone, however, is not enough, for what is novel may be arbitrary, or down-right misleading. Evidently, to be appropriate is also a necessary condition for intelligence." In PURR–PUSS, novelty controls hypothesis formation and several levels of appropriateness are made possible by her multiple context. (See UC-DSE/7, page 24).

10. In the Appendix I take a first step to derive a physiological model from PURR–PUSS. The need for a dual model of the brain was argued in note 2.

There has been a great deal of argument about the relevance of machine (computer) models to human thought and about the possibility of machines thinking. Two stimulating books on the subject are "What Computers Can't Do" by Dreyfus (1972) and "The Nature of Mind" by Kenny, Longuet-Higgins, Lucas and Waddington (1972). See also Feigenbaum and Feldman (1963), Anderson (1964), Elithorn and Jones (1973), and Arbib (1972).

11. The design of PURR–PUSS has followed the strategy employed with her predecessor, STeLLA (Andreae and Cashin, 1969):—

14 THINKING WITH THE TEACHABLE MACHINE

(i) Try out a design.
(ii) Find classes of problem that it cannot tackle which, as humans, we feel it ought to be able to tackle.
(iii) Modify the design so that it can tackle one or more of these additional classes of problem.
(iv) With this new design, return to (i).

However, we have now reached the stage at which the above strategy has to be applied to the body, world and teaching of PURR–PUSS as much as to her design and structure because her behaviour is found to be so dependent on all these factors. (See UC-DSE/4, page 100, for the first realization of the importance of her body).

12. For information about reward and pain centres, see Magoun's (1963) "The Waking Brain", Campbell's (1973) "The Pleasure Areas", and Grossman's (1973) "Essentials of Physiological Psychology".

13. The reason for starting PURR–PUSS "from scratch" with nothing in her memories is simply to help us to see what she has learned. If her memories were primed with information, how would we distinguish what she had learned from what she had been given? It is true that she is given certain built-in "reflexes" (e.g. mimic-speech and pauses) and "discriminations" (e.g. speech patterns) as features of her body or the way in which her body is connected, but she begins with no information about what these reflexes and discriminations do.

14. Teachability is dangerously close to gullibility and one of the educational challengers ahead is to teach PURR–PUSS not to accept everything she is told!

15. A common reaction to PURR–PUSS is that she is only a kind of programmable system, which we program by a rather stilted form of teaching. After all, it is often said that computers can only do what they are told, so PURR–PUSS couldn't be anything else. Such a critic could go on and say that he notices we are gradually introducing "rules" by our MEDEATOR program to make the system easier to interact with. He might sling a final shot by asking whether this process won't lead us eventually to BASIC?! Such a criticism underlines the important fact that we are starting from the "no rules" end. I know of no one else who has, except Mother Nature. Babies and PURR–PUSS do not mind what language you teach them in, so long as you start at the very beginning. (UC-DSE/6, page 1).

16. See, for example, the prescription of the human information processing system given by Newell and Simon (1972) and discussed in note 4 of Chapter 6.

17. This book describes a machine and its interactive behaviour. The machine is precisely and formally defined by its algorithms and by the computer programs which implement them. The isolated machine is a formal system, closed and finite. We can describe its parts in a systematic and formal way; this is done in Chapters 2 and 5.

The interactive behaviour of the machine is another matter. For, when it is used, the machine becomes an interactive and integral part of its body and world. The world of PURR–PUSS includes Teacher, so PURR–PUSS becomes part of an open system that is no more a formal system than is Teacher in his world. The same is true of other machines, once we allow them to operate outside the formal, idealized situation in which they are usually conceived. A runaway motor can can be most informal!

All this explains why I cannot describe PURR–PUSS as an interacting system in the same systematic manner as I can her formal, isolated self. All I can do is show you the little that I have discovered about her so far. The inadequacy of my effort is not necessarily related to inadequacies in her. Her inadequacies are not necessarily revealed by my effort.

18. The implications of Gödel's theorem for machine intelligence is clearly stated by Lucas (1961) for the case of the isolated machine acting as a closed, formal system. Dreyfus (1972, page 148) suggests "that what distinguishes persons from machines, no matter how cleverly constructed, is not a detached, universal, immaterial soul but an involved, self-moving, material body." Narasimhan (1969) recognized that a natural language system is open and criticised work in artificial intelligence for its formal limitations. He argues powerfully for the paradigmatic mode of behaviour.

How much and what kind of interaction with the world is needed to turn a formal system into a non-formal system? I would guess that the interaction must be sufficient to affect the syntactic structure of the system.

19. PURR–PUSS has been taught to behave like a universal Turing machine (UCDSE/6; Andreae and Cleary, 1976). The significance of this result deserves elaboration. A universal Turing machine (see, for example, Minsky, 1967 and Manna, 1974) might be described as a particular finite state machine that is given as much memory and information as it needs (on a tape). With this unlimited memory and exactly-what-it-needs information, the universal Turing machine can (not surprisingly) do anything! To teach PURR–PUSS to behave like a universal Turing machine, I did no more than teach her to behave like a particular finite state machine (Minsky, 1967, page 279) and provide her with the appropriate information and unlimited memory. Personally, I look upon the universal Turing machine as no more than an "open" system comprising a simple machine (finite state) and a rich, infinite environment. To have taught PURR–PUSS to behave like that simple machine does not give her arbitrary powers. However, the way PURR–PUSS was taught established that she could be taught to behave like *any* finite state machine, given a large enough PUSS memory and echo-speech. Therefore, she can compute any function that a Turing machine can compute if she is taught the Turing machine structure and provided with the appropriate tape.

A related point is the claim of Anderson and Bower (1973) that "there is one feature which tends to haunt associative theories, which can be given precise statement, and which can be proven in error. This is the Terminal Meta-Postulate (TMP) ... may be divided into three statements, one statement corresponding to each of three associative meta-features.

1. Sensationalist Statement. The only elements required in a psychological explanation can be put into a one-to-one correspondence with potentially observable elements. . . .
2. Connectionistic Statement. The elements in Statement 1 become connected or associated if and only if they occur contiguously.
3. Mechanistic Statement. All observable behaviour can be explained by concatenating the associative links in Statement 2." (Page 12).

The teaching of PURR–PUSS to behave like a universal Turing machine seems to disprove their disproof and support the TMP. The reason is clear: even the human is treated as a closed system by Anderson and Bower!

2. The Basic Mechanism: PUSS

> Pussy can sit by the fire and sing,
> Pussy can climb a tree,
> Or play with a silly old cork and string
> To 'muse herself, not me.
>
> Rudyard Kipling
> "The Cat That Walked By Himself"

The Prediction of Events

PUSS is a mechanism for remembering events and for recalling them. Events are recalled by a process of prediction based on the principle "What happened in the past is likely to happen again". To predict what will happen after a given context of events, we recall those events which occurred in the past after the same context.

Suppose that the weather on consecutive days is as given in Fig. 2.1. The 16th day is today. What will be the weather tomorrow, the 17th day?

```
1st  day    Snow
2nd  day    Fine
3rd  day    Cloudy
4th  day    Rain
5th  day    Gale
6th  day    Fine
7th  day    Fine
8th  day    Cloudy
9th  day    Rain
10th day    Fine
11th day    Cloudy
12th day    Rain
13th day    Gale
14th day    Fine
15th day    Cloudy
16th day    Rain
```

Figure 2.1

In this example, each day is an "event". We can abbreviate the sequence of events by
$$S - F - C - R - G - F - F - C - R - F - C - R - G - F - C - R - ?$$
with:
S standing for the event: a day with Snow,
F standing for the event: a Fine day,
C standing for the event: a Cloudy day,
R standing for the event: a day with Rain,
G standing for the event: a day with Gale,
? standing for the unknown event that will be tomorrow.

Let us predict with a PUSS having a "window" or context of three events. Once the weather (rain) has been determined for today, the 16th day, the window will contain F − C − R, the last 3 events. This is the context with which we predict tomorrow's weather. Comparing the sequence of events in the window with the earlier events, it is noticed that F − C − R also occurred on the 2nd, 3rd and 4th days. The 5th day was Gale so, on that occasion, F − C − R was followed by G. However, F − C − R also occurred on the 7th, 8th and 9th days with F following on the 10th. Again, we notice that F − C − R appeared a third time on the 10th, 11th and 12th days with G following on the 13th day.

Summarising this information we have recalled:
F − C − R on days 2 − 3 − 4 was followed by G on day 5,
F − C − R on days 7 − 8 − 9 was followed by F on day 10, and
F − C − R on days 10 − 11 − 12 was followed by G on day 13.

Now we can predict tomorrow's weather. If what happened in the past happens again, then we shall have G or F. PUSS predicts "Gale or Fine".

To check that this method of prediction is fully understood, the reader may like to confirm that a PUSS with a window of 2 events would predict the same, while a PUSS with a window of 4 events would make no prediction of the weather on the 17th day.

Remembering Events

There have been several versions of PUSS.[1] In all of them the events of the past are stored in such a way that the whole sequence of past events is *not* stored and yet the predictions of PUSS are the same as if the whole sequence of past events *were* stored. This is achieved quite easily by storing for each context that occurs all the different events which have immediately followed the context. If a particular event follows a particular context twice, then it is stored (remembered) only once.

Let me illustrate this storage process with the sequence of events in Fig. 2.1. We extract each context from the sequence and associate with it the events which immediately follow it. If a prediction were made from a

18   THINKING WITH THE TEACHABLE MACHINE

particular context, then the events which immediately followed it would be the predicted events. In other words, we remember the predictions associated with the contexts. Figure 2.2 lists the contexts and associated predictions for the sequence of Fig. 2.1.

Contexts	Predictions
S-F-C	R
F-C-R	G,F
C-R-G	F
R-G-F	F,C
G-F-F	C
F-F-C	R
C-R-F	C
R-F-C	R
G-F-C	R

Fig. 2.2

To remember the predictions associated with a context, we must have a memory in which to record the predictions and we must have a way of telling which predictions are associated with which contexts. In the process to be described, we use each context to determine the addresses in memory where its predictions are to be recorded. The special features of the process (like storing each prediction three times and like dividing by prime numbers to get

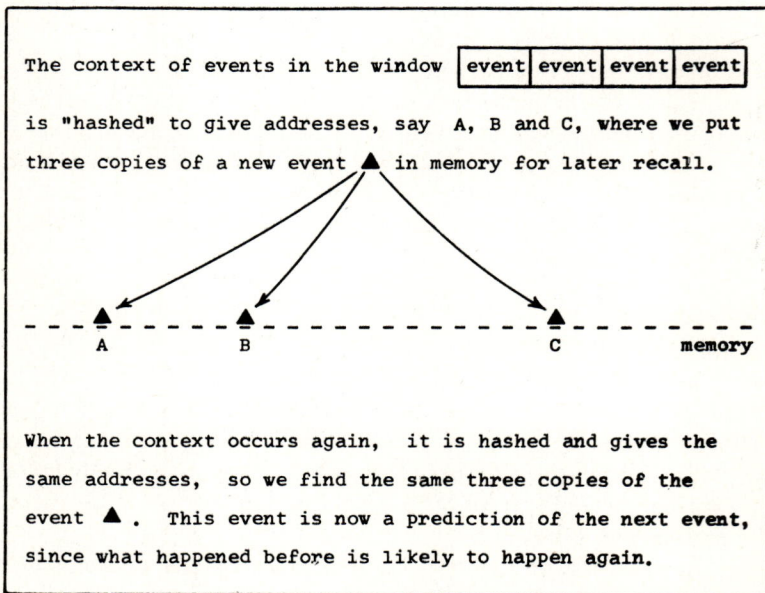

Fig. 2.3 A rough idea of the PUSS memory process

THE BASIC MECHANISM: PUSS   19

remainders) are standard techniques ("hashing")[2] for making the process work when there is not enough memory for each possible context to have its own part of memory for its associated predictions. Figure 2.3 gives a rough idea of what is done.

Fortunately, the mechanics of the storage (remembering) process are simple arithmetic and they can be described in detail without trouble*. Suppose that the sequence of events in Fig. 2.1 is being stored by a PUSS into a memory of 47 locations. The state of this memory on 12 consecutive days is shown in the right half of Fig. 2.4. Notice that the locations have addresses from 0 to 46, *not* 1 to 47.

The storage occurs event by event, but nothing is stored until the arrival of the 4th event. The first, second and third events arrived before the window was filled so there was no context with which to store them. Notice that in the right half of Fig. 2.4 the memory remains empty for the first three days.

On the 4th day, the first three events (S – F – C) are filling the window and provide the context for storing the new event (R). The procedure for storing an event will be stated and then explained.

To store an event

Step 1. Code the context into a number.
Step 2. Calculate the address of a location in memory. (This is done by dividing the context number by the next largest prime number that is not larger than the size of memory and by taking the remainder.)
Step 3. If the location (addressed by the remainder) is empty, store the event and the number of the prime (e.g. "1" for the first, "2" for the second, and so on).
Step 4. If the event has now been seen in or put into 3 of the addressed locations, stop; if not, repeat from step 2.

This procedure is illustrated in Figs 2.4 and 2.5 for the first 12 days of Fig. 2.1.

On the first day, referring to Figs 2.1 and 2.4, there is nothing in memory and there is no context in the window of the PUSS when the new event S (Snow) arrives, so nothing can be done. On the second day the context becomes S, which does not fill the window, and the new event F arrives. On the third day the context becomes S–F and the new event C arrives.

On the 4th day, the process of storage begins with a context S – F – C in the window of PUSS and a new event R to store. Step 1 of the procedure can be carried out as follows. The context is S – F – C. S is the 19th letter of the alphabet, F the 6th and C the 3rd. Using two digits for each letter, we can code S - F - C into 19 – 06 – 03, or just 190603. The context is coded[3] into the number 190603.

* The hurried reader may skip to page 23.

20 THINKING WITH THE TEACHABLE MACHINE

Day	Context and Number	New Event	Prime Numbers and Remainders	Memory locations (0–45)
1		S		
2	S		F	
3	S–F		C	
4	S–F–C 190603	R	47 43 41 18 27 35	R 1 — R 2 — R 3
5	F–C–R 060318	G	47 43 41 17 32 7	G 3 — GR 11 — R 2 — G 2 — R 3
6	C–R–G 031807	F	47 43 41 37 31 35 30 32 24 1	F 5 — G 3 — GR 11 — F 4 — R 2 — F 2 — G 2 — R 3
7	R–G–F 180706	F	47 43 41 38 20 19	F 5 — G 3 — GRFF 1132 — F 4 — R 2 — F 2 — G 2 — R 3
8	G–F–F 070606	C	47 43 12 0 4	CF 25 — C 3 — G 3 — GRFF 1132 — F 4 — R 2 — F 2 — G 2 — R 3 — 1
9	F–F–C 060603	R	47 43 41 37 20 16 5 34	CF 25 — CR 33 — G 3 — RGRFF 21132 — F 4 — R 2 — F 2 — G 2 — RR 43 — F 1
10	F–C–R	F	. . 37 31 29 23 19 17 8 23 27 12 12 2	CFF 259 — CR 33 — GF 34 — C 1 — RGRFF 21132 — FF 54 — R 2 — F 2 — G 2 — RR 43 — F 1
11	C–R–F	C	47 43 41 37 31 29 34 29 31 23 0 22	CFF 259 — CR 33 — GF 34 — C 1 — RGRFF 21132 — CFF 654 — R 2 — CFCG 2232 — RR 43 — F 1
12	R–F–C 180603	R	47 43 41 37 29 3 39 6	CFFRCRRGF 259233434 — C 1 — RGRFF 21132 — CFF 654 — R 2 — CFCG 2232 — RR 43 — FR 13

Fig. 2.4. Illustrating the storage of events.

The first time we carry out step 2 in storing an event, we take the largest prime number less than or equal to the size of memory. Having chosen a memory size of 47 locations, we take 47 as the first prime number. This prime is divided into the context number 190603. We are not interested in the fact that it goes 4055 times, only that it leaves a remainder of 18. Location 18 is the one we want and is where we put the new event R. By step 3 of the procedure, since the whole of the memory is empty, the new event R is stored with the number (1 for the first) of the prime used. It can be seen in Fig. 2.4 that R/1 is stored in location 18 on the 4th day.

By step 4, it is not time to stop, so step 2 is repeated with the next largest prime (43) giving location 27 for storing a second copy of the new event R with the number (2) of the prime. On the next repetition of step 2, the third prime (41) gives location 35. Now, as can be seen in Fig. 2.4, the new event has been stored 3 times and the procedure is completed. Notice that the location addresses calculated for the three primes are underlined in Fig. 2.4 to show that locations 18, 27 and 35 were found to be empty and the new event was stored in them on the 4th day. On the 4th day the memory contains R/1 in location 18, R/2 in location 27, and R/3 in location 35.

With the arrival of the event F on the 6th day, the window holds the context C – R – G which codes into 031807. Dividing by the first prime (47) yields 35 and when location 35 is examined it is found to contain R/3 already. We leave R/3 there and divide the code by the next largest prime (43) to get location 30 which is empty and into which we put the new event F with 2, the number of the prime. (Notice how location 35 was *not* underlined in Fig. 2.4 because we did not store the new event in it. 30 is underlined because we have put the new event in it.) The third prime (41) also gives a full location and so the 4th (37) and 5th (31) primes have to be used to obtain empty locations 24 and 1 for storing F/4 and F/5, respectively.

On the 10th day there is the same context F – C – R as on the 5th day, but with a different new event F, so nine primes have to be used in order to find three empty locations (8, 23 and 2) into which the event can be stored. The small illustrative memory of Fig. 2.4 is filling up. Figure 2.5 further illustrates the storage procedure for the 12th day.

Looking at the top of the memory in Fig. 2.4 for the 12th day, it will be noticed that locations 40 to 46 are empty. These locations are wasted because the remainders from the primes cannot exceed the values of the primes. Thus, the prime 47 can only give remainders up to 46, the prime 43 can only give remainders up to 42, the prime 41 up to 40, and so on. For this reason the top locations have a small chance of being filled. However, in a very large memory, the wasted locations near the top become a negligible proportion of the total memory. For a memory of about 60,000 events, as used for the work reported in this book, even the 50th prime wastes only 1% of memory.

22 THINKING WITH THE TEACHABLE MACHINE

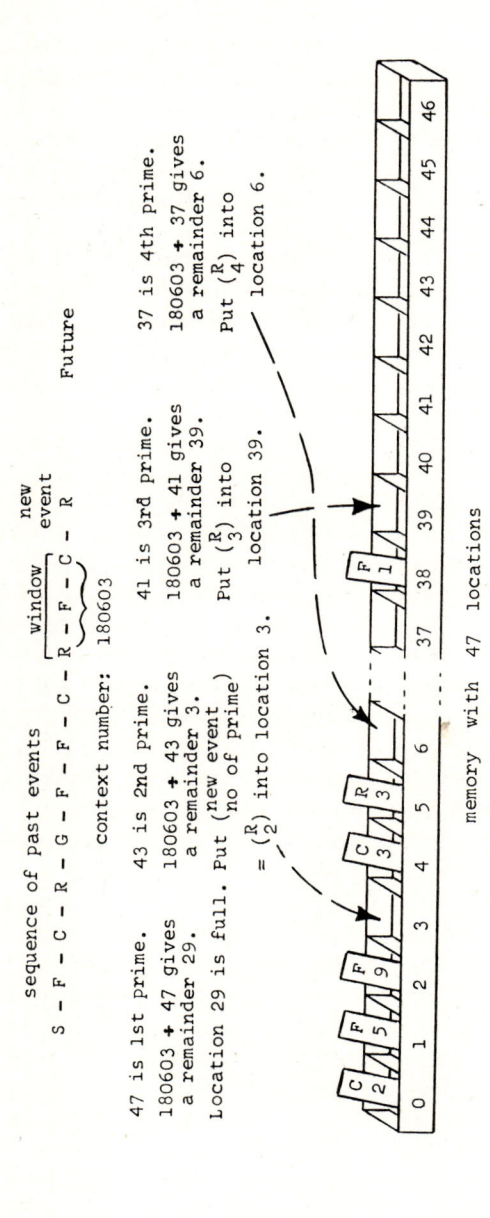

```
                          window    new
                         ┌───────┐  event
sequence of past events  │       │
S - F - C - R - G - F - F - C - R - F - C - R
              context number:
                         180603
```

47 is 1st prime.
180603 ÷ 47 gives a remainder 29.
Location 29 is full. Put $\binom{\text{new event}}{\text{no of prime}}$ = $\binom{R}{2}$ into location 3.

43 is 2nd prime.
180603 ÷ 43 gives a remainder 3.
Put $\binom{R}{3}$ into location 3.

41 is 3rd prime.
180603 ÷ 41 gives a remainder 39.
Put $\binom{R}{3}$ into location 39.

Future

37 is 4th prime.
180603 ÷ 37 gives a remainder 6.
Put $\binom{R}{4}$ into location 6.

memory with 47 locations

Fig. 2.5. Illustrating the storage of event R on the 12th day. (Compare this with Fig. 2.4, day 12).

(Other "hashing" methods do not have this peculiarity, but they tend to have other disadvantages.[2])

Three aspects of this memory storage process are worth emphasising. First, it can be seen that events are distributed randomly throughout memory. Biologists and others have pointed out that the memory process in the brain probably has this "holographic" property.[4] Secondly, it should be noticed that there is no searching of memory to find predictions from a context (next section) or to store events for a context. The context tells us where to look. Only rarely will we have to look beyond the locations addressed by the first few primes. This means that the storage and prediction processes have a speed independent of memory size. Memories of millions of events are feasible.[5] Thirdly, when several PUSSes are being used in a PURR-PUSS, they can all share the same memory.[6] In this case, each event is stored with the number of the prime and the number of the PUSS to ensure that the probability of error is negligible.

Recalling Events

The word "remember" is commonly used both for the storage of information and for its subsequent recall, so we shall avoid it. The recall of events in PURR–PUSS is always carried out as a prediction from context,[7] so the words "recall" and "prediction" will be used equivalently.

The procedure for recalling an event is the reverse of that for storing an event.* Instead of putting events into the locations prescribed by the remainders from dividing the context number by the primes, we look into those locations to see what has already been put there. If anything is seen three times (with the appropriate number of prime and PUSS), it is a prediction. The following procedure uses a "list" which is empty at the start and contains the predictions at the end:—

To recall an event (prediction)

Step 1. Code the context into a number (as for storage).
Step 2. Calculate the address of a location in memory. (This is done as for storage.)
Step 3. If the addressed location is empty, go to step 5.
Step 4. If the event in the addressed location has the appropriate number for the prime (and for the PUSS being used if there is more than one), put it on the list; repeat from step 2.
Step 5. Remove from the list all events that do not appear on it at least three times. The list now contains the predicted (recalled) events. Stop.

This procedure may be illustrated by applying it to the situation at the end of the sequence shown in Fig. 2.4. With the memory as indicated at the end of

* The hurried reader may skip to the next section.

24   THINKING WITH THE TEACHABLE MACHINE

the 12th day, we predict the weather for the 13th day. Taking each prime number in turn, we examine the contents of the calculated locations:—

> The 1st prime 47 gives location 17 which contains G/1
> so put it on the list;
> The 2nd prime 43 gives location 32 which contains G/2
> so put it on the list;
> The 3rd prime 41 gives location 7 which contains G/3
> so put it on the list;
> The 4th prime 37 gives location 8 which contains F/4
> so put it on the list;
> The 5th prime 31 gives location 23 which contains F/5
> so put it on the list;
> The 6th prime 29 gives location 27 which contains R/2
> so the prime is wrong;
> The 7th prime 23 gives location 12 which contains C/1
> so the prime is wrong;
> The 8th prime 19 gives location 12 also;
> The 9th prime 17 gives location 2 which contains F/9
> so put it on the list;
> The 10th prime 13 gives location 11 which is empty
> so predict "G or F".

A PUSS Net Memory

The memory shown in Fig. 2.4 for the 12th day is much more difficult to think about than the equivalent information in Fig. 2.2, where predictions and contexts are shown together. However, even Fig. 2.2 lacks an appearance of sequential behaviour. By turning the original sequence of events in Fig. 2.1 into a PUSS "net", we can retain the sequential appearance of the events while imposing the fixed context restriction of the storage process. (Previous versions of PUSS had memories like the net to be described.) Later I shall need to refer to the different representations of memory, so the memory given in Fig. 2.4 will be called a "mew-gram" or just a "mew".[8]

To form a PUSS net, take the original sequence of Fig. 2.1,

$$S-F-C-R-G-F-F-C-R-F-C-R-G-F-C-R-,$$

and twist it around like a string so that, wherever the same context of three events occurs in two places, the most recent event of each context is combined into a single occurrence (a "node" of the net). The steps of this process are illustrated in Fig. 2.6. Dotted lines indicate which two events are going to be merged next.

THE BASIC MECHANISM: PUSS 25

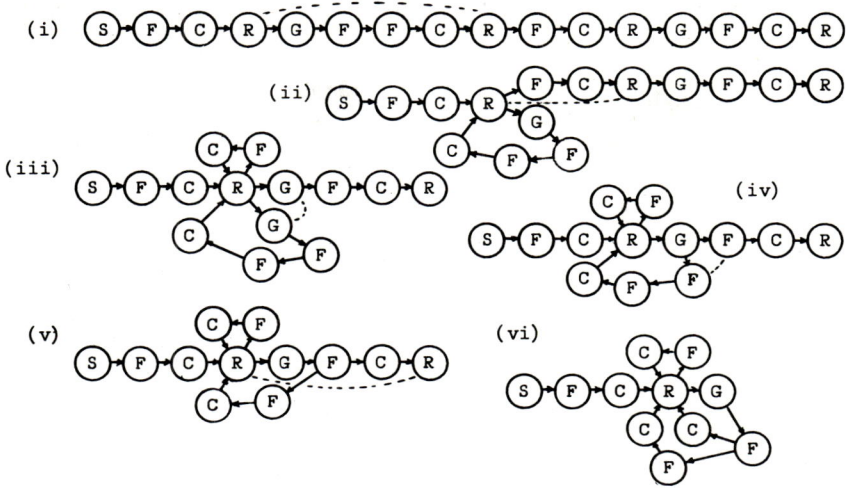

Figure 2.6. Fashioning a sequence into a PUSS net. (Each event of the net is a "node".)

By looking at the PUSS net (stage (vi) of Fig. 2.6), we can observe five general features of a PUSS memory that would be difficult to see in the equivalent mew:—

(1) The generating sequence of Fig. 2.1 can be traced through the net. It is still in memory.

(2) Other sequences that did *not* occur can also be traced through memory, such as $S - F - C - R - F - C - R -$. In other words, the PUSS memory contains novel sequences.

(3) All sequences up to a length of 4 events (window plus one) *did* occur in the generating sequence.

(4) No sequence of length 3 (window length) or more is duplicated in memory.

(5) The last context to occur ($F - C - R$ is the context on the 16th day) points to what would happen next (F or G) if we went on tracing through the net from there. In other words, predictions are made as though the existing PUSS memory were a model of what was happening.

The PUSS net is an easier representation for thinking about what is in a PUSS memory, but it is less efficient than a mew-gram for implementing a PUSS memory. An implementation in terms of a PUSS net requires the memory to be searched for each new event, to find the location of its context. The larger the memory, the longer it will take to perform this search. In the case of the mew, the mew context points directly to where we have to look in memory and no search is needed. The speed of the operation of a mew can be maintained with memories up to the largest available.

We shall use the PUSS net to clarify what is going on, but the real PUSSes will use a mew.[9]

The PUSS mechanism enables PURR–PUSS to learn. All learning by PURR-PUSS takes place in PUSSes.[10] In the next chapter, we shall see the importance of a collection of PUSSes acting together.

Examples of PUSS*

As stated in Chapter 1, the primary message of this book is the simple mechanism of PUSS. Chapters that follow this one will suggest some of the things that can be done with several PUSSes acting together, but first we must understand the operation of a single PUSS acting on its own.

Example 1. Letters as Events
Consider the sentence

"when-the-sun-does-not-shine-we-play-in-tne-house."

as a sequence of "letter events":—

w h e n - t h e - s u n - d o e s - n o t - s h i n e - w e - p l a y - i n - t h e - h o u s e

The first event is the letter "w", the second the letter "h", the third the letter "e", the fourth the letter "n" and the fifth is the word separator "-". Right at the end of the sentence is the full stop, or period, ".". It would have been confusing to use spaces as word separators since nothing appears on the paper when a space is printed.

Feed the sentence, event by event, into a PUSS having a window of 2 events. Each time an event is fed in, a prediction is attempted. The predictions, if any, are shown as capital letters below the original sentence:—
w h e n - t h e - s u n - d o e s - n o t - s h i n e - w e - p l a y - i n - t h e - h o u s e .
        N   T   U   S   S   ETHE-S
                  W   D NW
                                         P

The first prediction comes after "when-the" because the two events "h" and "e" are in the window of the PUSS and this context of two events has already been followed by event "n" in the first word "when". The prediction of "n" is shown by a capital "N" below the next event, which happens to be "-". The prediction was wrong. The next prediction of "T" after "when-the-sun-" is also wrong. After " . . . not-shine-we-" there are two predictions "S"

---
* The hurried reader may skip these examples and go on to Chapter 3.

THE BASIC MECHANISM: PUSS   27

and "W", because the two events "e-" in the window were previously followed by "s" and "w". Both of these predictions are wrong. The first correct prediction is the "T" after " . . . play-in-", but it is accompanied by a wrong prediction "D". The next "h" is predicted correctly and uniquely, as is the "e" that comes after it. Instead of the "h" of "house", we get the predictions "S", "W" and "P".

If we look at the PUSS memory after the last event of the sentence, ".", has been fed in, we can draw the memory as the PUSS net of Fig. 2.7.

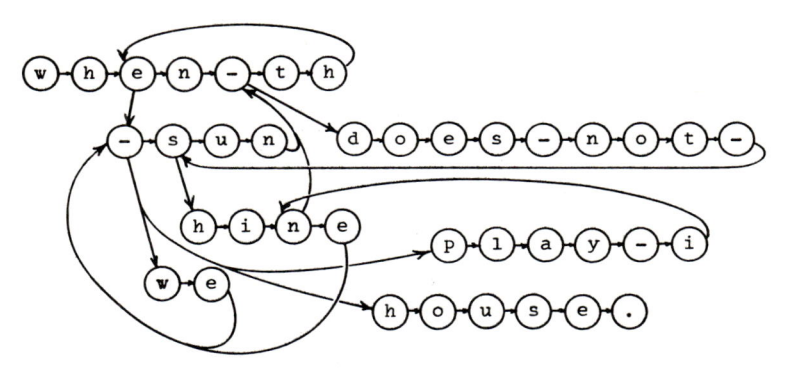

Fig. 2.7. PUSS net after one sentence fed in as letters.

To show how the PUSS net grows, another sentence is fed in:—
w e - d o - n o t - p l a y - i n - t h e - h o u s e - w h e n - t h e - s u n - i s - o u t .

```
-SOE OT-SLAY-IN-THE-HOUSE.WEEN-THE-SUN-TN N S
 W           ED   NS    P  —  D  NHH  D
 P                W     H        W
 H                P     S        P
                  D     D        D
```

It can be seen that with this small window length of 2 events, there are many ambiguous predictions. The PUSS net has grown to the extent shown in Fig. 2.8

The reader is asked to trace the two sentences through the PUSS net of Fig. 2.8. Also, it should be noticed that each node of the net is a unique head of a 2-event sequence, except the initial "w" which had nothing before it. Thus, there are four nodes containing "s", one for the 2-event sequence "-s", one for "es", one for "is" and one for "us".

As an exercise, the reader might care to repeat this example for a PUSS with a 3-event window.

28   THINKING WITH THE TEACHABLE MACHINE

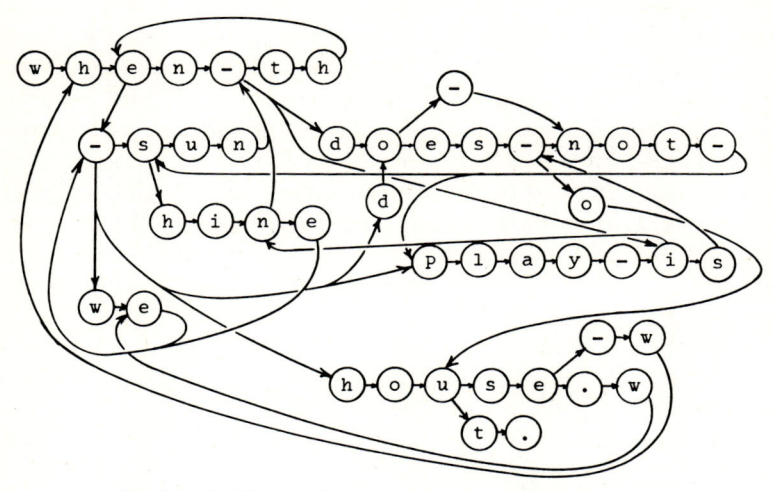

Fig. 2.8. PUSS net after two sentences fed in as letters.

A fundamental learning property of a PUSS enables it to accept any sequence of events: No existing node or connection has to be changed in a PUSS net to insert a new prediction — all learning is achieved by the *addition* of nodes and connections. Each node represents a unique context, each connection a unique event-in-context. To see this, compare Fig. 2.7 with Fig. 2.8.

Before leaving Fig. 2.8, the reader should follow through the memory net to find some of the sequences that are represented by the PUSS net, but did not occur in the input sequence of two sentences, e.g. "whe-shin-does-ouse.". Even after this short input, the memory has become too complicated to think about clearly. After a long sequence of input, the structure in memory becomes too complicated even to draw as a PUSS net. One can always inspect the memory of a PUSS, because it is stored in a digital computer, but this is not necessarily of any help in understanding what is there! The memory of PURR–PUSS, comprising several PUSSes, is even more inaccessible.

There is a kind of forgetting, which might be called "loss of recall", that does not depend upon "loss of memory" (the actual disappearance of events from memory). At the moment depicted by Fig 2.7 the context is " e. " and nothing can be predicted. There is a complete loss of recall, but no memory is lost. With the arrival of the first two letters of the second sentence, the context becomes " we " and all contexts but one in memory become accessible to prediction (see next example for wandering through memory by prediction). Which context is not accessible? When does it become accessible?

THE BASIC MECHANISM: PUSS   29

Example 2. Words as Events[11]

The whole of the book "The Cat in the Hat" by Dr Seuss (Hutchinson) and part of the book "Ant and Bee" by Angela Banner (Edmund Ward Ltd) were fed into a PUSS with a window of 3 events, each event being a word or a full stop ".". All punctuation in the original texts was removed or changed into full stops.

A program was then written to take the predictions of the PUSS after each event, choose one of the predictions at random, and feed that prediction back into the PUSS as its next event. In this way, the PUSS was made to wander through its own memory. The predicted events fed back into PUSS were as follows:—

THAT HAD WRITTEN ON IT THE WORD EXIT . BEE SAID EXIT MEANT WAY OUT . BEE SAID IT WAS . THE SAILOR TOLD ANT AND BEE GOT INTO THE COAT POCKET SO THAT THEY COULD SEE WHAT WAS HAPPENING . THE MAN WALKED ABOUT ON THE DECK OF THE BOAT FOR A LITTLE WHILE . THEN HE SHUT UP THE THINGS IN THE BOX WITH THE HOOK . AND THE CAT WENT AWAY WITH A SAD KIND OF LOOK . THAT IS GOOD SAID THE FISH . AND HE PUT THEM AWAY . . . .

This sequence was certainly not in either of the books. However, if we look for common 3-event contexts in the following extracts, it is quite easy to see how the sequence given above appeared in the PUSS memory. Here are the extracts:

. . . WHAT A SHAME . THEN HE SHUT UP THE THINGS IN THE BOX WITH THE HOOK . AND THE CAT WENT AWAY WITH A SAD KIND OF LOOK . THAT IS GOOD SAID THE FISH . HE HAS GONE AWAY . . . .

. . . AND THE SHIP AND THE FISH . AND HE PUT THEM AWAY . . . .

. . . BEE SAID THEIR GARDEN WAS NOT THE HOTTEST PLACE IN THE WORLD . BEE SAID IT WAS MUCH HOTTER IN ANOTHER PART OF THE WORLD . . .

. . . THE SAILOR SAID IT WAS . THE SAILOR TOLD ANT AND BEE TO FIND SOMEWHERE COSY TO SIT OR THEY WOULD BE BLOWN AWAY . . .

. . . BEE TOLD ANT THAT THE POCKET OF THE COAT WOULD BE A NICE PLACE FOR THEM TO GO . SO VERY QUICKLY ANT AND BEE GOT INTO THE COAT POCKET . THE POCKET OF THE COAT WAS BIG . THE MAN DID NOT SEE THEM GET INSIDE . THEY JUST PEEPED OUT OF THE COAT POCKET SO THAT THEY COULD SEE WHAT WAS HAPPENING . THE MAN

30 THINKING WITH THE TEACHABLE MACHINE

WALKED ABOUT ON THE DECK OF THE BOAT FOR A LITTLE
WHILE . THEN HE WALKED THROUGH A SMALL DOOR . . . .
. . . IN THE ROOM THERE WAS A DOOR THAT HAD WRITTEN
ON IT THE WORD EXIT . DEE SAID EXIT MEANT WAY OUT .
BEE SAID IF THE MAN . . .

In Fig. 2.9, partial construction of a PUSS net from the extracts shows how the different segments of text became connected through common 3-event contexts to produce the route through memory taken by the randomly selected predictions.

```
... THAT HAD WRITTEN ON IT THE WORD EXIT . BEE SAID EXIT MEANT
WAY OUT . BEE          IF THE MAN ...
... THE WORLD . BEE SAID IT        MUCH HOTTER ...
    ... THE SAILOR SAID IT WAS . THE SAILOR
            TOLD ANT AND      TO FIND SOMEWHERE COSY ...
    ... SO VERY QUICKLY ANT AND BEE GOT INTO
            THE COAT        . THE POCKET OF THE COAT ...
... JUST PEEPED OUT OF THE COAT POCKET SO THAT THEY COULD SEE
WHAT WAS HAPPENING . THE MAN WALKED ABOUT ON THE DECK OF THE
BOAT FOR A LITTLE WHILE . THEN     WALKED THROUGH A SMALL ...
        ... WHAT A SHAME . THEN HE SHUT UP THE THINGS IN THE
BOX WITH THE HOOK . AND THE CAT WENT AWAY WITH A SAD KIND OF
LOOK . THAT IS GOOD SAID THE FISH    HE HAS GONE AWAY . ...
    ... AND THE SHIP AND THE FISH . AND HE PUT THEM AWAY . ...
```

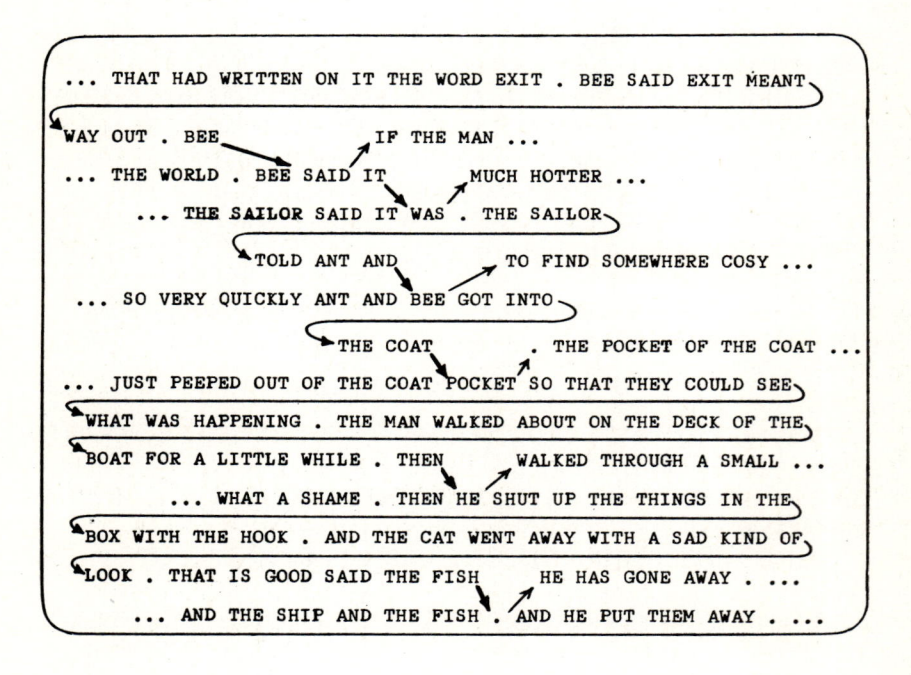

Fig. 2.9. Partial construction of a PUSS net. Each word and full stop is an event. Each context is 3 events long.

In the above example, we have allowed a PUSS to "wander through its own memory" to show us a little of what is stored there. In a similar way, we shall have to interact with PURR-PUSS in order to find out what she has learned. It is not possible to analyse what is in memory after she has had but a modest amount of experience. This is not stated as a virtue of the system, but as an inescapable fact.

THE BASIC MECHANISM: PUSS

Example 3. Bill and Ben, the Power Plot Men.[12]

An acquaintance of mine, Phil Broad by name, runs a gambling den. The other day he was approached by a fellow calling himself Ken Brook, who tried to sell Phil an electronic coin-tossing machine. Phil was quite attracted by the machine because it was cheap and easy to use; when a button was pushed, one of two panels lit up, the first showing a "head" and the second a "tail". Phil was suspicious as always, but particularly because he had got wind of a plot to take over his den. A couple of months earlier he had seen me demonstrate my PUSS predictor so Phil arranged to borrow the coin-tossing machine for a day to try it out, brought it over to me and asked me to test it. If PUSS could predict what the machine would show next in a sequence of heads and tails, it would certainly be no good.

Unfortunately, I was unable to book time on the computer to run my PUSS program so I had to resort to the kit set which I keep at home for working out simple things with PUSS. The kit set consists of nothing more than a pad of ruled paper with 64 equally-spaced horizontal lines and 12 vertical columns.

It is so easy to make mistakes with the kit set that one needs to be meticulously methodical. Choosing a window of 3 events, I thickened the line to the right of the third vertical column. Window events would be drawn to the left of the thick line, predictions to the right. While Phil pushed the button of the coin-tossing machine, I wrote H's or T's on the pad, according to whether the machine showed "head" or "tail".

The first four pushes gave head, head, head, tail, so I wrote H H H T in the first four positions of the first line. The three H's were to the left of the thick line as they represented the first context. The T on the right of the line would be a prediction if the context H H H ever occurred again. See (a) of Fig. 2.10.

```
(a) H H H|T           (f) H H H|T           (i) H H H|T
                          H H T|T               H H T|T H
(b) H H H|T               H T T|H               H T T|H T
    H H T|                 T T H|T               T T H|T H
                          T H T|                 T H T|T
(c) H H H|T                                      T T T|H
    H H T|T           (g) H H H|T                T H H|T
                          H H T|T                H T H|
(d) H H H|T               H T T|H T
    H H T|T               T T H|T           (j) H H H|T H
    H T T|                T H T|T                H H T|T H
                                                 H T T|H T
(e) H H H|T           (h) H H H|T                T T H|T H
    H H T|T               H H T|T                T H T|T
    H T T|H               H T T|H T              T T T|H T
    T T H|                T T H|T                T H H|T H
                          T H T|T                H T H|H
                          T T T|
```

Fig. 2.10.

32 THINKING WITH THE TEACHABLE MACHINE

Now I copied the new context H H T from the 2nd, 3rd and 4th positions of the first line to the 1st, 2nd and 3rd positions of the second line. See (b) of Fig. 2.10. Phil pushed and obtained another tail, so T was written in the 4th position of line 2. See (c). The HTT of columns 2, 3 and 4 of line 2 are copied into line 3. See (d). The next push gave a head, hence (e) of Fig. 2.10.

Phil's next push of the button (the seventh event) was a tail and by then the pad looked as in (f) of Fig. 2.10. When the 8th event was a T, the new context H T T was already in line 3 so we could say that PUSS predicted H, a head. This was wrong because the 9th event was a T, so the alternative prediction T was written in position 5 of line 3 as in (g) of Fig. 2.10. Now the most recent context is T T T from the 2nd, 3rd and 5th positions of line 3 and this is copied into the first 3 positions of line 6 as in (h) of Fig. 2.10.

The 10th, 11th and 12th events were H, H and T. The prediction was T, but the 13th event was H. No prediction right yet and the situation is shown in (i) of Fig. 2.10. Every possible context has occurred, since there are only eight ways in which heads or tails can be placed in a context of 3 events.

The next eight events were H H H H T T T T. All predictions had been ambiguous or wrong! The pad of the kit set now looked like (j) of Fig. 2.10 so it seemed only a matter of time before PUSS would be predicting head-or-tail for all contexts. Phil was beginning to lose interest, but we agreed to go on until each context was predicting head-or-tail.

The 34th event made the context T H T as in line 5 so the prediction was T and the next push gave a tail. The 43rd event made the context H T H as in line 8 so the prediction was H and the next push gave a head! The 47th event was predicted correctly as a head.

Button-push	1000				1005					1010		
Event	H	H	T	H	H	H	H	H	T	T	T	T
Prediction	H	H/T	H/T	H	H/T	H/T	H	H/T	H/T	H/T	H/T	H/T

Button-push			1015				1020					1025
Event	T	H	T	T	T	H	H	H	H	T	H	H
Prediction	H/T	H/T	T	H/T	H/T	H	H/T	H/T	H/T	H/T	H	H/T

Button-push					1030					1035		
Event	H	T	T	T	H	H	T	T	T	H	H	T
Prediction	H/T	T	H/T	H/T	H/T	H/T	H/T	T	H/T	H/T	H/T	H/T

Fig. 2.11. PUSS predictions of heads and tails.

It wasn't much, but it was enough. The next day I managed to get on the computer and ran a longer sequence through a PUSS with a window of 6 events. As PUSS received more and more of the behaviour of the coin-tossing machine, its predictions took on the semblance of a pattern. Fig. 2.11 shows what they looked like from the 1000th button-push. A single prediction of H or T was always a multiple of 3 pushes from the previous single prediction. The "penny" dropped. I listed the events in threes

(Fig. 2.12). In each case, the first two events of a triple were the same. The coin-tossing machine was giving a repeat followed by two random patterns. No wonder it was difficult to spot.

Phil bought the machine and had the repeat step removed. I have heard no more from him, so doubtless he is profitting.

```
H H T    H H T
H H H    H H H
H H H    H H H
T T T    T T H
T T H    T T H
T T T    T T T
H H H    H H H
H H T    H H T
H H H    H H H
T T T    T T T
H H T    H H T
T T H    T T H
H H T    H H T
```

Fig. 2.12.

The kit set used for this example employed the storage process which we first met in Fig. 2.2. The example shows that a PUSS can sometimes extract regular behaviour (the repeating of heads and tails by the coin-tossing machine) even when it is mixed with randomness.

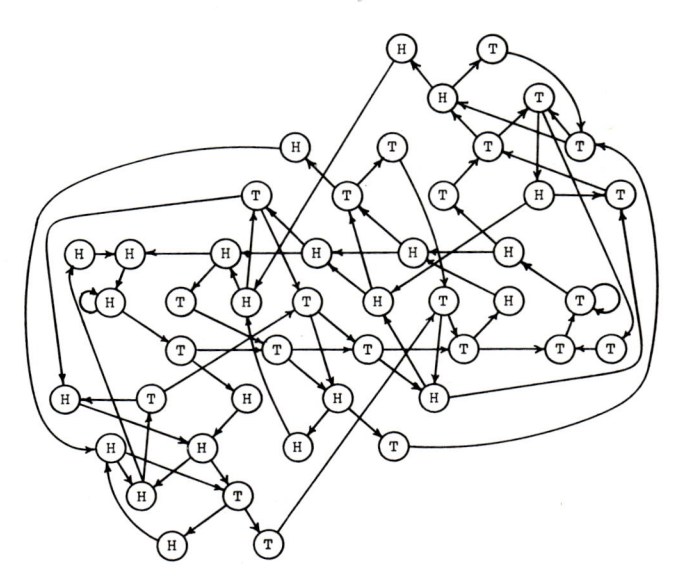

Fig. 2.13. PUSS net for coin-tossing machine. Context in window is 6 events.

34   THINKING WITH THE TEACHABLE MACHINE

The example can also be used to show the effect of increasing window length. The PUSS with a window of length 3 had only 8 contexts, which means that the PUSS net corresponding to (j) of Fig. 2.10 would have only 8 nodes. It is an easy exercise to draw this net. Not so easy to draw is the 46-node PUSS net shown in Fig. 2.13 for the PUSS with a window of length 6. It would not have been easy to deduce what was wrong with the coin-tossing machine by looking at this net.

In general, one PUSS on its own is a very limited predictor useful only for a few problems appropriate to its window length. By having several PUSSes operating together, we achieve a multiple context which is so much more powerful than its constituent fixed contexts as to recall Robert Browning's famous words in Abt Vogler:—

And I know not if, save in this, such gift be allowed to man,
That out of three sounds he frame, not a fourth sound, but a star.

Multiple contexts are discussed in the next chapter.

Example 4. A Simple Teachable Machine.

To turn a single PUSS predictor into a teachable machine, we must give it a decision strategy for choosing actions. Suppose we give it the following mechanism:—

(1) If a single action is predicted, do it.
(2) If more than one action is predicted, choose one of the predicted actions at random and do it.
(3) If no action is predicted, Teacher provides an action.
(4) If Teacher presses the "disapproval button" after an action has been chosen, then the stored prediction corresponding to that action is deleted from memory.

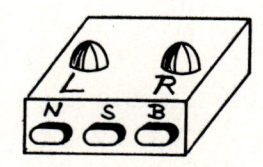

Fig. 2.14. The counting problem.

Now let us teach this "ONE–PUSS" machine the counting problem[13] embodied in the box shown in Fig. 2.14. The box has two lights (L and R) and three buttons (N, S and B). The left light (L) is not affected by button B, but button N causes it to come ON or go OFF at random. The aim of the game is to make the light R (think of it as "reward") flash ON as often as possible. Now, the light R flashes ON only after the button S is pressed and, then, only if the following conditions have been met:

S is pressed; light L will be OFF.
N is pressed as many times as is needed to bring light L ON.
B is pressed the *same number* of times. Light L stays ON.
S is pressed; light R now flashes ON (it doesn't stay ON); light L is OFF.

Each time that ONE–PUSS selects a button (or Teacher selects one for it) and the lights are seen, an event comprising the selected button (N, S or B) and the seen light (L or R) is fed into the PUSS memory. Each event will be written as an equals sign " = ", followed by N, S or B for the button and then L or R or nothing for the lights. Thus, " =NL" means the event comprising a push of button N followed by the left light L being ON. "=B" would mean a push of button B followed by both lights being OFF.

In the following teaching session, events in which the Teacher pushed the button will be written with an underline. This does not mean that the events are stored any differently from those in which ONE–PUSS pushes the button. We assume that the PUSS has a window of 3 events.

For the first four steps, there is nothing in the memory and so no predictions can be made and so Teacher has to push the button each time:

step:	1	2	3	4
event:	=S	=N	=N	=NL

The event =NL is stored in the PUSS memory with context " =S =N =N ". Teacher now pushes buttom B three times to match the three times button N was pushed before the light L came ON:

step:	1	2	3	4	5	6	7
event:	=S	=N	=N	=NL	=BL	=BL	=BL

No context has been repeated so no prediction has been made and ONE-PUSS has taken no action. Teacher now pushes button S and the reward light R flashes ON. Teacher starts pushing button N again, but this time five pushes are required to bring light L ON:

step:	1	2	3	4	5	6	7
event:	=S	=N	=N	=NL	=BL	=BL	=BL
	8	9	10	11	12	13	
	=SR	=N	=N	=N	=N	=NL	

36 THINKING WITH THE TEACHABLE MACHINE

At last, ONE-PUSS can make a prediction since the context occurred before on steps 2, 3 and 4. Therefore, ONE–PUSS selects the action B from the predicted event =BL (it was stored in memory when event =BL occurred on step 5). ONE–PUSS selects the action B three times (instead of five) because of its predictions and so when it selects button S the reward light does not flash on. The whole sequence is shown in Fig. 2.15.

step	event	step	event
1	=S	10	=N
2	=N	11	=N
3	=N	12	=N
4	=NL	13	=NL
5	=BL	14	=BL
6	=BL	15	=BL
7	=BL	16	=BL
8	=SR	17	=S
9	=N		

Fig. 2.15.

The reader is advised to check the steps carefully so as to follow the way the predictions determine the actions selected by ONE–PUSS.

It is quite clear that ONE-PUSS cannot learn the task of pushing button B the same number of times as button N when taught in this way. With the same context in the window of its single PUSS it is required to do different actions: on step 8 it was right to push button S, but on step 17 with the same context " =BL =BL =BL " in the window the right button to push was B. If ONE–PUSS is to be taught this task, it must be given additional actions which it can make quite separately from the actions on the box. We shall give ONE–PUSS "speech" actions.

Speech actions will be words and these words will be "echoed" in the patterns that follow the actions. Thus, if the action is "START", the next pattern to ONE-PUSS will also be "START" and the event comprising the action and pattern will be written "START". (This is less clumsy than writing "START START" for the action folowed by the echo pattern.)

With speech added to its repertoire, ONE–PUSS can be taught the counting problem quite easily. Fig. 2.16 shows the same sequence of button and light events as before but with speech inserted to produce unambiguous contexts. The speech distinguishes the first, second, third, ... button pushes so that the context in the window is sufficient to determine what should be done.

THE BASIC MECHANISM: PUSS   37

Step	Event	Context → Prediction (added to memory)
1	=S	–
2	=N	–
3	ONE	–
4	=N	=S =N ONE → =N
5	TWO	=N ONE =N → TWO
6	=NL	ONE =N TWO → =NL
7	THREE	=N TWO =NL → THREE
8	=BL	TWO =NL THREE → =BL
9	THREE	=NL THREE =BL → THREE
10	=BL	THREE =BL THREE → =BL
11	TWO	=BL THREE =BL → TWO
12	=BL	THREE =BL TWO → =BL
13	ONE	=BL TWO =BL → ONE
14	=SR	TWO =BL ONE → =SR
15	=N	=BL ONE =SR → =N
16	ONE	ONE =SR =N → ONE
17	=N	=SR =N ONE → =N
18	TWO	–
19	=N	ONE =N TWO → =N
20	THREE	=N TWO =N → THREE
21	=N	TWO =N THREE → =N
22	FOUR	=N THREE =N → FOUR
23	=NL	THREE =N FOUR → =NL
24	FIVE	=N FOUR =NL → FIVE
25	=BL	FOUR =NL FIVE → =BL
26	FIVE	=NL FIVE =BL → FIVE
27	=BL	FIVE =BL FIVE → =BL
28	FOUR	=BL FIVE =BL → FOUR
29	=BL	FIVE =BL FOUR → =BL
30	THREE	=BL FOUR =BL → THREE
31	=BL	FOUR =BL THREE → =BL
32	TWO	
33	=BL	
34	ONE	
35	=SR	
..	...	

Fig. 2.16. Counting with speech

ONE–PUSS is not only an example of the operation of a single PUSS, but it is preparation for the more interesting PURR–PUSS. The reader is urged to understand this example by attempting the following exercises:—

(1) ONE–PUSS chooses the action on steps 18, 19, 32, 33, 34 and 35. Explain why in each case. Who will push the button on step 36?

(2) Teacher selects the action on steps 17 and 20. Explain why ONE–PUSS was not able to choose these actions.

(3) There is an addition to memory when Teacher selects an action, but only sometimes when ONE–PUSS selects an action. Why?

(4) If Teacher gives the wrong action, what should he do? Explain with an illustration.

(5) The reader is urged to continue the teaching session of Fig. 2.16. Whenever button N is pushed by ONE–PUSS or by Teacher, toss a coin and make the next event =N if heads come up and =NL if tails come up. ONE–PUSS will soon be selecting the actions most of the time.

(6) Draw a PUSS net for the memory after step 35 in Fig. 2.16 or, better still, for the memory after completing exercise 5.

(7) The PUSS memory in ONE–PUSS can never store more than one predicted action per context. Explain why this is so.

38 THINKING WITH THE TEACHABLE MACHINE

(8) ONE–PUSS is strictly deterministic. In other words, it cannot be taught alternative decisions. Justify this statement.

*Example 5. Variety of PUSS Structures.**

We have already met three ways of representing a PUSS: the mew, the net, and the context-prediction table of Figs 2.2 and 2.10. In this example, I shall take the specific memory shown as a PUSS net in Fig. 2.13 (heads and tails) and describe several different ways of storing the same information.

Trace Method[14]

Each context and prediction is treated as a separate string of events of length window-plus-one and is stored individually. Recall that any sequence of events in a PUSS net one event longer than the window corresponds to a unique connection in the net. Such a sequence is called a "trace" and comprises a context and prediction. For the PUSS net of Fig. 2.13, 7-event traces are stored by this method. Although the method is quite uneconomical in its use of memory, it is a very useful way of thinking about PUSS memory. It can be seen from the table of traces for Fig. 2.13 given in Fig. 2.17 that the memory needed in this case is the number of traces (=74) multiplied by the window length plus one (=7) "bits" of storage. (A bit, or binary digit, is the smallest element of computer memory and allows the storage of a single alternative, like H or T.) Altogether, the memory takes 74 × 7 =518 bits.

HHHHHHH	HHTHHHH	HTHHTTT	THHHHTT	TTHHHHT	TTTHTTH
HHHHHHT	HHTHHHT	HTTHHHH	THHHTHH	TTHHHTH	TTTHTTT
HHHHHTH	HHTHHTH	HTTHHHT	THHHTTH	TTHHHTT	TTTTHHH
HHHHHTT	HHTHHTT	HTTHHTH	THHHTTT	TTHHTHH	TTTTHHT
HHHHTHH	HHTHHHH	HTTHTTT	THHTHHH	TTHHTTT	TTTTHTT
HHHHTTH	HHTTHTT	HTTTHHH	THHTHHT	TTHTTHH	TTTTTHH
HHHHTTT	HHTTTHH	HTTTHHT	THHTTHH	TTHTTHT	TTTTTHT
HHHTHHH	HHTTTHT	HTTTHTT	THHTTTT	TTHTTTH	TTTTTTH
HHHTHHT	HHTTTTH	HTTTTHH	THTTHHH	TTHTTTT	TTTTTTT
HHHTTHH	HHTTTTT	HTTTTTH	THTTHTT	TTTHHHH	
HHHTTHT	HTHHHHH	HTTTTTT	THTTTHH	TTTHHHT	
HHHTTTH	HTHHHTT	THHHHHH	THTTTTT	TTTHHTH	
HHHTTTT	HTHHTHH	THHHHHT	TTHHHHH	TTTHHTT	

Fig. 2.17. Traces.

Context and Prediction Method

This is the method of Figs 2.2 and 2.10. There are many ways of storing contexts and predictions so that less memory is used than if all traces are stored separately. For the case of Fig. 2.13, we can store a context (6 events or 6 bits) and the maximum of two predictions (2 events or 2 bits) in 8 bits of storage. There are 46 different contexts, so 46 × 8 = 368 bits of storage are needed.

* This example is a little technical.

THE BASIC MECHANISM: PUSS

The memory of contexts and predictions can be derived directly from the traces in Fig. 2.17 and it is shown in Fig. 2.18.

Notice that if there had been fewer than 7 contexts with both predictions, H and T, the trace method of Fig. 2.17 would have taken up less storage space than the context and prediction method of Fig. 2.18.

```
HHHHHH·HT    HHTHHT·HT    HTHHTT·T     THHHHT·T     THTTTT·T     TTTHHT·HT
HHHHHT·HT    HHTTHH·H     HTTHHH·HT    THHHTH·H     TTHHHH·HT    TTTHTT·HT
HHHHTH·H     HHTTHT·T     HTTHTT·HT    THHHHT·HT    TTHHHT·HT    TTTTHH·HT
HHHHTT·HT    HHTTTH·HT    HTTTHH·HT    THHTHH·HT    TTHHTH·H     TTTTHT·T
HHHTHH·HT    HHTTTT·HT    HTTTHT·T     THHTTT·HT    TTHHTT·T     TTTTTH·HT
HHHTTH·HT    HTHHHH·H     HTTTTH·H     THTTHH·H     TTHTTH·HT    TTTTTT·HT
HHHTTT·HT    HTHHHT·T     HTTTTT·HT    THTTHT·T     TTHTTT·HT
HHTHHH·HT    HTHHTH·H     THHHHH·HT    THTTTH·H     TTTHHH·HT
```

Fig. 2.18. Contexts and predictions

Event and Transition Method (PUSS Net)

When a context (e.g. HHTTTH) has a prediction (e.g. T), then a trace comprising context and prediction (e.g. HHTTTHT) is implied. Also a context to context transition (e.g. HHTTTH→HTTTHT) is implied, as illustrated in Fig. 2.19.

```
                    trace:   H H T T T H T
context·prediction:          H H T T T H·T

context→context
     transition:   H H T T T H
                              H T T T H T
```

Fig. 2.19.

This third way of looking at the information in a PUSS memory allows us to store the memory as a list of events (the head events, or most recent events, of the contexts) and a list of transitions (which context, or node of the PUSS net, is connected to which). If the nodes in Fig. 2.13 are numbered from left to right of the top row, the next row and on to the bottom row, the lists of events and transitions will be as in Fig. 2.20.

Now, if we work out how much storage is required for the lists of Fig. 2.20, it comes out as nearly 1000 bits which is much more than the 518 bits for Fig. 2.17 and the 368 bits for Fig. 2.18. However, this is mainly due to unusual features of the example we have taken (there are only two events, H and T, and a large proportion of the possible contexts actually occur) and usually the event and transition method will work out to be more economical than the first two.

40 THINKING WITH THE TEACHABLE MACHINE

List of Events		Context to Context Transitions			
1) H	24) H	1→22	16→21	29→30	43→35
2) T	25) T	2→8	17→9	29→37	44→45
3) H	26) H	3→1	17→16	30→31	44→46
4) T	27) T	3→2	18→10	30→38	45→39
5) H	28) T	4→12	18→17	31→26	46→25
6) T	29) T	4→33	19→11	31→32	
7) T	30) T	5→39	19→18	32→27	
8) T	31) T	6→25	20→20	33→32	
9) T	32) T	7→3	20→28	34→40	
10) T	33) T	7→4	21→29	35→23	
11) T	34) H	8→3	22→9	35→34	
12) H	35) T	8→4	22→16	36→40	
13) T	36) H	9→23	23→30	37→41	
14) H	37) H	9→34	23→37	37→42	
15) H	38) H	10→5	24→10	38→13	
16) H	39) H	10→6	24→17	38→24	
17) H	40) H	11→7	25→31	39→43	
18) H	41) H	12→13	25→38	39→44	
19) H	42) T	12→24	26→18	40→43	
20) H	43) H	13→7	27→19	40→44	
21) T	44) T	14→15	27→27	41→22	
22) H	45) H	15→20	28→29	42→8	
23) T	46) T	16→15	28→36	43→14	

Fig. 2.20. Events and transitions

Event and Flag Method (Cleary)[15]

A neat method of storing a PUSS memory is illustrated by the sequence of events in Fig. 2.21, which corresponds to a path through the net of Fig. 2.13 starting with the top left node.

HHTHHHTTHHHHHHHTHHTHHHHHHTTHTTTHHTTTHTTTTTTTHTTHTT

HHHTHHHTHHTTTTTHHTHHTTTTHHHHTTTHHHTTTTTTHTTTHT

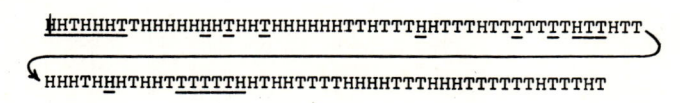

Fig. 2.21.

The whole memory is a list of events, each of which can be underlined or not (the underlining is the "flag"). Every new event as it enters memory adds a head event to the trace formed by it and the last 6 events. If any other event in memory heads the same trace, that event is underlined. If 7 events in succession are underlined, the oldest one of the seven is deleted and memory is shifted up to close the gap. In the sequence above only the first event of the whole sequence had to be deleted. Since one bit is required to store the event (H or T) and one bit is required to store the flag (underlined or not), the 96 events of the sequence (which includes all transitions in the net) uses only 2 × 96 = 192 bits. This is much less than for the previous methods but is mainly due to the fact that the example strongly favours this method. When events are more numerous and a smaller fraction of traces occur, the event and flag method turns out to be no better than the event and transition method.

THE BASIC MECHANISM: PUSS   41

Tree Method (Cleary)[16]

When a PUSS memory is stored by any of the first four methods, the finding of a context or trace involves a long search through memory. The tree method avoids this long search by arranging for all events that can occur as the first event of a context to be on a "first-event-list" joined to the root of the tree. In Fig. 2.22, the horizontal first-event-list from the root has H and T, only, on it because these are the only events that can begin a context.

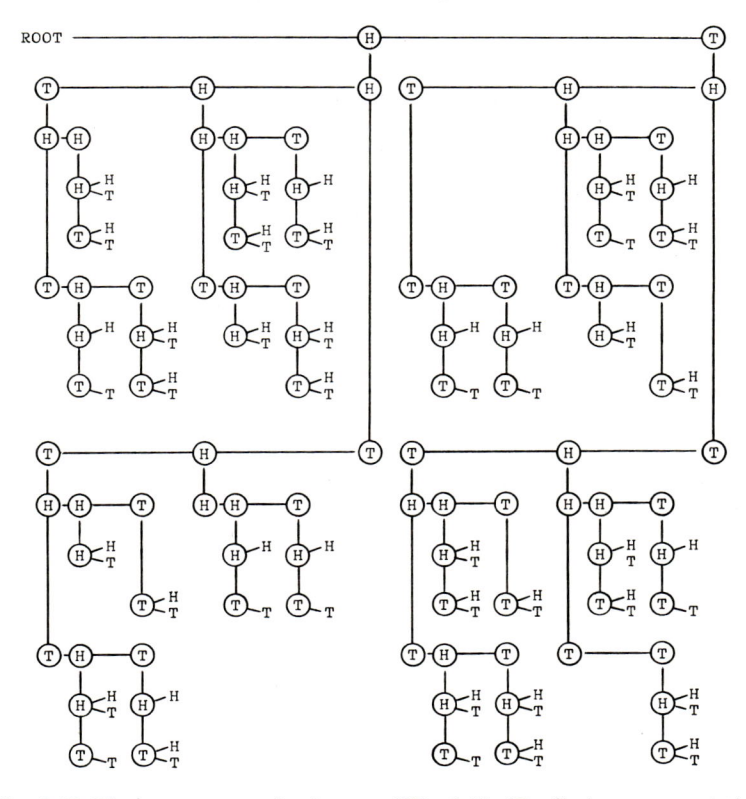

Fig. 2.22. The tree memory for the net of Fig. 2.13. (Predictions are uncircled.)

Each event of the first-event-list is joined to a second-event-list which has all events that can be second in a context for that first event. Each event on a second-event-list starts a third-event-list, and so on. Each event on the sixth-event-lists represents a complete context and it is connected to the predictions for that context (uncircled in Fig. 2.22).

Each context and its predictions can be reached from the root by searching the first-event-list for the first event, the appropriate second-event-list for the

42   THINKING WITH THE TEACHABLE MACHINE

second event, the appropriate third-event-list for the third event, ... the appropriate sixth-event-list for the last event of the context.

In the present case, where there are only two events (H and T) on each list, the tree method is very efficient. If there are many possible events and the lists become long, then this method will become inferior to the mew-gram method described earlier in the chapter. Indeed, it is worth giving the mew-gram method again here because of the special features of the coin-tossing problem.

The Mew-gram Method

The essential idea behind the mew-gram method is that the context determines where its predictions will be stored. In the PUSS memory of Fig. 2.13, this can be done in a particularly simple way. Code the context into an address by replacing H by 0 and T by 1. The result is treated as a binary number and can be turned into its decimal equivalent (000000 = 0, 000001 = 1, 000010 = 2, etc.). There will be 64 (=2^6) possible addresses and for each context we shall need 2 bits of storage for the possible predictions H and T. The total memory required by the mew-gram is 64 × 2 = 128 bits, the least of all the methods. The mew-gram of Fig. 2.23 is obtained directly from Fig. 2.18 by using the contexts as addresses as explained above.

0	HT	8	HT	16	H	24	HT	32	HT	40	–	48	HT	56	HT
	HT		HT		T		–		T		–		HT		HT
	H		–		H		–		H		–		H		–
	HT		–		T		HT		HT		–		T		HT
	HT		H		–		HT		HT		H		–		HT
	–		T		–		T		–		T		–		T
	HT		HT		–		H		–		H		HT		HT
	HT		HT		–		HT		HT		T		HT		HT

Fig. 2.23. The mew-gram method for Fig. 2.13.

Each of the above six methods of representing a PUSS memory throws a different light on the nature of PUSS[17]. The trace method emphasises the important feature of a PUSS that it is a *collection of separate elements* and the elements are traces. The context and prediction method explains the use of a PUSS for prediction. The event and transition method is the basis of the PUSS net and applies only to sequential contexts. The event and flag method is an interesting linear equivalent of the PUSS net for sequential contexts. The tree method recognizes the cause of the slow operation of the previous methods as being the finding of contexts in memory by exhaustive searching. It is the most elegant of all the methods and was the first to show that we could use PUSS memories of unlimited size at reasonable speeds. However, with the mew-gram came the realization that contexts need not be found at all if one could go straight to the predictions from a given context.

Notes on Chapter 2

1. Early versions of PUSS employed a variable length window mechanism that was economical and efficient in deterministic environments (see UC-DSE/5, page 72). The present PUSS with fixed window length is simpler than the variable one and it learns faster in non-deterministic environments. The mew memory cannot be used with PUSSes having variable length windows. Since real environments are hardly ever deterministic, all the advantages are with the fixed length window.

2. Division by a prime number and use of the remainder as an address is a form of "hashing" (Knuth, 1973). We store the connection between the context and the event without having to store the context. The disadvantage of this forward hashing method is that we cannot move backwards through memory. All processing must be done by predicting forwards. Backward processing was made use of in the earlier PUSS net memories (UC-DSE/6; Andreae and Cleary, 1976), but this would be too slow for large memories and serial computation, even if hashing were done in the backward direction as well.

3. The coding of an event into a number is more elaborate in practice because events are not usually as simple as single letters. In the programs used for this book, each different event that occurs is assigned a different number and it is these numbers that are concatenated to give the number that is divided by the primes. Recently, we have transferred this process of coding events into numbers to the mew memory. That is, the character strings are hashed into addresses and the addresses are used to represent the strings. Because we have to be able to get back to the character strings from the addresses, the strings are stored at the addressed locations.

4. The advantages of ascribing an holographic memory to the brain have been discussed by Van Heerden (1963), Pribram (1969a), Willshaw *et al.* (1969), and Arbib (1972). The mew-gram is holographic in two senses. First, the storage and retrieval of information is effected by means of a reference, which is the context. Secondly, storage of information is spread over the whole memory area so that damage to one area need not prevent retrieval of the lost information from other areas. I have hypothesised in UC-DSE/7 that a neural network could be based on the mew-gram such that the pseudorandom addressing (hashing) in the mew corresponded to genetically-controlled neuron-to-neuron connections in the network. A tentative neural network organization was described there, but Mew-Brain, described in the Appendix, is much more complete.

5. Terabit (10^{12} bit) memories are already in use (Wildmann, 1975) with disc storage not essentially different from the million times smaller memory used at present for PURR-PUSS. With the simple addressing requirements of the mew-gram, a terabit memory with the same access time as our small fixed-head disc (about 20

milliseconds) is within the state of the art. Cost and justification are another matter! It is interesting to note that if the brain has a terabit memory (100 bits per neuron), computer memories are within a factor of ten of the brain in access time (taking the access time of the brain to be 2 milliseconds from the speed of travel of a nerve impulse), but are probably not within a million of the brain in physical size.

6. John Cleary suggested that several PUSSes should use the same mew-gram. He has analysed the mew mathematically in UC-DSE/7.

7. Miller, Galanter and Pribram (1960) discussed the relationship between recall and prediction in an interesting way (p. 173): "Is there an alternative to the search paradigm of thinking? Of course, there are several. For example, instead of discussing every problem as a search for an object, or a concept, or a Plan, we might just as well have discussed them as attempts to *predict* what is going to happen. . . . The prediction paradigm for thinking and problem-solving tends to direct our attention more to the Image than to the Plan, . . . " PURR-PUSS uses the prediction paradigm.

8. The first version of the mew-gram was probabilistic and new events were allowed to replace stored events in memory (UC-DSE/7). Such a probabilistic procedure would be particularly appropriate in biological systems where the memory "hardware" is likely to be unreliable. The storage procedure used for the results in this book is simpler in that it involves no displacement of already stored events. At the time of writing, the storage procedure has been changed again (i) to make it faster and (ii) to prevent the mew memory from becoming overloaded. The first is achieved by storing each event from a context once only, but storing with it two additional remainders. The second is achieved by allowing new events with a given context to displace the oldest events with that context when there is insufficient room for both. The latter has been programmed by Alex Palfi.

9. Four features of a mew memory suggest a biological equivalent. The holographic nature of the hashing (especially the probabilistic version) would provide reliable operation from unreliable biological "hardware". Genetically-determined neuron growth could do the same job as the pre-determined hash addresses. The alternative destinations offered by the several prime numbers in the hashing process could be carried out by synaptic connections in a neural network. Finally, the particulate and independent collection of PUSS productions suggests a "pool" of RNA molecules in a group of cells or in the blood stream. Could a neuron-synapse network be instrumental in coding and decoding context-to-event sequences into and from RNA molecules? Neurobiologists (e.g. Hydén, 1970) have already made suggestions like these, but without our working memory system as a guide. Mew-Brain, described in the Appendix, is a first attempt to draw some of these ideas together into a coherent and practical system.

We can speculate on how a biological mew might evolve from a small memory with specific neuron connections (for the responses, say, of a primitive animal) to a large memory with unspecific connections. The initial increase in numbers of connections could be favoured because of the additional reliability that they would give to a species entirely dependent on its pre-determined responses. However, these redundant connections could then give additional benefits of extra flexibility and adaptation to new responses. As the process continued and the mew grew in size, the flexibility of the evolved connections would begin to dominate in importance over the specificity of the original connections.

10. Newell and Simon (1972), summing up their work on the human information

processing system (IPS) say (p. 866): "The human IPS must grow itself to its adult normal state, starting from a primitive neonatal state that is not yet well understood. . . . and we have made the rather strong proposal that all increments of knowledge are cast in the form of productions. But we have not examined the acquisition process, and the acquisition mechanisms for productions that have been proposed (for example, Waterman's (1970) learning production system for poker) are not specific enough to answer the important psychological questions about the process." My strong proposal is that the productions must be simplified to the form of several PUSS memories, each of which *is* a production system, for the acquisition process to satisfy psychological requirements. Further, I see the work of Newell and Simon on adult problem-solving as providing a most important guide for establishing the acquisition process through teaching. In particular, we can attempt to acquire the more sophisticated (but well-defined) productions listed by them from the simpler PUSS productions. See the recent paper by Hedrick (1976).

11. The results used in this example first appeared in UC-DSE/5, page 86.

12. Bill and Ben first appeared in UC-DSE/4, section A.3.1, with an earlier version of PUSS using slide and strings. The example has been used recently by Gaines (1976b) to illustrate the operation of his "ATOM" algorithms. His paper is a good starting point for the reader interested in PUSS-like and more sophisticated string predictors, grammatical inference and behaviour-to-structure transformations.

13. This counting problem was first proposed as a problem for a PUSS in UC-DSE/2 (p. 89). Then in UC-DSE/3 (pp. 35-37) some unconvincing results were given. It was not until UC-DSE/4 (p. 117) that the "solution" with echo speech was presented. The problem is a standard one in automata theory for distinguishing finite state systems from context-free systems (e.g. Manna, 1974). Of course, any real system, like PUSS, will be finite state and therefore be unable to solve the counting problem for *any* number of button N pushes in a row. As with the infinite tapes and pushdown stores of automata theory, we are using the sequence of spoken numbers (ONE, TWO, THREE, . .) as a potentially infinite structure. We may note here that ONE-PUSS would be an excellent pupil for learning to behave like a Turing machine. If taught like PURR-PUSS in Andreae and Cleary (1976) or UC-DSE/6, ONE-PUSS would be obedient and continue to do as instructed for as long as Teacher wished. This would not be the case for PURR-PUSS, who gets bored easily!

14. John Cleary introduced the concept of a trace in his article in UC-DSE/5.

15. The event and flag method was devised by John Cleary and first reported under the name "Simple" in UC-DSE/5.

16. The tree structure was first reported in UC-DSE/5 by John Cleary who devised the method and named it Tree Felix. He suggested the use of hash coding for speeding up the tree search.

17. What are the memory sizes needed for the six different methods of representing a PUSS? Even knowing the ratio R of the number T of traces to the number C of contexts (i.e. $R = T/C$) and knowing the number E of different events which might occur, meaningful estimates of memory requirements are difficult to obtain. John Cleary has calculated memory requirements in his articles in UC-DSE/5 and UC-DSE/7. The results are not straightforward, but, assuming a window length W, the memory size M for each case is *roughly* as follows:—

trace method:
$$M = T(W+1)\log_2 E \text{ bits}$$
context and prediction:
$$M = CW.\log_2 E + T(\log_2 C + \log_2 E) \text{ bits}$$
event and transition:
$$M = C.\log_2 E + 2T.\log_2 C \text{ bits}$$
event and flag;
$$1.5T.\log_2 E < M < 3T.\log_2 E \text{ bits}$$
tree structure;
$$M = (T+C)\log_2 E \text{ bits}$$
mew-gram:
$$M = T.\log_2 E \text{ bits}$$

Note. $\log_2 E$ is the number of bits needed to code the E events and $\log_2 C$ is the number of bits needed to code the C contexts.

3. Multiple Context

We shall meet the Morning Spiders,
The fairy cotton riders,
Each mounted on a star's rejected ray;
With their tiny nets of feather
They collect our thoughts together,
And on strips of windy weather
Bring the Day . . .

> Algernon Blackwood
> "A Prisoner in Fairyland"

Threaded Contexts

A single PUSS provides limited context for an event by means of its window. If, for example, the window is of length 4, the most recent event to be entered into the PUSS memory is associated with the previous 4 events in the window to form a unique sequence in memory.

Suppose now that we have two PUSSes, each with a window of length 2, and that the first of these PUSSes, PUSS–1, receives each event from the sequence a – A – b – c – B – a – C – b – c – A – a – B – b – c – C – a – A – b – c –. By the end of the sequence the PUSS–1 net would appear as in Fig. 3.1 (a). It can be seen that PUSS–1 is predicting "A or B or C" from the last context (b–c).

The second PUSS, PUSS–2, receives only the "capital" events so its sequence is A – B – C – A – B – C – A – and its PUSS net in Fig. 3.1 (b) shows a prediction of "B".

At this point in time, then, PUSS–1 has a context of b–c in its window, while PUSS–2 has a context of C–A. Past occurrences of b – c – B, b – c – A and b – c – C recorded in the memory of PUSS–1 (Fig. 3.1 (a)) make it predict "A or B or C". For PUSS–2, the context C – A has been followed in the past only by the event B, so it makes an unambiguous prediction of "B". The "intersection" of the two sets of predictions is the event B. The event B is common to the two predictions. The prediction of PUSS–2 can be said to resolve the ambiguity in the prediction of PUSS–1.

A way of showing a sequence as it appears to two or more PUSSes is by means of "threads". In Fig. 3.1 (c) the sequence used above is re-drawn with a dotted line thread indicating the sequence of events which go to PUSS–2.

48   THINKING WITH THE TEACHABLE MACHINE

Note. Heavier arrows indicate predictions.

(a) PUSS-1 net

(b) PUSS-2 net

a-A-b-c-B-a-C-b-c-A-a-B-b-c-C-a-A-b-c-

(c) Generating sequence with PUSS-2 thread.

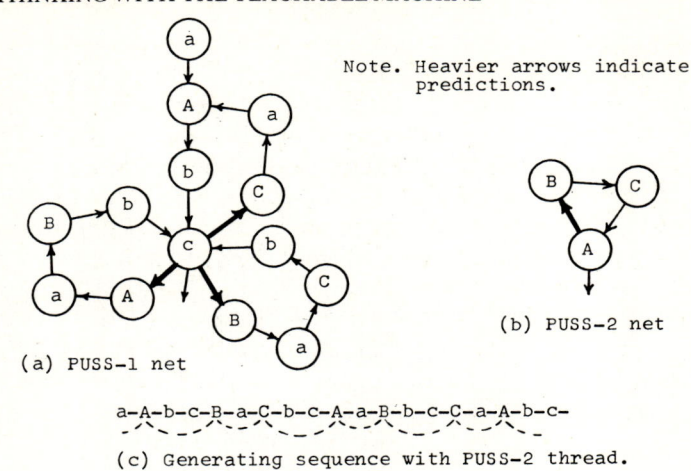

Fig. 3.1.

Continuing from the example illustrated in Fig. 3.1, suppose that the predicted event B happens. The PUSS nets become updated to those shown in Fig. 3.2, from which the predictions can be seen to be "a" from PUSS-1 and "C" from PUSS-2. The intersection of these sets of predictions is empty (i.e. they have no common events). However, in this simple case it is easy to see why the prediction of PUSS-1 is to be preferred. PUSS-1 receives every event

(a) PUSS-1 net

(b) PUSS-2 net

a-A-b-c-B-a-C-b-c-A-a-B-b-c-C-a-A-b-c-B-

(c) Generating sequence with PUSS-2 thread.

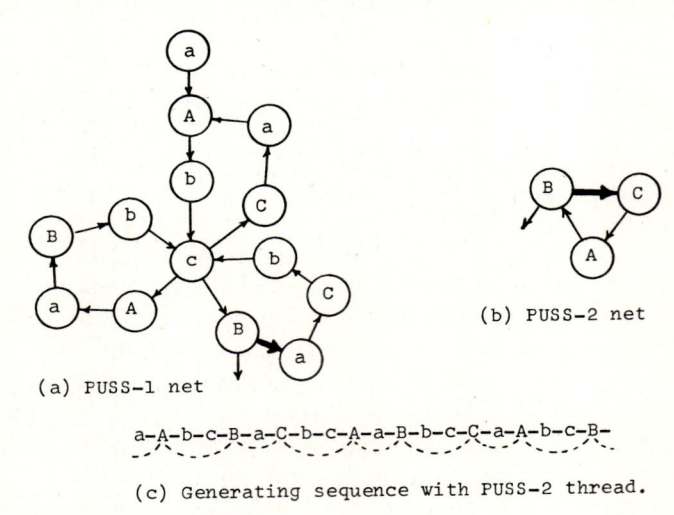

Fig. 3.2.

MULTIPLE CONTEXT 49

and is predicting the next event. PUSS—2, however, receives only the capital events and so it is predicting the next capital event. At the time represented by Fig. 3.1, the next event was predicted to be a capital event by PUSS–1 (but it couldn't predict which capital event) and PUSS–2's prediction of the next capital event removed the ambiguity. At the time represented by Fig. 3.2, a capital event is not expected so PUSS–2 cannot help PUSS–1.

In the above example, the context of PUSS–2 threaded the context of PUSS–1. This was indicated quite simply in the generating sequence of Fig. 3.1 (c). Unfortunately, there does not seem to be any useful way of showing this threading in the PUSS nets of Figs 3.1 (a) and (b). The complexity generated by the threading of contexts is a strength of PURR–PUSS, but, at present, our understanding of her potential is severely limited by the lack of good descriptions of a memory with threaded contexts.

Schedules of Events

A generating sequence may have special features that affect the way it is stored in a PUSS memory. Suppose the generating sequence is: A – B – C – Q – A – B – C – P – A – B – C – P – A – B – C – S – A – B – C – R – A – B – C – Q – A – B – C . . . where every fourth event is one from the set P, Q, R or S, while the three events between are always A – B – C –. Writing down the sequence is a clumsy way of showing what is happening because a very long sequence is needed to establish its features. The same information can be conveyed compactly by the "schedule" of events in Fig. 3.3(a).

(a) Schedule.   (b) PUSS net for window of 2 events.   (c) PUSS net for window of 3 events.

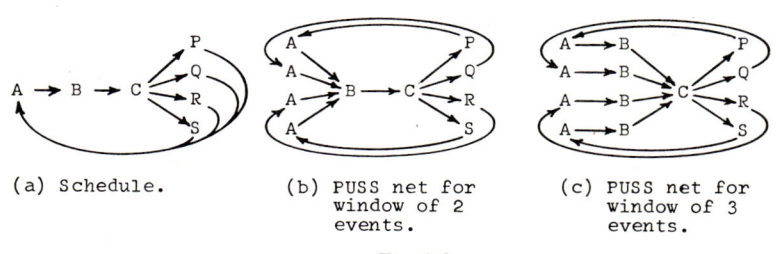

Fig. 3.3.

The schedule of Fig. 3.3(a) happens to be the PUSS net for a window of length 1. This is unusual. The corresponding PUSS nets for PUSSes with windows of length 2 and 3, respectively, are drawn in Figs 3.3(b) and (c). The PUSS net for a window of length 4 is left as an exercise for the reader. Remember that the same window-length context never appears in two parts of a PUSS net without sharing the same final event. These final or "head" events of the contexts are the nodes of the net. Each context has a unique node in the net.

50   THINKING WITH THE TEACHABLE MACHINE

The following is a straightforward way of drawing a PUSS net from a schedule:

Step 1. List all the window-length contexts from the schedule. Fig. 3.4(a) does this for the schedule of Fig. 3.3(a) and a window of length 3 events.

Step 2. Each head event (most recent event) of the contexts is made a node of the net. Head events are underlined in Fig. 3.4(a).

Step 3. Note all the transitions between contexts which are permitted by the schedule. Allowed transitions are indicated by dotted lines in Fig. 3.4(b).

Step 4. Join up the nodes according to the transitions, as in Fig. 3.4(c).

Step 5. Tidy up the net, if necessary. Figure 3.4(c) and Fig. 3.3(c) are the same.

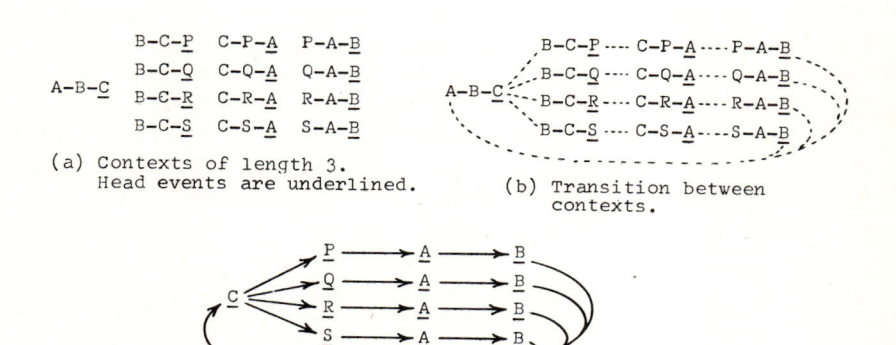

```
                 B-C-P    C-P-A    P-A-B                B-C-P ···· C-P-A ···· P-A-B
                 B-C-Q    C-Q-A    Q-A-B                B-C-Q ···· C-Q-A ···· Q-A-B
         A-B-C   B-C-R    C-R-A    R-A-B        A-B-C   B-C-R ···· C-R-A ···· R-A-B
                 B-C-S    C-S-A    S-A-B                B-C-S ···· C-S-A ···· S-A-B

         (a) Contexts of length 3.
             Head events are underlined.             (b) Transition between
                                                         contexts.
```

(c) PUSS net (same net as Figure 3-3 (c)).

Fig. 3.4. Deriving a PUSS net from the schedule of Fig. 3.3(a) for a window length of 3 events.

Why do we not use schedules instead of PUSS memories? Schedules are more compact and they never contain sequences that cannot occur. However, you can construct a schedule only if you know exactly what is going to happen. If you *do* know what is going to happen then you do not need a learning system with PUSSes. A PUSS copes with any sequence no matter how that sequence varies in the future. It is less compact than a schedule because it has to allow for future additions to its structure. Schedules have been introduced solely for the purpose of explaining the behaviour of PURR–PUSS. They provide a compact way of describing complex, but known, behaviour.

Sparse and Dense Events

In the schedule of Fig. 3.3(a) there is a repetitive cycle of four events, the fourth of which takes several forms, P, Q, R and S. The events A, B and C are called "sparse" events because they only appear in a single form, but the fourth event in the cycle will be referred to as a "dense" event because of its many forms.

Dense events are important because they are usually information-bearing events. However, they are liable to take excessive storage in a PUSS memory. Notice how A – B has to be duplicated in Fig. 3.4(c) in order to represent the contexts P – A – B, Q – A – B, R – A – B and S – A – B. If a window of length 5 were used in deriving a PUSS net from the schedule of Fig. 3.3(a), the resulting net would be much more complex than the net of Fig. 3.4(c) because the dense event would appear in its own context. The PUSS net tends to "blow up" as will be illustrated in a moment.

Sparse events provide a framework for the dense events and can keep the dense events out of each other's contexts. Sparse events play a controlling role. To illustrate how a PUSS net blows up when dense events get in each other's contexts and how sparse events can relieve this situation, we consider the schedule of Fig. 3.5(a).*

With this schedule, even a PUSS with a window of only two events requires

(a) Schedule.

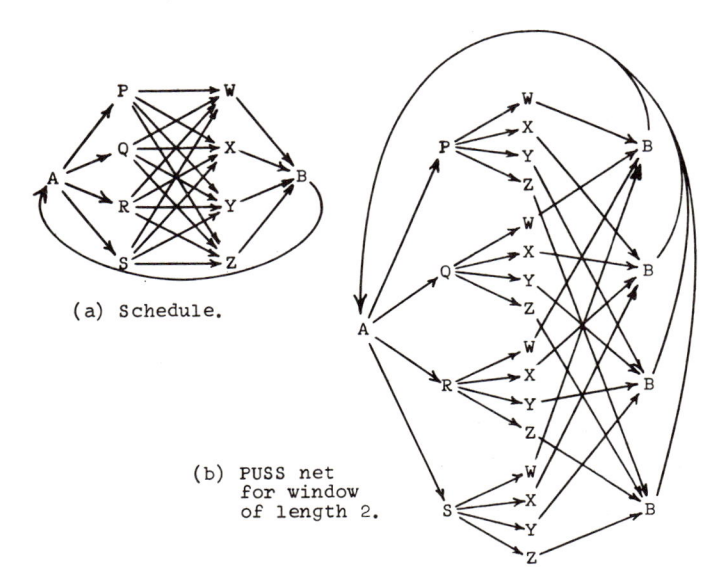

(b) PUSS net for window of length 2.

Fig. 3.5.

*The hurried reader may skip the remainder of this section.

52 THINKING WITH THE TEACHABLE MACHINE

the 25 contexts:

A – P	P – W	Q – W	R – W	S – W	W – B	
A – Q	P – X	Q – X	R – X	S – X	X – B	B – A
A – R	P – Y	Q – Y	R – Y	S – Y	Y – B	
A – S	P – Z	Q – Z	R – Z	S – Z	Z – B .	

The corresponding PUSS net is drawn in Fig. 3.5(b).

From the point of view of a mew memory, the storage requirements of a PUSS net depend only on the total number of events associated with contexts. This number is the number of arrows in the PUSS net, since each arrow (connection) points from a context to an event. The amount of memory needed to store the PUSS net of Fig. 3.5(b) is, therefore, proportional to the number of arrows, which is 40.

Now change the schedule of Fig. 3.5(a) by having a sparse event B between the two dense events, as shown in Fig. 3.6(a). The number of contexts for a window of length 2 drops to 17:

A – P	P – B	B – W	W – C	
A – Q	Q – B	B – X	X – C	C – A
A – R	R – B	B – Y	Y – C	
A – S	S – B	B – Z	Z – C .	

The corresponding PUSS net, which appears in Fig. 3.6(b), has only 32 arrows. Adding the sparse event has reduced the storage requirements by 20 per cent.

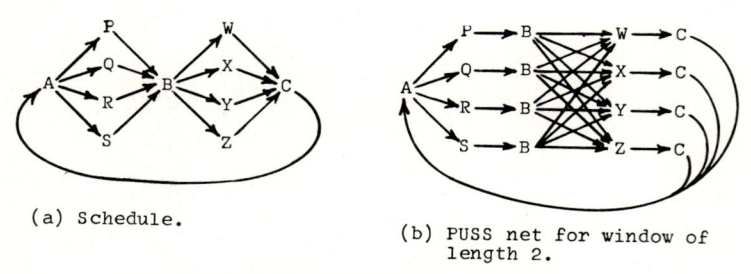

(a) Schedule.

(b) PUSS net for window of length 2.

Fig. 3.6. One sparse event between two dense events.

Two sparse events between the dense events yields a further improvement, as illustrated by Fig. 3.7. The number of contexts increases by one to 18, but the number of arrows falls to 24. When the window is of length 2, the two sparse events effectively separate the dense events.

In the general case we may have windows of length greater than 2, we may have more than two dense events in the one context, and we may have dense events with more than 4 forms. When dense events occur in each other's contexts, the number of arrows depends upon the *product* of their numbers of forms. When out of each other's contexts, the number of arrows depends

(a) Schedule.

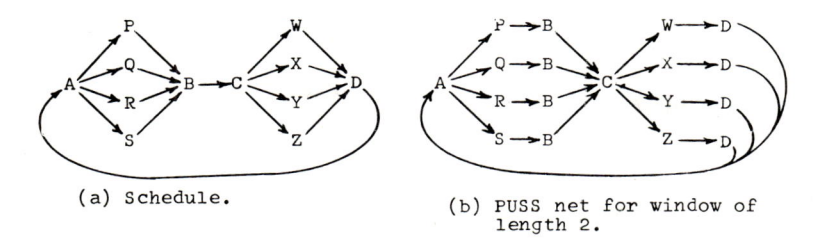

(b) PUSS net for window of length 2.

Fig. 3.7. Two sparse events between two dense events.

upon the *sum* of their numbers of forms. The sum will usually be much smaller than the product, which is why there is such a saving of memory by interposing sparse events between dense events. The saving in learning time may be even more spectacular since each arrow (i.e. each prediction) must occur to be learned.

Parallel Contexts

At this point I should like to be able to present a concise "theory of context" that would lay down what can and what cannot be done.[1] I know of no such theory and so we must be content with the few general ideas that have been learned with PURR–PUSS.

When two or more sequences of context progress in parallel, we can describe the relationships between them.[2] One context threads another if the first comprises only some of the events of the second. Fig. 3.1(c) illustrated a sequence of "upper case events" threading a stream of "upper and lower case events". The former is referred to as a "sequence" because there are gaps of variable time duration between its events. The latter is called a "stream" because its events are assumed to arrive in regular time sequence. The prediction of an event in a stream says "when the next" as well as "what next". In the case of a sequence that is not a stream, a prediction only says "what next".

Two sequences or streams are concurrent if their events occur at the same time. In the two concurrent streams

$$a - A - b - c - B - a - C - b - c - A - a - B - b - c - C - a - \ldots$$

and

$$p - 1 - q - p - 2 - q - 3 - p - q - 2 - p - 1 - q - p - 2 - q - \ldots$$

the threaded sequences $A - B - C - A - B - C - \ldots$ and $1 - 2 - 3 - 2 - 1 - 2 - \ldots$ are concurrent.

One sequence or stream is coupled to a second sequence or stream if some events in the first can be derived from simultaneous or earlier events in the second, or vice-versa. If a stream has a dense event, then by coupling to a

54 THINKING WITH THE TEACHABLE MACHINE

second stream before the dense event and coupling back after the event, it is possible to predict events just past the dense event. This kind of situation will be illustrated and explained more readily when we are discussing specific behaviours of PURR–PUSS in later chapters.

Two streams or sequences of events interleave if the events of one occur at times between the times at which the events of the other occur. We may combine two streams or sequences into a single stream or sequence of composite events.

Some features of parallel contexts are pictured in Fig. 3.8. Many other ways of combining, dividing, merging, coupling and interleaving of sequences and streams are possible.[3]

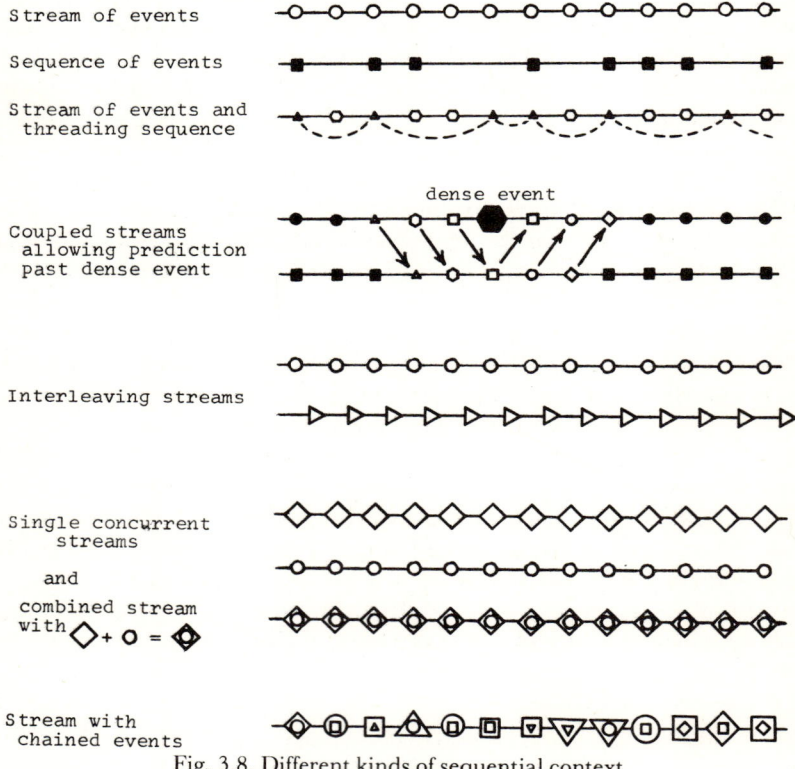

Fig. 3.8. Different kinds of sequential context.

The events of a context need not be in time sequence since they could represent a spatial context.[4] Events in one part of a visual space could be acting as context for events in another part of that space. This great potential variety in the kind of information that can be stored in a mew-gram is understandable if the mew is seen as an associative memory of quite general form.[5]

Examples of Contexts[*]

The interaction between Teacher and PURR–PUSS described in detail in Chapters 6 and 7 was carried out at a particular stage of the development of PURR–PUSS. The research was "frozen" for 3 months to allow the whole system to be recorded precisely and the frozen system is described in Chapters 4 and 5. Here, at a much more superficial and intuitive level, some of the ideas suggested by a multiple context will be illustrated by a variety of teaching examples. Details will be omitted because some of the examples were not taken from the "frozen" period and I do not wish to confuse the reader with minor variants of the PURR–PUSS program.

Example 1. Raising Fingers for an Object

PURR–PUSS says "ANY MORE OBJECTS". Teacher says "YES". PURR–PUSS says "OBJECT PLEASE". Teacher types in object "<FISH>". PURR–PUSS has never "seen" this object before, but because it does not disturb the speech context she is able to carry on saying "RAISE FINGER FOR OBJECT". The detailed mechanics of this interaction are discussed in Chapter 6, but here we just notice how the speech context can carry on past the non-speech object just because the object is not part of the speech context. This is indicated in Fig. 3.9.

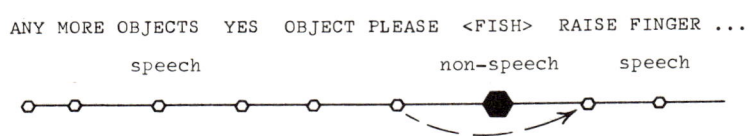

Fig. 3.9. Speech context continues past a dense event.

In the next example, we see how the speech context can extend its influence across a longer non-speech context.

Example 2. Drawing Open and Closed Boxes

Teacher says (by typing) "PUSS DRAW AN OPEN BOX". PURR–PUSS draws an open box on the screen[6] using the actions %S (to clear screen and start in top left-hand corner), %ME (to move east unit distance), %DS (to draw south a unit line), %DE (to draw east a unit line), %DE, and %DN (to draw north a unit line). The effect of these actions is illustrated in Fig. 3.10(a). Now PURR–PUSS says "OPEN BOX IS DRAWN".

*The hurried reader may skip these examples and go on to Chapter 4.

56   THINKING WITH THE TEACHABLE MACHINE

The above sequence may be contrasted with what happens if Teacher says "NOW DRAW A CLOSED BOX". Because of the way PURR–PUSS was taught, she now goes through the same sequence of drawing actions as above (that is, %S %ME %DS %DE %DE %DN) but, this time, she goes on to say "NOW CLOSE BOX", draws two lines to the west %DW %DW and ends with "CLOSED BOX IS DRAWN".

The only point that I am making here is that the initial request of Teacher is still remembered at the end of the first drawing sequence because the speech context, established by Teacher, is still predicting the appropriate next section of speech. This is illustrated in Fig. 3-10(b).

Example 3. Drawing Poles and Counting Down

This example is similar to the last, but it shows how the controlling speech context can impose a counting sequence. In example 4 of Chapter 2 speech was used for counting but we were limited to a single PUSS and the context in its window.

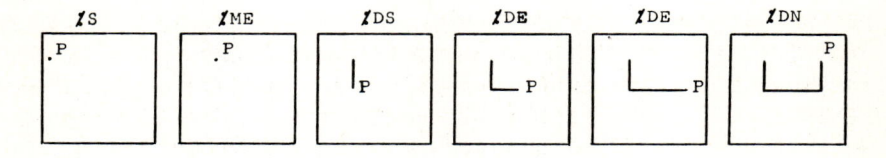

(a)   Drawing an open box on the screen. "P" shows the position of PURR–PUSS on the screen.

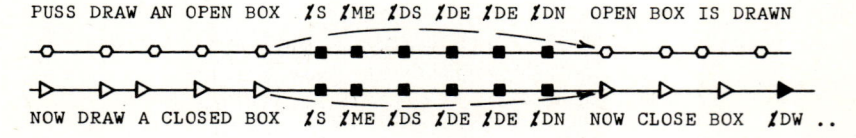

(b)   Speech context controls the continuation of the task.

Fig. 3.10. Drawing open and closed boxes.

Teacher says "DRAW SOME VERTICAL POLES PUSS". PURR–PUSS wipes the screen and initializes her position with a %S action. Then PURR–PUSS says "HOW MANY??". Teacher says "THREE POLES TO DRAW THREE POLES". PURR–PUSS draws one "pole" with the actions %ME %DS %MN. That is, she moves east without drawing, draws a pole by drawing a line south and then moves north without drawing to be ready for drawing the next pole, if there is one. The sequence is illustrated in Fig. 3.11.

MULTIPLE CONTEXT   57

Having drawn the first pole, PURR–PUSS says "TWO POLES TO DRAW TWO POLES" and draws another pole. Then she says "ONE POLE TO DRAW ONE POLE" and draws a third pole. PURR–PUSS ends by saying "NO MORE POLES TO DRAW". The condition of the screen after the second and third poles have been drawn is indicated in Fig. 3.12.

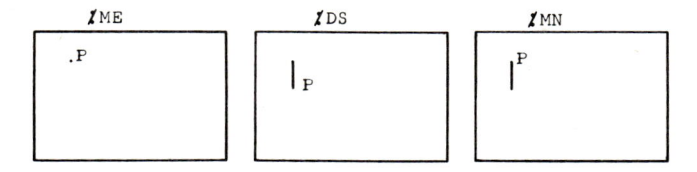

Fig. 3.11 Drawing the first pole.

This task was taught to PURR–PUSS by Teacher going once through the sequence for six poles, the maximum number that could be drawn on the screen. The "counting down" speech segments not only connect each pole-drawing sequence with the next and ensure that the right number of poles are drawn, but the speech segments also provide entry contexts for any number of poles up to six. By providing the appropriate speech segment (as we did above with "THREE POLES TO DRAW THREE POLES"), the appropriate entry for the task is established. A schematic diagram of the speech and drawing contexts with the possible entries is given as a schedule in Fig. 3.13.

Two Poles Drawn

Three Poles Drawn

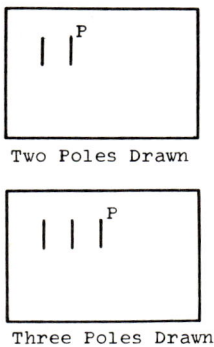

Fig. 3.12.

Example 4. Rubbing Out a Line
In the last example, the thread of speech contexts controlled the counting down process, each speech segment determining the next one to follow it.

58   THINKING WITH THE TEACHABLE MACHINE

```
        DRAW SOME VERTICAL POLES PUSS  /S  HOW MANY  ??
    ┌→ SIX POLES TO DRAW SIX POLES      /ME /DS /MN
    ┌→ FIVE POLES TO DRAW FIVE· POLES   /ME /DS /MN
    ┌→ FOUR POLES TO DRAW FOUR POLES    /ME /DS /MN
    ┌→ THREE POLES TO DRAW THREE POLES  /ME /DS /MN
    ┌→ TWO POLES TO DRAW TWO POLES      /ME /DS /MN
    ┌→ ONE POLE TO DRAW ONE POLE        /ME /DS /MN
    └→ NO MORE POLES TO DRAW
```

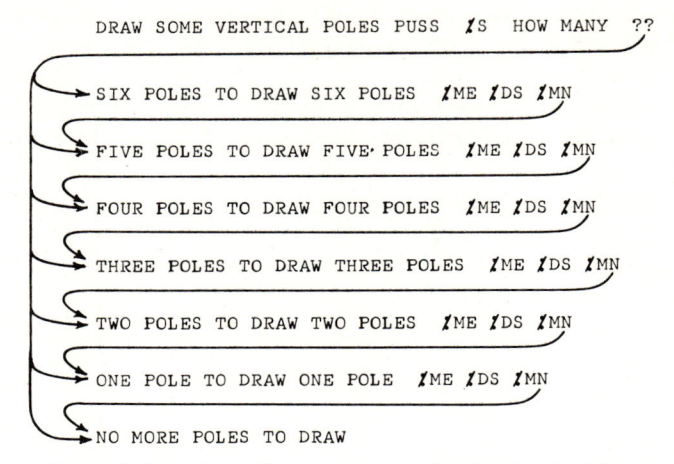

Fig. 3.13. Drawing different numbers of poles. A schedule.

Here we illustrate the situation in which each speech segment determines that it should be followed by itself until a final terminating condition is reached. Rubbing out a line is an example of "recursive" behaviour, an important concept in Computer Science.[7]

Teacher has already instructed PURR–PUSS to draw a line on the screen. One by one she was asked to draw 6 lines to the east, 3 lines south, 1 west, 2 north, 2 west, 1 south, 1 east, 1 south, 2 west, 1 north, 1 west and 1 north. The resulting line is shown in Fig. 3.14(a).

(a)   (b)

Fig. 3.14. Rubbing out a line.

Now Teacher says "RUB OUT THE LINE" and PURR–PUSS does the actions %X %X %X %L. The three %X actions have no effect, but she has been taught to do these to separate the dense events associated with the look action %L. After the look action, PURR–PUSS sees the pattern %S, indicating that there is a line going from where she is in a direction south. PURR–PUSS does the action %ES to "erase south". The line is erased and she is now in the position indicated by Fig. 3.14(b). PURR–PUSS says "RUB OUT THE LINE" herself, does %X %X %X %L and sees the pattern %E because of the line going to her east. She does the erase action %EE and another piece of the line has been rubbed out. This goes on until the whole line is rubbed out, when the look action %L will result in the pattern % meaning that there is no line from where PURR–PUSS is. She then says "NO MORE LINE" and the task is completed.

It is quite possible to teach PURR–PUSS this task without the dummy actions %X, but it will take much longer because many more window-length contexts will have to be learned. The details of this argument will be skipped here because they have already been given in the section on Sparse and Dense Events.

Notes on Chapter 3

1. Although I have no theory of context, sharper definitions of some of the terms used in the text can be given for the mathematical reader as follows:—

A *behaviour* B is an ordered set or sequence ($b_1, b_2, \ldots, b_n$) of happenings.

A *happening* b ∈ B is an ordered set of *events* from the set, E, of events.

A *PUSS predictor* is a quintuple (w, P, C, M, A), where w is a non-zero positive integer called the *window length;*

P is a set of *predictable events*, $P \subseteq E$;

C is a set of w-tuples, called *contexts;*

M is a set of < context, predictable event > pairs;

A is an *algorithm* that updates the memory M when given a happening b. (The algorithm may, or may not, generate from the happening a < context, predictable event > pair to be added to M.)

Note. To make a prediction with a PUSS predictor, supply a context c and receive the set of predictions { p | <c, p> ∈ M }.

To update a PUSS with a behaviour B, the happenings of B are presented to the algorithm A one at a time.

A *sequential PUSS,* or just a "PUSS", is a PUSS predictor having an algorithm A equipped with a w-event memory $W = (e_1, e_2, \ldots e_w)$, called the *window,* and with an event store q, the algorithm operating as follows:—

1. If there is an event in q, shift it into the window:—

$e_1 \leftarrow e_2, e_2 \leftarrow e_3, \ldots e_{w-1} \leftarrow e_w, e_w \leftarrow q, q \leftarrow \{\ \}$.

2. Extract a predictable event, A(b), from the happening b and put it into q: q ← A(B). If no predictable event is obtained, stop.

3. Add the pair <W, q> to the map M (the memory) if not already in M: M ← MU <(e₁, e₂, .. e_w), A(b)>

A *threading PUSS* is a sequential PUSS for which A(b_i), where b_i ∈ B, produces no predictable event for some i.

A *spatial PUSS* is a PUSS predictor having an algorithm that extracts a context, c, directly from a happening. The associated predictable event, p, (that forms with c a < context, predictable event > pair in M) may be obtained by the algorithm from the same or a later happening.

A sequence of events derived from a behaviour is called a *stream* of events if it contains one event from each happening.

Two or more sequential PUSSes provide a *multiple context* if their algorithms derive different sequences of events from the same behaviour.

One sequence of events *threads* a second sequence of events if both are derived from the same behaviour and if the first does not derive an event from every happening from which the second derives an event.

An event p derived from a happening b by the algorithm A of a sequential PUSS is a *dense (sparse)* event if the associated context c can (cannot) be found in some member of M, say <c, p'>, with p ≠ p'.

2. Lashley's (1951) "multiplicity of integrative processes", needed in temporal organizations like speech, may be seen in the multiple contexts of PURR–PUSS. However, the latter can also be seen as an extension of the associative chain theories that Lashley was criticising. In a similar way, the multiple contexts of PURR–PUSS can be seen as a counter-example to the paper of Halwes and Jenkins (1971) entitled "Problem of Serial Order in Behaviour is Not Resolved by Context-Sensitive Associative Memory Models". However, PURR–PUSS offers a different solution to those of Wickelgren (1969).

The work of Anderson and Bower (1973) is an impressive combination of a theoretical associative memory model "HAM" and the psychological data to support it. Their structure is probably too formal to allow learning in a natural way.

3. Music is a phenomenon in which threaded multiple contexts seem to occur naturally as rhythm, stress, melody, harmony etc. Application of PURR–PUSS in this area is being explored with Martin Lamb, Richard Bates and John Cousins. One of the PUSSes being used by Martin Lamb stores (and predicts) "root pitch" from a context of melody notes. There are possible advantages in using a similar spatial-sequential context in PURR–PUSS with contexts of patterns storing (and predicting) actions. Another example of spatial-sequential contexts is to be found in mew-Brain (in the Appendix) where there are two sequential events and two parallel (spatial) events in a three event context. See UC–DSE/10.

4. PUSS nets can be used to describe a mew only if the contexts are sequential. See the paper by Andreae and Cleary (1976) and UC–DSE/6 for illustrations of PUSS net memories. Spatial contexts can be handled by a mew-gram but cannot be described by PUSS nets.

5. Dalenoort (1976) has picked out "three phenomena of many that it would be "nice" to be able to explain:—

(1) the more or less immediate recognition of patterns (human faces, words, music), excluding sequential or exhaustive search,

(2) the more or less immediate realization that a piece of information is not present in memory . . .

(3) the relative insensitivity of certain kinds of information processing to damage of the neural tissue".

The last is explained by the holographic storage of events in PURR–PUSS. PUSS predictions satisfy the first by enabling recognition without sequential or exhaustive search. The second phenomenon is more difficult, but a similar problem is encountered in the HELLO task (Chapter 7) when PURR–PUSS has to distinguish between a known and unkown stranger. She is taught to use the difference between prediction and no prediction. I doubt if the human does more than find no prediction from a reasonable sample of related contexts in order to judge that something is not in memory. To the extent that we understand what needs to be explained, PURR–PUSS seems to offer a reasonable explanation.

6. The drawing environment used for examples 2, 3 and 4 was developed by David Bakker (1976) while the research on PURR–PUSS was frozen, so it did not come into use until afterwards. It has proved to be a useful environment for illustrating different kinds of task. A separate PUSS handles the threading context from the drawing environment.

7. For the importance of "recursion" see Minsky (1967) or Manna (1974).

4. Teaching PURR–PUSS

"Kitty, can you play chess? Now, don't smile, my dear, I'm asking it seriously. Because, when we were playing just now, you watched just as if you understood it: and when I said "Check"! you purred! Well, it *was* a nice check, Kitty, and really I might have won, if it hadn't been for that nasty Knight, that came wriggling down among my pieces. Kitty, dear, let's pretend —"

Lewis Carroll
"Through the Looking-Glass"

At the Console Typewriter

Imagine that you are sitting at the console typewriter of a small computer.[1] You type in an instruction which brings the MEDEATOR program into operation.[2] The computer types back to you:—
MEDEATOR AT YOUR SERVICE
TYPE NAME/DATE/TIME:

You oblige by typing in your name, the date and the time. This ensures that all interactions with PURR–PUSS are recorded properly. The "space" character which is typed by touching the "space bar" will be taken to mean that you have finished your message, so don't put spaces in your message! MEDEATOR then types:—

WHOLE MEMORY OF PURR–PUSS IS EMPTY
TCHR ←

The MEDEATOR program has now asked you, the Teacher (TCHR), to type in a "pattern" for PURR–PUSS.[3] This will be what you want her to "see" or "hear" or "feel". You may type in a string of characters of any length and terminated by a space. Nearly all characters are allowed, but the five characters # ↑ , ( ) must not be used because they have a special significance for the MEDEATOR program. Suppose that you type:—

=START

The MEDEATOR program passes your pattern to PURR–PUSS and then, finding that she cannot decide upon an action, comes back to you with a request to provide the next action.

ACTN ←

Whenever PURR–PUSS fails to choose an action, MEDEATOR will ask Teacher for an action in this way. Again you are allowed to type in any string of allowed characters ending with a space. Suppose that you type:—

=DOONE

MEDEATOR hands over this action to PURR–PUSS and then comes back to you for the next pattern. Now you have to say what pattern she should receive next as a result (or not) of the action. (Recall that MEDEATOR is an auxiliary program which handles the interaction between Teacher, PURR–PUSS and various problem environments. It operates in an entirely mechanical fashion according to instructions from Teacher).

Things will go on in this way until PURR–PUSS can choose an action for herself. Starting with absolutely no knowledge of what is going on or of what actions she can do or what patterns she might receive, PURR–PUSS has to have several actions chosen for her before displaying any activity.

Before continuing with the interaction, we should be clear about the strings of characters that are typed in as patterns or actions. Each string of characters ending with a space is an indivisible whole to PURR–PUSS, who sees nothing of the individual characters that you type. (However, the first character of a string sometimes determines which of several PUSSes a pattern or action goes to). When teaching PURR–PUSS we need to remember what we have taught so it is as well to choose easy-to-remember patterns and actions. "=DOONE" sounds like an action (do one) and it is easily associated in our minds with the pattern "=ONE" that follows it. The " = " at the beginning of these strings is a neutral character that prevents them from being treated as "speech" or "physical". An action like "/B – Z = 9<" would be more difficult for Teacher to remember, though just as easy for PURR–PUSS. The simple patterns of behaviour we are about to see demonstrate all the main features of the PURR decision strategy, but the patterns and actions used are not significant. More interesting tasks are taught in Chapters 6 and 7.

Continuing with the interaction, suppose that you type (including the pattern and action already given) the following sequence which begins to repeat itself after step 6:—

Step 1. TCHR ← = START   ACTN ← = DOONE
Step 2. TCHR ← = ONE   ACTN ← = DOTWO
Step 3. TCHR ← = TWO   ACTN ← = DOTHREE
Step 4. TCHR ← = THREE   ACTN ← = DOFOUR
Step 5. TCHR ← = FOUR   ACTN ← = DOFIVE
Step 6. TCHR ← = FIVE   ACTN ← = ANYTHING
Step 7. TCHR ← = START   ACTN ← = DOONE
Step 8. TCHR ← = ONE   ACTN ← = DOTWO
Step 9. TCHR ← = TWO   ACTN ← = DOTHREE

64   THINKING WITH THE TEACHABLE MACHINE

At this point, main-PUSS predicts the event "=THREE =DOFOUR." (Main-PUSS is one of the 5 PUSSes in PURR–PUSS. Glance ahead to Fig. 5.1). In other words, main-PUSS is predicting the pattern =THREE and the action =DOFOUR. We can find this out by asking MEDEATOR to tell us what main-PUSS is predicting or we can deduce it as follows. Notice that the prediction is what we would expect.

Main-PUSS has a window of length 3 and each event that it receives is a composite pattern-action, or "p–a". The first event given to main-PUSS was the first pattern =START and the first action =DOONE combined into the p–a "=START =DOONE". This did not fill the window, so the next event could not be stored by the procedure of Fig. 2.4. The second event, "=ONE =DOTWO", did not fill the window either; but when the third event, "=TWO =DOTHREE", arrived, the window was full with the context "=START =DOONE =ONE =DOTWO =TWO =DOTHREE". With this context, the fourth event "=THREE =DOFOUR" was stored by main–PUSS in the mew memory using the storage procedure of Fig. 2.4.

In a similar way, the fifth event "=FOUR =DOFIVE" was stored with the context "=ONE =DOTWO =TWO =DOTHREE =THREE =DOFOUR", which were the previous three events, or p–a's. Each new event is stored by means of the current context of three events which are in the window.

However, there will be a short time interval between the storing of an event and the arrival of the next event. In this time, the event that has just been stored is shifted into the window and the oldest event in the window is shifted out. Also, with the new context in the window, the next event can be predicted before it arrives. This is illustrated in Fig. 4.1 for the situation at the end of the sequence that we were discussing above.

We showed that when the fourth event "=THREE =DOFOUR" arrived it was stored with the context comprising the 1st, 2nd and 3rd events. At the

```
window holds:      { =START  =DOONE
                     =ONE    =DOTWO
                     =TWO    =DOTHREE

main-PUSS predicts:   =THREE  =DOFOUR

Teacher provides:     =THREE

PURR-PUSS chooses:            =DOFOUR

main-PUSS stores:     =THREE  =DOFOUR

window now holds:  { =ONE    =DOTWO
                     =TWO    =DOTHREE
                     =THREE  =DOFOUR
```

Fig. 4.1.

top of Fig. 4.1 this same context is in the window and so the prediction procedure for recalling events (see section "Recalling Events" in Chapter 2) will find the stored fourth event and make it the prediction of main–PUSS. What happened before is likely to happen again. Now, we suppose that you, as Teacher, type in for the second time the pattern =THREE. That PURR–PUSS chooses the =DOFOUR action is hardly unexpected. MEDEATOR reports this choice as follows:—

TCHR ← = THREE   PUSS: =DOFOUR

where "PUSS:" should be read as PURR–PUSS chooses the action:". After PURR–PUSS has chosen this action, the event "=THREE =DOFOUR" is stored and is then shifted into the window (as indicated in Fig. 4.1), ready for the next prediction.

It will be easier to explain exactly how PURR–PUSS chooses an action when we have seen more situations in which she does and does not choose an action. While going through these illustrative teaching sequences (interactions between Teacher and PURR–PUSS), an attempt will be made to indicate some of the reasons for PURR–PUSS's behaviour at an intuitive level. The imprecision in these interpretations will be removed in the next chapter where the PURR procedure for choosing actions is prescribed in detail.

The teaching that we started above is shown again in Fig. 4.2 together with a continuation of several steps. PURR–PUSS continues to repeat the actions first given by Teacher until "all the novelty is gone" (step 16).

The patterns of behaviour we teach PURR–PUSS in this chapter serve to illuminate the basic process of action selection, but do no more. The reader should not seek any significance in the patterns and actions used. In the examples at the end of Chapter 3, patterns and actions represented definite aspects of the world outside PURR–PUSS. Here, significance is avoided so that basic patterns of activity can be emphasised. Before going into detail, let me anticipate some of the points that will be made.

In Fig. 4.2 an initial sequence (steps 1 to 6) is repeated (steps 7 to 12) and we have already seen how this enables main–PUSS to predict what is coming. With these predictions and an "hypothesis" PURR–PUSS starts to act on her own (steps 10 to 15). We shall see, shortly, how "novelty" comes and goes, and how hypotheses are formed. During the second repetition of the initial sequence, PURR–PUSS stops choosing actions (step 16) because "novelty has run out" and she has no working hypothesis.

From step 19 to step 24 a new sequence is introduced and this also is repeated twice. Square brackets ([) in the actions and patterns of the new sequence cause another PUSS, a "threading" PUSS called physical–PUSS, to receive information. With the extra confirmation from this PUSS, PURR–PUSS is able to continue choosing actions on steps 34, 35 and 37

66   THINKING WITH THE TEACHABLE MACHINE

```
 1 TCHR←  =START   ACTN←  =DOONE
   TCHR←  =ONE     ACTN←  =DOTWO
   TCHR←  =TWO     ACTN←  =DOTHREE
   TCHR←  =THREE   ACTN←  =DOFOUR
   TCHR←  =FOUR    ACTN←  =DOFIVE
   TCHR←  =FIVE    ACTN←  =ANYTHING
   TCHR←  =START   ACTN←  =DOONE
   TCHR←  =ONE     ACTN←  =DOTWO
   TCHR←  =TWO     ACTN←  =DOTHREE     mP: =THREE
10 TCHR←  =THREE   PUSS:  =DOFOUR      mP: =FOUR       hy: =FOUR     2
   TCHR←  =FOUR    PUSS:  =DOFIVE      mP: =FIVE       hy: =FIVE     2
   TCHR←  =FIVE    PUSS:  =ANYTHING    mP: =START      hy: =START    2
   TCHR←  =START   PUSS:  =DOONE       mP: =ONE        hy: =ONE      2
   TCHR←  =ONE     PUSS:  =DOTWO       mP: =TWO        hy: =TWO      2
   TCHR←  =TWO     PUSS:  =DOTHREE     mP: =THREE      hy: =THREE    2
   TCHR←  =THREE   ACTN←  =DOFOUR      mP: =FOUR
   TCHR←  =FOUR    ACTN←  =DOFIVE      mP: =FIVE
   TCHR←  =FIVE    ACTN←  =ANYTHING    mP: =START
   TCHR←  =START   ACTN←  [DOONE
20 TCHR←  [ONE     ACTN←  [DOTWO
   TCHR←  [TWO     ACTN←  [DOTHREE
   TCHR←  [THREE   ACTN←  [DOFOUR
   TCHR←  [FOUR    ACTN←  [DOFIVE
   TCHR←  [FIVE    ACTN←  =ANYTHING
   TCHR←  =START   ACTN←  [DOONE
   TCHR←  [ONE     ACTN←  [DOTWO
   TCHR←  [TWO     ACTN←  [DOTHREE    mP: [THREE
   TCHR←  [THREE   PUSS:  [DOFOUR     mP: [FOUR    [P: [DOFOUR   hy: [FOUR    1
   TCHR←  [FOUR    PUSS:  [DOFIVE     mP: [FIVE    [P: [DOFIVE   hy: [FIVE    1
30 TCHR←  [FIVE    PUSS:  =ANYTHING   mP: =START   [P: [DOONE    hy: =START   2
   TCHR←  =START   PUSS:  [DOONE      mP: [ONE                   hy: [ONE     1
   TCHR←  [ONE     PUSS:  [DOTWO      mP: [TWO     [P: [DOTWO    hy: [TWO     1
   TCHR←  [TWO     PUSS:  [DOTHREE    mP: [THREE   [P: [DOTHREE  hy: [THREE   1
   TCHR←  [THREE   PUSS:  [DOFOUR     mP: [FOUR    [P: [DOFOUR                4
   TCHR←  [FOUR    PUSS:  [DOFIVE     mP: [FIVE    [P: [DOFIVE                4
   TCHR←  [FIVE    ACTN←  =ANYTHING   mP: =START   [P: [DOONE
   TCHR←  =START   PUSS:  [DOONE      mP: [ONE                                4
   TCHR←  [1       ACTN←  [DOTWO
   TCHR←  [2       ACTN←  [DOTHREE
40 TCHR←  [3       ACTN←  [DOFOUR
   TCHR←  [4       ACTN←  [DOFIVE
   TCHR←  [5       ACTN←  =ANYTHING
   TCHR←  =START   ACTN←  [DOONE
   TCHR←  [ONE     ACTN←  [DOTWO
   TCHR←  [TWO     ACTN←  [DOTHREE    mP: [THREE
   TCHR←  [THREE   PUSS:  [DOFOUR     mP: [FOUR    [P: [DOFOUR                1
                                          hy: [FOUR,[FIVE,=START,[1
   TCHR←  [FOUR    PUSS:  [DOFIVE     mP: [FIVE    [P: [DOFIVE                1
                                          hy: [FIVE,=START,[1
   TCHR←  [FIVE    PUSS:  =ANYTHING   mP: =START   [P: [DOONE                 2
                                          hy: =START,[1
   TCHR←  =X       PUSS:  [DOONE      hy: [1                                  3
50 TCHR←  [1       PUSS:  [DOTWO                   [P: [DOTWO                 4
   TCHR←  [2       PUSS:  [DOTHREE                 [P: [DOTHREE               4
   TCHR←  [3       PUSS:  [DOFOUR                  [P: [DOFOUR                4
   TCHR←  [4       PUSS:  [DOFIVE     mP: [5       [P: [DOFIVE   hy: [5       1
   TCHR←  [5       PUSS:  =ANYTHING   mP: =START   [P: [DOONE    hy: =START   2
```

Abbreviations used:-   mP: means main-PUSS predicts
                       [P: means physical-PUSS predicts
                       hy: means hypothesis is
The number on the far right of each line indicates the priority level.

Fig. 4.2. Illustrative interaction.

after novelty has run out. Step 37 heralds a third sequence (steps 38 to 42) introduced to provide novelty and followed by the second sequence. Then a "surprise" pattern "=X" is given to PURR–PUSS on step 49. We shall see how PURR–PUSS copes with this unexpected occurrence by means of information from yet another PUSS, called action–PUSS.

In this way, the three sequences of Fig. 4.2 provide a concise illustration of most of the behaviour of PURR–PUSS. Her several PUSSes provide information to enable PURR (the action-selecting part of PURR–PUSS) to select an action. This information is classified under different "priority levels". PURR always selects an action at the highest priority level available.

A short continuation of the interaction, in Fig. 4.7, will be used to illustrate the importance of those events which refer specifically to pauses in time and to "speech". These aspects of the body and world which we have given to PURR–PUSS contribute significantly to her overall capability. It is not sensible to talk about the capabilities of PURR–PUSS in isolation from a body and world. In discussing the details, we have to mention items, like square brackets, that are as much a property of the body and world as they are of PURR–PUSS.

Novelty

On the right hand side of Fig. 4.2 three kinds of information are listed. Thus, for step 9, the comment "mP: =THREE" records the prediction of pattern =THREE by main–PUSS, as discussed in the last section with reference to Fig. 4.1. On step 10 in Fig. 4.2, there is a prediction of =FOUR by main–PUSS but, also, an hypothesis =FOUR is recorded and the number "2" gives the priority level at which PURR–PUSS chose the action =DOFOUR. The numbers on the far right of Fig. 4.2, like the "2" just mentioned, can be 1, 2, 3 or 4. All of these values appear in Fig. 4.2. They refer to the priority level at which PURR–PUSS selects an action. The significance of each value is explained in Table 4.1 and in Fig. 4.3.

On step 10 of Fig. 4.2, PURR–PUSS's choice of the action =DOFOUR was made at a priority level of 2 indicating from Table 4.1 that there was an

Table 4.1.

Priority Level	Action is chosen because of:
1	Hypothesis match and pattern match and thread match
2	Hypothesis match and pattern match
3	Hypothesis match and thread match
4	Pattern match and thread match or
4	Action match

68   THINKING WITH THE TEACHABLE MACHINE

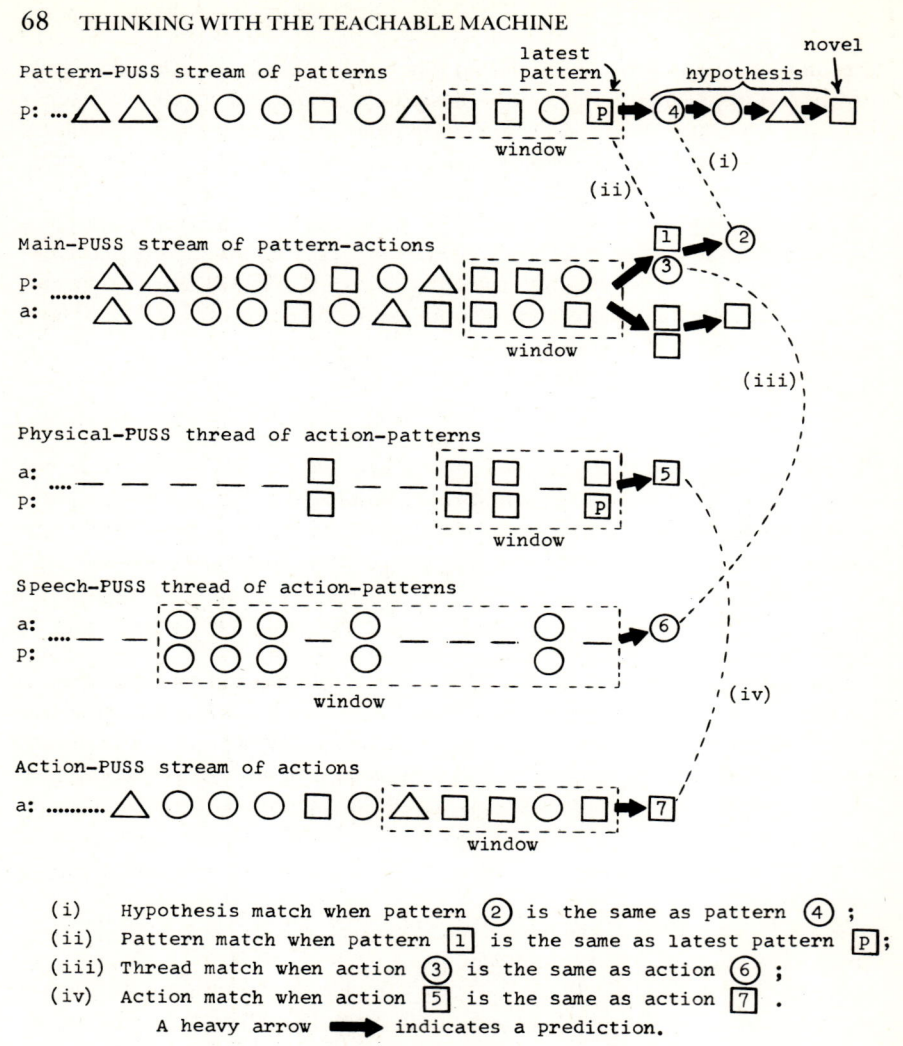

Fig. 4.3. Illustrating the choice of action by PURR (Table 4.1).

"hypothesis match and pattern match". "Pattern match" can be explained immediately with the help of Fig. 4.1. When main–PUSS predicts the event "=THREE =DOFOUR", the predicted pattern =THREE is received from Teacher thus confirming the associated action =DOFOUR. The pattern from Teacher matches the predicted pattern. The pattern match is one factor in the choice of the action =DOFOUR by PURR–PUSS. We shall see later that PURR–PUSS can choose an action when there is no pattern match (step 49 of Fig. 4.2). On the other hand, a pattern match by itself is insufficient for a decision by PURR–PUSS. There always has to be some additional evidence from an hypothesis match or from a thread match. Pattern match is further illustrated in Fig. 4.3 under (ii).

"Hypothesis match" is the primary factor in the choice of an action by PURR–PUSS, but it also is insufficient on its own. To explain hypothesis match, we must introduce pattern–PUSS and "novelty". The stream of events which goes to pattern–PUSS comprises the patterns that PURR–PUSS receives (see Fig. 4.3). If there is no hypothesis already, pattern–PUSS is used to construct a sequence of patterns forwards in time (by successive predictions) to the first pattern in pattern–PUSS that is marked as "novel". This sequence of patterns is then treated as a "working hypothesis" for the decisions of PURR–PUSS. A short hypothesis to a novel pattern is indicated in Fig. 4.3. Actions are selected so as to obtain, consecutively, the patterns of the hypothesis.

For example, on step 46 of Fig. 4.2, the hypothesis "[FOUR, [FIVE, =START, [1" is formed and the next few actions selected by PURR–PUSS carry her along the hypothesis. The action [DOFOUR takes her to [FOUR, [DOFIVE takes her to [FIVE, =ANYTHING takes her to =X! She expected the pattern =START but actually received =X on step 49. Nevertheless, the hypothesis is still followed as though *it* were true and the received pattern not.* The precise way in which all of this is accomplished will be described in the next chapter. Fig. 4.3 provides a pictorial summary of the action selection procedure.

PURR–PUSS is novelty-seeking.[4] The hypothesis leads to novelty and she tries to follow the hypothesis. But what is "novelty"? Any pattern received by pattern–PUSS that was not predicted by pattern–PUSS is marked as "novel" when it is stored.[5] This "novelty mark" is removed (i) when an hypothesis is constructed up to the marked pattern, or (ii) when the pattern is predicted and happens.

Referring again to Fig. 4.2, everything stored in pattern–PUSS up to step 10 is marked as novel because it has not been stored before. Pattern–PUSS has a window of 4 events so the first four patterns, =START, =ONE, =TWO and =THREE, were not stored (the window of pattern–PUSS was not full). The pattern–PUSS net after the arrival of the 10th pattern is shown in Fig. 4.4(a). Predicting from the context "=START =ONE =TWO =THREE", the first pattern predicted is =FOUR and that has a novelty mark so the hypothesis on step 10 is just =FOUR (check with Fig. 4.2). The novelty mark is removed from =FOUR.

On the 11th step, an hypothesis is constructed to the next novel pattern, =FIVE, and its novelty mark is removed. Fig. 4.4 shows the pattern–PUSS nets for steps 10, 11 and 12 of Fig. 4.2 to illustrate how the novelty marks are gradually removed.

*The advantage of "seeing what she wants to see" is illustrated by step 143 in Figure 6.6 when a never-seen-before object <DOLL> is shown her by Teacher.

70   THINKING WITH THE TEACHABLE MACHINE

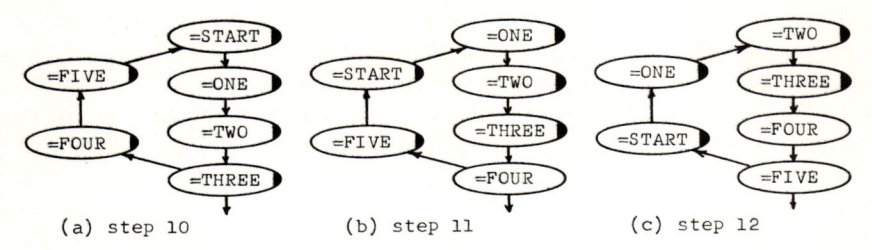

```
        =START                    =ONE                      =TWO
  =FIVE   =ONE       =START   =TWO         =ONE   =THREE
  =FOUR   =TWO       =FIVE    =THREE       =START  =FOUR
          =THREE              =FOUR                 =FIVE

   (a) step 10           (b) step 11            (c) step 12
```

Fig. 4.4. The removal of novelty. Novel events are marked with a "black nose".

On step 16, no novel events remain in pattern–PUSS and so no hypothesis can be constructed[6]. As remarked at the end of the last section, all the novelty is gone. Teacher has to provide the actions even though PURR–PUSS "knows where she is", as can be verified from her predictions recorded in Fig. 4.2.

Physical–PUSS
The behaviour of PURR–PUSS on steps 1 to 15 of Fig. 4.2. is superficially the same as her behaviour on steps 19 to 33, yet on step 16 she fails to select an action while on the corresponding step 34 she chooses an action at priority level 4. The difference is attributable to physical–PUSS, which receives as events all actions beginning with [and the patterns that follow. (These are the actions that act on the "physical" parts of PURR–PUSS's body and world, like HAND, ABACUS and SQUARES, which we discuss in Chapter 5). Thus, on step 19, the action [DOONE is provided by Teacher and this is followed by the pattern [ONE, so physical–PUSS receives its first event "[DOONE [ONE". Notice that an event of physical–PUSS is an action-pattern (a-p) and that the pattern does not have to begin with [, only the action. (The symbol [is chosen quite arbitrarily, but once Teacher has instructed MEDEATOR to pass all actions beginning with [and the patterns that follow to physical–PUSS, MEDEATOR will do so infallibly).

Physical–PUSS is a threading PUSS which receives a sequence, not a stream, of events that threads the stream of main–PUSS. Its predictions are action-patterns, of which only the actions are used by PURR–PUSS. Physical–PUSS predicts actions for PURR–PUSS. When physical–PUSS predicts an action that confirms a choice of PURR–PUSS, the priority level is raised, in accordance with Table 4.1. Now we can see why the decision on step 10 of Fig. 4.2 was taken at a priority level of 2 (hypothesis match and pattern match), while the corresponding decision on step 28 was at a priority level 1 (hypothesis match and pattern match and thread match). On step 28, physical–PUSS confirmed the hypothesis match and pattern match with a thread match (compare with (iii) in Fig. 4.3). The prediction of physical–PUSS, which provided this confirmation, is recorded on step 28 of Fig. 4.2 by "[P: [DOFOUR". Notice that the prediction was made by physical–PUSS *after* receiving the pattern [THREE but *before* PURR–PUSS chose the action [DOFOUR. It is recorded on the right of the figure to keep these details away from the interaction listed on the left. In the same way, the hypothesis recorded on the right is actually constructed between the pattern and the action of the interaction.

Action–PUSS

The illustrative interaction of Fig. 4.2 lists a number of steps on which PURR–PUSS chooses an action at priority level 4. The first is step 34. Novelty has run out and so no hypothesis can be formed, but both pattern match and thread match (from physical–PUSS) favour the action [DOFOUR. This represents a selection at priority level 4, as stated in Table 4.1. The same situation is encountered on step 35, but on step 36 physical–PUSS is predicting ahead to [DOONE so Teacher has to provide the action. Pattern match is insufficient on its own for the decision. On step 37, the prediction of physical–PUSS is relevant again and PURR–PUSS chooses [DOONE at priority level 4. Notice how the prediction of the threading physical–PUSS remains valid from step 36 to step 37 because "=ANYTHING =START" is not a physical event.

The next priority 4 decision is taken on step 50 just after a priority 3 decision. The priority 4 decision is taken with the help of action–PUSS. Action–PUSS receives a stream of actions as events and has a window[7] of length 5, as shown in Fig. 4.3.

On step 49, a new pattern =X is given by Teacher so that the priority level 3 of the action [DOONE is determined by an hypothesis match and a thread match from physical–PUSS, but not a pattern match. The new pattern also prevents main–PUSS from predicting the next pattern and at the same time the hypothesis comes to an end. A new hypothesis cannot be constructed because the pattern =X was novel to pattern–PUSS. In this situation, the only remaining possibility is a priority 4 decision by an action match (Table 4.1 and Fig. 4.3 (iv)). Action–PUSS is predicting [DOTWO (not shown in Fig. 4.2) and physical–PUSS (the threading PUSS) is predicting [DOTWO also, so there is an action match and PURR–PUSS selects the action. The next two actions are selected in the same way, by which time main–PUSS is predicting again and an hypothesis can be constructed to give a priority 1 decision.

To help the reader visualize the context carried by each of the four PUSSes introduced so far, Fig. 4.5 shows the interaction of Fig. 4.2 broken up into four contexts. The streams of main–PUSS, pattern–PUSS and action–PUSS contrast with the threading sequence of physical–PUSS. Since the

72   THINKING WITH THE TEACHABLE MACHINE

main-PUSS		pattern-PUSS	action-PUSS	physical-PUSS	
=START	=DOONE	=START	=DOONE		
=ONE	=DOTWO	=ONE	=DOTWO		
=TWO	=DOTHREE	=TWO	=DOTHREE		
=THREE	=DOFOUR	=THREE	=DOFOUR		
=FOUR	=DOFIVE	=FOUR	=DOFIVE		
=FIVE	=ANYTHING	=FIVE	=ANYTHING		
=START	=DOONE	=START	=DOONE		
=ONE	=DOTWO	=ONE	=DOTWO		
=TWO	=DOTHREE	=TWO	=DOTHREE		
=THREE	=DOFOUR	=THREE	=DOFOUR		
=FOUR	=DOFIVE	=FOUR	=DOFIVE		
=FIVE	=ANYTHING	=FIVE	=ANYTHING		
=START	=DOONE	=START	=DOONE		
=ONE	=DOTWO	=ONE	=DOTWO		
=TWO	=DOTHREE	=TWO	=DOTHREE		
=THREE	=DOFOUR	=THREE	=DOFOUR		
=FOUR	=DOFIVE	=FOUR	=DOFIVE		
=FIVE	=ANYTHING	=FIVE	=ANYTHING		
=START	[DOONE	=START	=ANYTHING		
[ONE	[DOTWO	[ONE	[DOONE	[DOONE	[ONE
[TWO	[DOTHREE	[TWO	[DOTWO	[DOTWO	[TWO
[THREE	[DOFOUR	[THREE	[DOTHREE	[DOTHREE	[THREE
[FOUR	[DOFIVE	[FOUR	[DOFOUR	[DOFOUR	[FOUR
[FIVE	=ANYTHING	[FIVE	[DOFIVE	[DOFIVE	[FIVE
=START	[DOONE	=START	=ANYTHING		
[ONE	[DOTWO	[ONE	[DOONE	[DOONE	[ONE
[TWO	[DOTHREE	[TWO	[DOTWO	[DOTWO	[TWO
[THREE	[DOFOUR	[THREE	[DOTHREE	[DOTHREE	[THREE
[FOUR	[DOFIVE	[FOUR	[DOFOUR	[DOFOUR	[FOUR
[FIVE	=ANYTHING	[FIVE	[DOFIVE	[DOFIVE	[FIVE
=START	[DOONE	=START	=ANYTHING		
[ONE	[DOTWO	[ONE	[DOONE	[DOONE	[ONE
[TWO	[DOTHREE	[TWO	[DOTWO	[DOTWO	[TWO
[THREE	[DOFOUR	[THREE	[DOTHREE	[DOTHREE	[THREE
[FOUR	[DOFIVE	[FOUR	[DOFOUR	[DOFOUR	[FOUR
[FIVE	=ANYTHING	[FIVE	[DOFIVE	[DOFIVE	[FIVE
=START	[DOONE	=START	=ANYTHING		
[1	[DOTWO	[1	[DOONE	[DOONE	[1
[2	[DOTHREE	[2	[DOTWO	[DOTWO	[2
[3	[DOFOUR	[3	[DOTHREE	[DOTHREE	[3
[4	[DOFIVE	[4	[DOFOUR	[DOFOUR	[4
[5	=ANYTHING	[5	[DOFIVE	[DOFIVE	[5
=START	[DOONE	=START	=ANYTHING		
[ONE	[DOTWO	[ONE	[DOONE	[DOONE	[ONE
[TWO	[DOTHREE	[TWO	[DOTWO	[DOTWO	[TWO
[THREE	[DOFOUR	[THREE	[DOTHREE	[DOTHREE	[THREE
[FOUR	[DOFIVE	[FOUR	[DOFOUR	[DOFOUR	[FOUR
[FIVE	=ANYTHING	[FIVE	[DOFIVE	[DOFIVE	[FIVE
=X	[DOONE	=X	=ANYTHING		
[1	[DOTWO	[1	[DOONE	[DOONE	[1
[2	[DOTHREE	[2	[DOTWO	[DOTWO	[2
[3	[DOFOUR	[3	[DOTHREE	[DOTHREE	[3
[4	[DOFIVE	[4	[DOFOUR	[DOFOUR	[4
[5	=ANYTHING	[5	[DOFIVE	[DOFIVE	[5

Notice that main-PUSS events interleave the others.
Fig. 4.5.

MEDEATOR messages "TCHR ← ", "ACTN ← " and "PUSS:" have been omitted for compactness, it has been necessary to introduce the convention that all actions provided by Teacher are underlined in main–PUSS. The vertical lines down the left hand side of each PUSS sequence mark the steps

TEACHING PURR-PUSS 73

at which a prediction is made or, if you prefer, where the context is "familiar".

Real Time

Time does not wait for Teacher.

For initial simplicity, the earlier description of how Teacher provides patterns and actions for PURR–PUSS was incomplete. After typing TCHR ← or ACTN← , MEDEATOR waits only a short time for Teacher to respond. If Teacher does not respond by touching the space bar within 3 seconds, then MEDEATOR types another arrow " ← " and waits another 3 seconds. If Teacher fails to respond in this period too, then MEDEATOR gives PURR–PUSS a null pattern or action. A null pattern or action is just a pattern or action with no characters (zero length). It is a pause.[8]

Figure 4.7 continues the interaction of Fig. 4.2. During the first four steps of Fig. 4.7, Teacher makes no response and so there is a series of null patterns and actions.

If Teacher *does* touch the space bar during one of the 3 second waits, then MEDEATOR waits (indefinitely) for Teacher to type in a string of characters as a pattern or action to PURR–PUSS.

This procedure is illustrated in Fig. 4.6. It may be noticed that the Teacher can force a null pattern or action without the six-second wait by touching the space bar twice.[9]

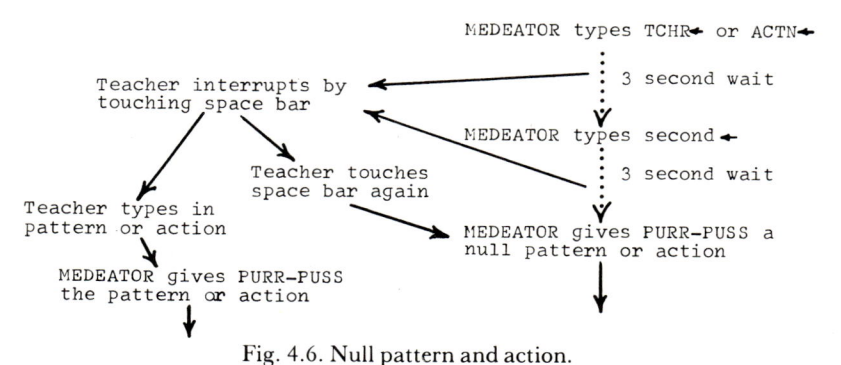

Fig. 4.6. Null pattern and action.

When a null pattern or action is predicted, it is recorded in Fig. 4.7 as a hyphen "-", since a zero-length character string cannot be printed.

Speech

The final example of a context in Fig. 3.8 illustrated the chaining of events. The inner shape (circle, square, triangle, etc.) of each event was the same as the outer shape of the next event. In this way, each event was linked to the

74   THINKING WITH THE TEACHABLE MACHINE

```
      TCHR◄ ◄       PUSS: [DOONE           4
      TCHR◄ ◄       ACTN◄ ◄
      TCHR◄ ◄       ACTN◄ ◄                Note. When a null pattern is
      TCHR◄ ◄       ACTN◄ ◄                      predicted it is shown
      TCHR◄ SAY     ACTN◄ ◄                      as "-", as in step 72.
  60  ACTN◄ ◄       ACTN◄ SHE
      ECHO: SHE     ACTN◄ SELLS
      ECHO: SELLS   ACTN◄ SEA              Abbreviations:
      ECHO: SEA     ACTN◄ SHELLS
      ECHO: SHELLS  ACTN◄ ON                   sP: speech-PUSS predicts
      ECHO: ON      ACTN◄ THE                  mP: main-PUSS predicts
      ECHO: THE     ACTN◄ SEA                  hy: hypothesis is
      ECHO: SEA     ACTN◄ SHORE
      ECHO: SHORE   ACTN◄ ◄
      TCHR◄ ◄       ACTN◄ ◄
  70  TCHR◄ ◄       ACTN◄ ◄
      TCHR◄ ◄       ACTN◄ ◄                mP: SAY
      TCHR◄ SAY     ACTN◄ ◄                mP: -
      TCHR◄ ◄       PUSS: SHE              mP: SHE   hy: SHE               2
      ECHO: SHE     PUSS: SELLS            mP: SELLS hy: SELLS             2
      ECHO: SELLS   PUSS: SEA              mP: SEA   hy: SEA               2
      ECHO: SEA     PUSS: SHELLS           mP: SHELLS hy: SHELLS           2
      ECHO: SHELLS  PUSS: ON               mP: ON    sP: ON    hy: ON      1
      ECHO: ON      PUSS: THE              mP: THE   sP: THE   hy: THE     1
      ECHO: THE     PUSS: SEA              mP: SEA   sP: SEA   hy: SEA     1
  80  ECHO: SEA     PUSS: SHORE            mP: SHORE sP: SHORE hy: SHORE   1
      ECHO: SHORE   ACTN◄ ◄                mP: -     sP: SAY
      TCHR◄ AND     ACTN◄ ◄
      TCHR◄ THE     ACTN◄ ◄
      TCHR◄ SHELLS  ACTN◄ ◄
      TCHR◄ SHE     ACTN◄ ◄
      TCHR◄ SELLS   ACTN◄ ◄
      TCHR◄ ARE     ACTN◄ ◄
      TCHR◄ SEA     ACTN◄ ◄
      TCHR◄ SHELLS  ACTN◄ ◄
  90  TCHR◄ I'M     ACTN◄ ◄
      TCHR◄ SURE    ACTN◄ ◄
      TCHR◄ ◄       ACTN◄ ◄
      TCHR◄ ◄       ACTN◄ ◄
      TCHR◄ ◄       ACTN◄ ◄                mP: SAY
      TCHR◄ ◄       ACTN◄ ◄                mP: SAY,-
      TCHR◄ SAY     ACTN◄ ◄                mP: -
      TCHR◄ ◄       PUSS: SHE              mP: SHE   hy: SHE,SELLS,SEA,SHELLS,   2
                                                        ON,THE,SEA,SHORE,-,-
      ECHO: SHE     PUSS: SELLS            mP: SELLS hy: SELLS,SEA,SHELLS,ON,     2
                                                        THE,SEA,SHORE,-,-
      ECHO: SELLS   PUSS: SEA              mP: SEA   hy: SEA,SHELLS,ON,THE,       2
                                                        SEA,SHORE,-,-
 100  ECHO: SEA     PUSS: SHELLS           mP:SHELLS hy:SHELLS,ON,THE,SEA,SHORE,-,- 2
      ECHO: SHELLS  PUSS: ON               mP: ON    sP: ON   hy: ON,THE,SEA,SHORE,-,- 1
      ECHO: ON      PUSS: THE              mP: THE   sP: THE  hy: THE,SEA,SHORE,-,-   1
      ECHO: THE     PUSS: SEA              mP: SEA   sP: SEA  hy: SEA,SHORE,-,-       1
      ECHO: SEA     PUSS: SHORE            mP: SHORE sP: SHORE hy: SHORE,-,-          1
      ECHO: SHORE   PUSS: AND                        sP: SAY,AND                      4
      ECHO: AND     PUSS: THE                        sP: THE                          4
      ECHO: THE     PUSS: SHELLS                     sP: SHELLS                       4
      ECHO: SHELLS  PUSS: SHE                        sP: SHE                          4
      ECHO: SHE     PUSS: SELLS                      sP: SELLS                        4
 110  ECHO: SELLS   PUSS: ARE                        sP: ARE                          4
      ECHO: ARE     PUSS: SEA                        sP: SEA                          4
      ECHO: SEA     PUSS: SHELLS                     sP: SHELLS                       4
      ECHO: SHELLS  PUSS: I'M                        sP: I'M                          4
      ECHO: I'M     PUSS: SURE                       sP: SURE                         4
      ECHO: SURE    ACTN◄ ◄                          sP: SAY
      TCHR◄ ◄       ACTN◄ ◄
```

Fig. 4.7. Illustrative interaction continued.

next. Knowing the inner shape of one event, we could deduce the outer shape of the next event. An important case of chaining is what I call "echo-speech".

Very little is known about the production and recognition of speech in spite of the enormous amount of research which has been carried out in that area, but we are all aware of the simple fact that we hear what we say. In other words, a speech action produces a heard sound pattern. This is a feature of our vocal apparatus, of the air which carries the sound waves and of our auditory apparatus.

To provide PURR–PUSS with a complex speech environment is out of the question, so I have given her a very simple substitute which contains little more than this direct connection from speech action to heard pattern. Any action which begins with a letter (A, B, . . Z) is treated as "speech" and the next pattern is made an "echo" of this action.[10] The echo pattern is the same string of characters as the speech action. PURR–PUSS "hears" the echo of her speech action.

Now it is impossible for Teacher always to remember to type in the echo pattern when PURR–PUSS chooses a speech action, so this is one of the chores given to MEDEATOR. This may be seen in Fig. 4.7. On step 60, Teacher gives PURR–PUSS the action SHE. This begins with a letter, S, so MEDEATOR identifies it as a speech action and types "ECHO: SHE" to record that it has been given to PURR–PUSS as the echo pattern. PURR–PUSS has been made to "say" SHE and then hears the echo SHE.

Echo-speech provides a sequence of chained events in main-PUSS, with each speech action determining the immediately following speech pattern. However, although a speech action is always echoed as a speech pattern, a speech pattern is not necessarily preceded by a speech action. For example, on step 59 of Fig. 4.7, Teacher provides the pattern SAY, which is a speech pattern but not an echo of the preceding null action.

The importance of speech to PURR–PUSS is such that a special PUSS, called speech-PUSS, is given as events all the speech action-patterns. When a speech pattern is not preceded by a speech action, but by a null action, that null action is treated as though it were the action which would give the pattern as an echo. It is, perhaps, simpler to see the events of speech-PUSS merely as the speech patterns preceded by identical speech actions, but we shall see in the next section that there is an important reason for turning a null action preceding a speech pattern into an identical speech action. Like physical-PUSS, speech-PUSS is a threading PUSS that is used to predict actions for thread matches and action matches.

Speech-PUSS is given a window of length 5 (see Fig. 4.3). Its predictions are recorded in Fig. 4.7 after "sP:" which should be read as "speech-PUSS predicts:". The first prediction from speech–PUSS occurs on step 77, when its window contains "SAY SHE SELLS SEA SHELLS". Here, as in Fig. 4.8,

76 THINKING WITH THE TEACHABLE MACHINE

main-PUSS		pattern-PUSS	action-PUSS	speech-PUSS
-	[DOONE	-	-	
-	-	-	[DOONE	
-	-	-	-	
SAY	-	SAY	SAY	SAY
-	SHE	-	-	-
SHE	SELLS	SHE	SHE	SHE
SELLS	SEA	SELLS	SELLS	SELLS
SEA	SHELLS	SEA	SEA	SEA
SHELLS	ON	SHELLS	SHELLS	SHELLS
ON	THE	ON	ON	ON
THE	SEA	THE	THE	THE
SEA	SHORE	SEA	SEA	SEA
SHORE	-	SHORE	SHORE	SHORE
-	-	-	-	
-	-	-	-	
SAY	-	SAY	SAY	SAY
-	SHE			
SHE	SELLS	SHE	SHE	SHE
SELLS	SEA	SELLS	SELLS	SELLS
SEA	SHELLS	SEA	SEA	SEA
SHELLS	ON	SHELLS	SHELLS	SHELLS
ON	THE	ON	ON	ON
THE	SEA	THE	THE	THE
SEA	SHORE	SEA	SEA	SEA
SHORE	-	SHORE	SHORE	SHORE
AND		AND	AND	AND
THE	-	THE	THE	THE
SHELLS	-	SHELLS	SHELLS	SHELLS
SHE	-	SHE	SHE	SHE
SELLS	-	SELLS	SELLS	SELLS
ARE	-	ARE	ARE	ARE
SEA	-	SEA	SEA	SEA
SHELLS	-	SHELLS	SHELLS	SHELLS
I'M		I'M	I'M	I'M
SURE	-	SURE	SURE	SURE
-	-	-	-	
-	-	-	-	
-	-			
SAY	-	SAY	SAY	SAY
-	SHE	-	-	-
SHE	SELLS	SHE	SHE	SHE
SELLS	SEA	SELLS	SELLS	SELLS
SEA	SHELLS	SEA	SEA	SEA
SHELLS	ON	SHELLS	SHELLS	SHELLS
ON	THE	ON	ON	ON
THE	SEA	THE	THE	THE
SEA	SHORE	SEA	SEA	SEA
SHORE	AND	SHORE	SHORE	SHORE
AND	THE	AND	AND	AND
THE	SHELLS	THE	THE	THE
SHELLS	SHE	SHELLS	SHELLS	SHELLS
SHE	SELLS	SHE	SHE	SHE
SELLS	ARE	SELLS	SELLS	SELLS
ARE	SEA	ARE	ARE	ARE
SEA	SHELLS	SEA	SEA	SEA
SHELLS	I'M	SHELLS	SHELLS	SHELLS
I'M	SURE	I'M	I'M	I'M
SURE	-	SURE	SURE	SURE
-		-		

Fig. 4.8.

the action-patterns of speech–PUSS have been written as single patterns and not as "SAY SAY SHE SHE SELLS SELLS...", so the reader is asked to remember that the prediction of "ON" from the above window actually represents the action ON of the predicted action-pattern "ON ON".

The importance of speech–PUSS is well illustrated by its provision of task-distinguishing threads for PURR–PUSS in Chapter 6 (see Fig. 6.8).

Mimic-speech

Imitation is important for learning, but very little is known about the actual processes of imitation.[11] Somehow, we *do* things that we see or hear. Mimicking a sound is making it (or something like it) after hearing it. This process is just the opposite of speech. In speech we hear what we say; in mimicking, we say what we hear!

The main justification for the way that I have given PURR–PUSS echo-speech and "mimic-speech" is that I have thought of nothing better. PURR–PUSS is an experiment. Others may think of more successful ways of equipping her with speech and the ability to imitate.[12]

In the last section, it was explained that, even when a speech pattern was preceded by a null action, the event fed into a speech–PUSS was a speech action and speech pattern: the speech action is made the same as the speech pattern so that the speech pattern appears like the echo of the action. This conversion of null action to speech action that would have produced an echo the same as the speech pattern is also applied to action–PUSS. If a null action is followed by a speech pattern (as on steps 58 and 59 of Fig. 4.7), then action–PUSS is given the speech pattern instead of the null action. Action–PUSS is, in effect, given the action that would have resulted in the speech pattern (as an echo) had PURR–PUSS chosen it.

The difference between echo-speech and mimic-speech is illustrated in Fig. 4.7. From step 60 to step 67, Teacher provides PURR–PUSS with the speech actions to say "SHE SELLS SEA SHELLS ON THE SEA SHORE". When Teacher sets the context again by typing SAY after a sequence of null events, PURR–PUSS repeats the sentence from step 73 to step 80. Teacher "put the words into her mouth", literally.[13] However, from step 82 to 91, Teacher types in the continuation "AND THE SHELLS SHE SELLS ARE SEA SHELLS I'M SURE", without giving PURR–PUSS any actions. Nevertheless, when the context is set for PURR–PUSS to repeat the saying, she goes right through from step 97, repeating as far as step 105 and mimicking (she wasn't given the actions) on to step 114. Notice that the mimicking is made possible by speech–PUSS and action–PUSS at priority level 4.

Figure 4.8 lists the events entering main–PUSS, pattern–PUSS, action–PUSS and speech–PUSS (only patterns, not action-patterns) during the interaction of Fig. 4.7, just as Fig. 4.5 did for Fig. 4.2. In Fig. 4.5, speech–PUSS was omitted because there was no speech. In Fig. 4.8,

78   THINKING WITH THE TEACHABLE MACHINE

physical–PUSS is omitted because "[DOONE –" is the only relevant event in Fig. 4.7.

Realism

The examples of interaction with PURR–PUSS used in this chapter were designed to illustrate the underlying formation of contexts in each of the five PUSSes. No attempt was made to teach PURR–PUSS realistic tasks, but some of the details of interaction were sketched. Only the reader's imagination can carry her or him to the console typewriter to receive MEDEATOR's messages, to type in patterns and actions, to anticipate some of PURR–PUSS's actions and to be surprised by others.

In the next chapter, a more complete description of PURR–PUSS, her body and her world is given so that we can go on to illustrate the teaching of more meaningful tasks.

Exercises

The reader is likely to have found this chapter the most difficult so far because in it we have met the full PURR–PUSS system for the first time. The jump from ONE–PUSS in Example 4 of Chapter 2 to PURR–PUSS is considerable. The exercises offered here have been designed to give the careful reader a chance to consolidate the material of the chapter by seeing it from different angles.

The hurried reader may like to go straight on to Chapter 6, using the figures of Chapter 5 for reference.

Exercise 1

Figure 4.9 is a schedule for the interaction of Fig. 4.2. Check that it is correct. Modify it for the case that Teacher had given the pattern =START instead of =X on step 49.

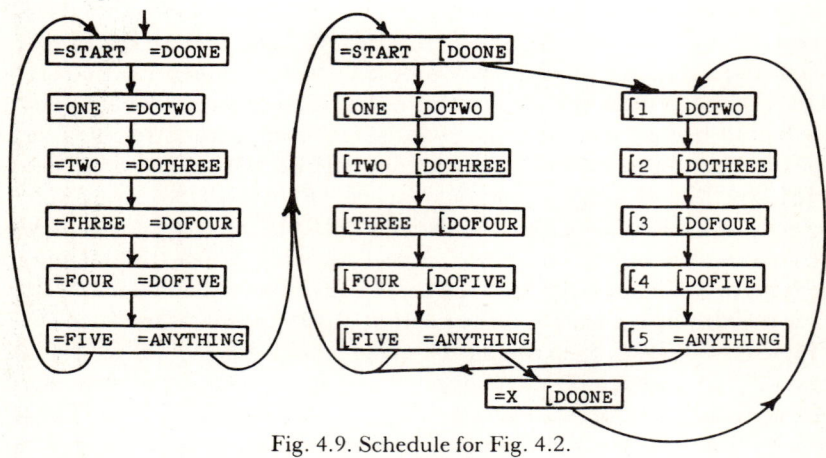

Fig. 4.9. Schedule for Fig. 4.2.

TEACHING PURR-PUSS 79

Exercise 2

Figure 4.10 is the pattern–PUSS net on step 54 of Fig. 4.2. Mark those events which are still novel on step 46 and thereby explain the hypothesis "[FOUR [FIVE =START [1" formed on that step. Now mark those events novel on step 54 and explain the hypothesis =START on that step.

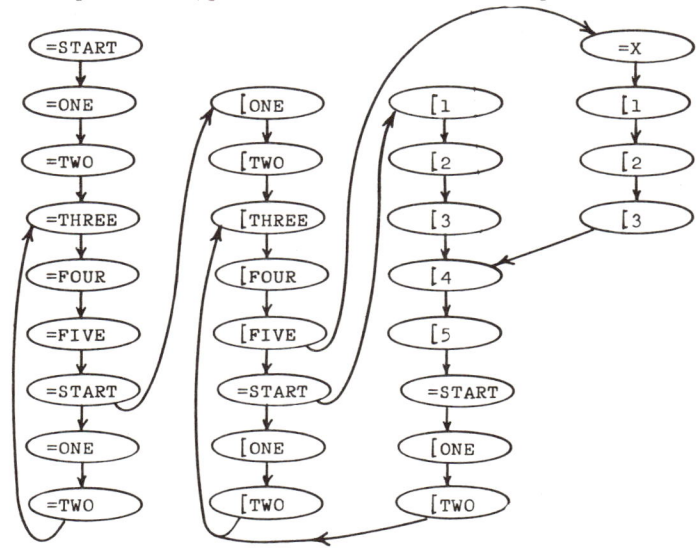

Fig. 4.10. Pattern–PUSS Net for Step 54 of Fig. 4.2.

Exercise 3

The priority 4 decision on step 34 of Fig. 4.2 can be made in two ways (pattern match and thread match *or* action match), while the priority 4 decision on step 50 can be made only one way. Which? How many ways can the priority 4 decision of step 52 be made?

Exercise 4

The action–PUSS net shown in Fig. 4.11 for step 97 of the interaction of Fig. 4.7 includes actions, like AND, which have not been performed. Explain this in terms of the way pauses can become speech actions. Explain also how the action–PUSS net remains unchanged from step 97 to step 116.

Exercise 5

Think of analogies of multiple context. Two were given in Chapter 1.

Think of the skates of a skater, threading each other's sequences of events. One skate momentarily holds its context to support the advance of the other.

Think of the paddles of a canoe threading the stream of events of the hull. Think of your own arms and legs co-operating to enable you to climb a tree

80 THINKING WITH THE TEACHABLE MACHINE

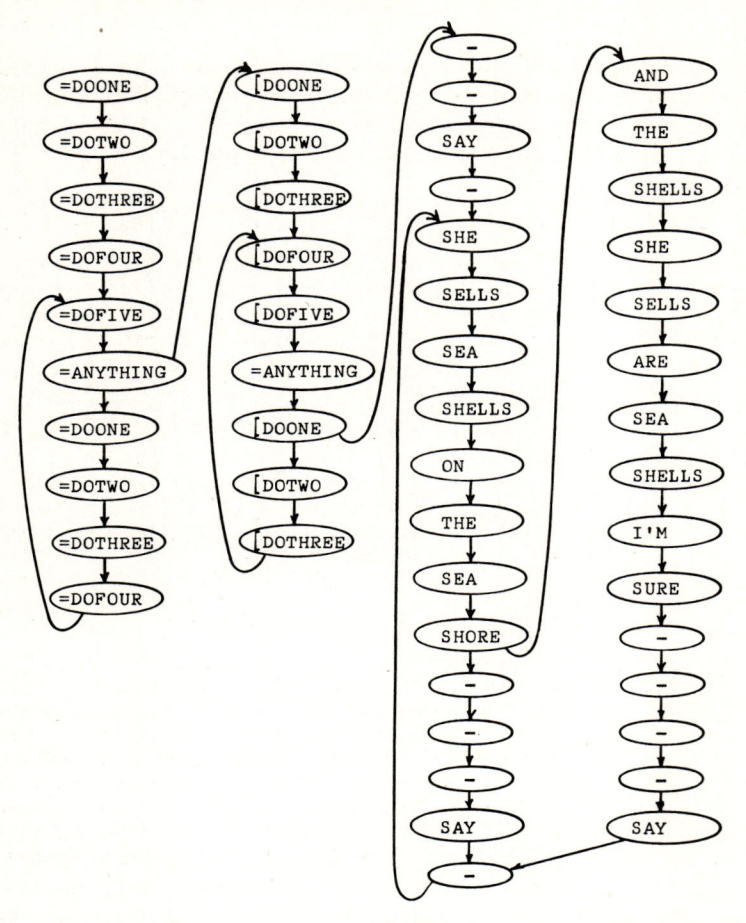

```
=DOONE      [DOONE      -           AND
=DOTWO      [DOTWO      -           THE
=DOTHREE    [DOTHREE    SAY         SHELLS
=DOFOUR     [DOFOUR     -           SHE
=DOFIVE     [DOFIVE     SHE         SELLS
=ANYTHING   =ANYTHING   SELLS       ARE
=DOONE      [DOONE      SEA         SEA
=DOTWO      [DOTWO      SHELLS      SHELLS
=DOTHREE    [DOTHREE    ON          I'M
=DOFOUR                 THE         SURE
                        SEA         -
                        SHORE       -
                        -           -
                        -           -
                        -           SAY
                        SAY
                        -
```

Fig. 4.11. Action–PUSS net from step 97 to step 116 of Fig. 4.7.

or a rock face. Think of the players of a football team anticipating and accepting the events of the game for a common goal.

Think of occasions when one person's speech guides another's actions, or when vision complements speech or touch. Think of line and colour and brightness in a picture, or melody and rhythm and harmony in music. Think of the threads of thought!

Notes on Chapter 4

1. All the work on PURR–PUSS reported in this book was carried out on an EAI640 digital computer with 16k of 16-bit word core memory and a single 360,000-word fixed-head disc memory. The mew-gram uses one third of the disc storage area, the remainder holding general system programs. The programs of PURR–PUSS occupy only 2200 words of core. The special environment programs for ABACUS, HAND and SQUARES take another 4000 locations. This leaves ample space in core memory for TRAC, an interpreter language.

2. The MEDEATOR program is written in the TRAC language (Mooers, 1966). TRAC is a flexible interpreter that is particularly suitable for supporting a developing system like PURR–PUSS on a small computer. Details are given in UC–DSE/5. The forbidden symbols have a special significance for TRAC and are used by Teacher to make changes to the MEDEATOR program.

3. Pattern and action correspond to the psychologist's stimulus and response. PURR–PUSS receives stimulus-response events into main–PUSS, stimulus events into pattern–PUSS, response events into action–PUSS and response-stimulus events into the threading PUSSes. This seems to be compatible with modern learning theory for, to quote Estes (1970, pp. 7, 8): "It should be recognized that the conception of the organism in modern association theory is considerably richer than a bundle of reflexes or stimulus-response bonds. The specific version which, I believe, now marshals broadest support is a stimulus-response formulation at the level of performance, but not at the level of learning, conceived as an inference from performance.... Now, I am persuaded that a wide variety of phenomena which had received little investigation at the time of those earlier formulations can be most simply interpreted in terms of a process more closely akin to the conception of S–S conditioning".

Chomsky (1972), though not supporting the stimulus-response view, sums it up in the following way (pp. 2, 3): "There was now little reason to question the conviction of Leonard Bloomfield, Bertrand Russell, and positivistic linguists, psychologists, and philosophers in general that the framework of stimulus-response psychology would soon be extended to the point where it would provide a satisfying explanation for the most mysterious of human abilities. The most radical souls felt that perhaps, in order to do full justice to those abilities, one must postulate little s's and r's inside the brain alongside the capital S's and R's that were open to immediate inspection, but this extension was not inconsistent with the general picture". However, Chomsky's opposition to stimulus–response theory is primarily (as I understand him) in its behavioural form of stimulus–response–reinforcement (see his famous criticism of Skinner's "Verbal Behaviour": Chomsky, 1959). His statement (1972, pp. 79, 80): "My own estimate of the situation is that the real problem for tomorrow is that of discovering an assumption regarding innate structure that is sufficiently rich, not that of finding one that is simple or elementary enough to be 'plausible'." does not altogether exclude a system like PURR–PUSS which generates richness by simple mechanisms!

4. The literature on the psychology of motivation is full of references to novelty. Here is one from Pribram (1971): "Feelings of 'interest', of motivation (appetites) and emotion (affects), stem from perturbations resulting when the organism faces novelty — novelty created by a continually changing World-Within immersed in an ever different World-Out-There" (p. 200).

5. Berlyne (1960, p. 20) sees only "two possible solutions" to "the crucial puzzle

about novelty": "But what do all novel stimuli have in common except the purely negative property of not having occurred earlier?" His first solution "(... the habituation hypothesis) is that novel stimuli owe their collective properties to the fact that they have not yet had a chance to lose effects that all stimuli originally possess. ... The second hypothesis is that novel stimuli are alike in inducing conflict". Somehow he misses the third possible solution (used in PURR–PUSS) that a novel stimulus is one that has not been predicted. Even though he emphasises the unexpectedness and surprisingness of stimuli, he does not seem to consider these as novelty-identifying properties. Thus, on page 22, in discussing how the novelty of a stimulus could be measured, he says "it would be discouraging if we could never determine how new a stimulus is for a given subject without a complete account of his past life". He does not include the possibility that the expectations of the subject *prior* to the novel stimulus (i.e. the subject's predictions) be studied, but only the responses *after* the novel stimulus. It is as if he assumed that the novelty of the stimulus cannot be measured without a complete account of the subject's past life. Luria (1973, p. 56) also requires that a novel stimulus be compared with old stimuli, rather than with predictions, when he says: "Each response to a novel situation requires, first and foremost, the comparison of the new stimulus with the system of old, previously encountered stimuli. Such a comparison alone can show whether a given stimulus is in fact novel. . . ." It is a special feature of PURR–PUSS that her predictions are based on a complete account of her past "life" without the need for that account (her memory) to be searched.

6. Millar (1968, p. 118) says: "To listen to what we know already becomes boring. Something too complicated to make any sense to the uninitiated is equally tiresome. But a familiar argument given a new twist, a common experience presented in a new light, unexpected variations on a theme, attract". In a similar way, both familiarity and too much novelty prevent PURR–PUSS from forming an hypothesis.

7. The choice of window length for each PUSS is not entirely arbitrary. Main–PUSS is required to provide alternatives for decision and it receives a large variety of events, so it is given a short window (3 events). Pattern–PUSS has a smaller variety of events than main–PUSS and is given a larger window of 4 events. Action–PUSS has an even smaller variety of events than main–PUSS or pattern–PUSS (because the repertoire of actions is smaller than the range of patterns) so it is given a long window of 5 events. The threading PUSSes are required to play a discriminating role, selecting between the actions suggested by main–PUSS or action–PUSS, so their windows should be long enough to produce unique predictions most of the time. Physical–PUSS has a considerable variety of events so a window of length 3 suffices, but speech–PUSS needs the long window of 5 events.

8. Null patterns and actions (pauses) improved the interaction with PURR–PUSS much more than expected. In addition to giving the impression that time is moving on, they provided points at which Teacher could inject commands to control the pattern of behaviour. Another bonus from the scheme was the way a sequence of null patterns and actions can behave like a "thinking focus," from which tasks begin and to which tasks progress. At the moment, Teacher is given the feeling that PURR–PUSS is waiting for him, but there is no such pressure in the opposite direction. The next advance towards the realization of time in the interaction should force PURR–PUSS to select actions "in time". There are tasks in which things have to be done fast enough, slowly enough or just at the right time. To ride a bicycle, PURR–PUSS would have to be able to control the moment at which her actions were

executed. In other tasks, PURR–PUSS may need to "hurry". I envisage a scheme whereby PURR–PUSS will select actions according to a priority which takes into account the computation time available. When an hypothesis has to be formed, an action may be selected without the hypothesis because there is not time for the formation of the hypothesis. In this case, a lower priority decision may take precedence.

9. As an example of "thinking with PURR–PUSS", we can speculate on the problem of fast and slow actions as follows. For many tasks, like hitting a swinging pendulum, riding a bicycle or playing the piano, sequences of actions must be performed at a variable but controlled rate. However, PURR–PUSS would learn very slowly if she had to learn the sequences separately at each speed until the right one was found. The control of speed must be independent of the action sequence. Suppose, therefore, that the rate of performance of all actions (and the sampling of patterns) is determined by a "clock rate" called the Tempo. PURR–PUSS is allowed two actions, one to increment and the other to decrement the Tempo by a small amount. The patterns that follow these actions need not provide a fine scale of Tempo, but only a coarse one such as "slow," "medium" and "fast". Many increments or decrements may be necessary to take Tempo from one coarse level to the next. In this way, speed control could be provided in both an incremental and an absolute sense with only three patterns and two actions.

Were we to decide upon this internal control of Tempo, we should meet the same kind of dilemma as caused the introduction of mimic–speech: we do not want Teacher to have direct control over Tempo and yet we need some way by which Teacher can influence the Tempo during teaching. (If PURR–PUSS were in a hostile environment, the direct access to her inner controls by external agents would leave her defenceless.) In this case, the simplest way of allowing the environment to influence the Tempo is through a "pulling-in" mechanism analogous to the pulling-in of an oscillator by a radio signal. We could arrange for the Tempo to be increased slightly by the arrival of a new pattern slightly ahead of the time predicted by the current Tempo; and slightly slowed down by a slightly late arrival of the new pattern.

There would be several interesting consequences of such an arrangement. First, notice that PURR–PUSS will be able to influence her Tempo indirectly by producing patterns not at the Tempo rate; she could do this if some of her actions acted on dynamic systems (e.g. arms with muscles and inertia) possessing their own response time constants. Secondly, there is the rather obvious analogy with the human tendency to pick up a rhythm. Thirdly, since a higher Tempo would demand a greater supply of power in a practical robot, the excitation of the system would vary with the Tempo. Indeed, an implementation of Tempo might generate a kind of emotion as an inevitable by-product. Fourthly, because an increased Tempo would allow less time for decision by PURR, action sequences would have to be learned slowly (with the time-consuming formation of hypotheses) and be well established before they could be performed at a higher Tempo.

Alex Palfi has started to explore and to extend these ideas in UC–DSE/9.

10. Echo-speech in PURR–PUSS may be seen as the final realization of years of work on a system called Monologue that never quite worked with my earlier learning machine, STeLLA (Andreae, 1963; Andreae and Joyce, 1965; Gaines and Andreae, 1966; Andreae, 1969; Andreae and Cashin, 1969; UC–DSE/1). A good example of the power of echo-speech was given in example 4 of chapter 2.

11. A general interest in psychology has made me aware of the main concepts and trends in the subject without giving me any depth of knowledge. However, on writing about PURR–PUSS I have felt some obligation to dig up references to the relevant psychological literature. In the case of "novelty" a brief search in my favourite works easily produced more than I could include. This was not the case with "imitation" which seems to be outside the normal run of psychological research. The classical work of Piaget (1951) on "Play, Dreams and Imitation in Childhood" is a treasure store of inspiration. The recent translation of Guillaume's (1926) "Imitation in Children" is the best account I have read. Susanna Millar's book "The Psychology of Play" (1968) is helpful. A remarkable argument of Lenneberg (1964) claims that, if babies imitate the sounds of their mothers, then the mothers can be expected to be able to imitate the sounds of their babies! I prefer Wolff's (1973): "The quality of an imitation can never be better than the elementary perceptual and motor skills from which it is built." (p. 112)

12. In the current computer program of PURR–PUSS, any speech pattern goes to speech–PUSS with the action preceding it unless that action is a null in which case the pattern replaces the null.

PURR–PUSS is given mimic-speech to improve our interaction with her. It is not because I think that imitation is instinctive. Guillaume (1926) has argued convincingly against that. Mimic-speech is a short-cut to enable us to interact with PURR–PUSS without going through the early stages of baby learning. As soon as we can give PURR–PUSS a voice and hearing, interest in the learning of imitation will return.

Whether or not "a special mechanism exists for language" (Montessori, 1949, p.121), there must certainly be an instinct to speak, and mimic-speech can be seen as a way of providing this economically. According to Penfield and Roberts (1959, p. 238), "The infant possesses a *speech mechanism,* but it is only a potential mechanism. It is a clean slate, waiting for what that infant is to hear and see. . . . man alone has an inborn control mechanism for vocalization in his cerebral cortex." Or, going back to Freud (1891): "We learn the language of others by endeavouring to equate the sound image produced by ourselves as much as possible to the one which had served as the stimulus for the act of innervation of our speech muscles, i.e. we learn to 'repeat'." (p. 33)

13. In teaching PURR–PUSS, words are used rather than, say, sounds or phonemes because it is easier for Teacher to detect errors or inconsistencies in sequences of words. A first step towards teaching elementary sounds like "MAA" and "MEE" was made in UC–DSE/6.

5. PURR–PUSS, BODY AND WORLD

> I asked the cat: "Pray tell me why
> You love to sing?" She blinked her eye.
> "My purr-puss, sir, as you can see,
> Is to a-mews myself," said she.
>   Nixon Waterman
>   "Tame Animals I have Known"

The Structure of PURR–PUSS

In this chapter, the structure and operation of PURR–PUSS will be defined. A "body" and "world" will also be described. To present a consistent picture, it has been necessary to freeze the research programme, in which PURR–PUSS is being developed, for long enough to record everything that is relevant. The temptation to talk about what was done in the past or what is going to be done in the future has been resisted strongly for the sake of clarity. Instead of a mass of past and future possibilities, there is a single coherent and consistent whole. The moment chosen for the freeze has turned out to be a good one. The work has reached a significant stage and yet it is still relatively uncomplicated. Nevertheless, in this situation it is inevitable that some things will be inadequately justified, some will be unconvincing, some will turn out to be poor choices and everything will appear arbitrary. The interaction with PURR–PUSS described in Chapters 6 and 7 offers "proof of the pudding".

PURR–PUSS comprises 5 PUSSes and a PURR strategy.[1] Main–PUSS, pattern–PUSS, physical–PUSS, speech–PUSS and action–PUSS all contribute to the decision strategy of PURR as indicated in Fig. 5.1. Each PUSS is fed with a different sequence of events, as described in the last chapter. The window sizes and events are summarized in Table 5.1.

The PUSS storage procedure described in Chapter 2 requires two additions to enable "novelty" and "disapproval" to be recorded. The marking of a stored event as novel was discussed in Chapter 4. Each new event that was not predicted must be stored and marked as novel. A "novelty marker" will hold this mark. Disapproval is a mild form of punishment which Teacher can give to PURR–PUSS by pressing a "disapproval button". An event stored while the button is pressed has to be marked as disapproved. A "disapproval marker" will hold this mark. If the same event occurs again without

86 THINKING WITH THE TEACHABLE MACHINE

Table 5.1. Window sizes and events of the PUSSes.

main-PUSS	3 events	each pattern and the action following. (p-a)
pattern-PUSS	4 events	each pattern (p).
physical-PUSS	3 events	each action beginning with [and the pattern following (a-p).
speech-PUSS	5 events	each pattern beginning with a letter preceded by an identical action (a-p).
action-PUSS	5 events	each action, except that a speech pattern following a null action becomes the event in place of the null action (a).

disapproval, the mark is deleted. Disapproval will be used in an interaction in the next chapter. The complete storage procedure for a PUSS is given in Fig. 5.2. It is suggested that the reader refer to Fig. 5.2 only when necessary to resolve a point of detail. The same is true of Fig. 5.3 which gives the complete PUSS prediction procedure. The explanation given in Chapter 2 should be quite adequate for a general reading.*

The Operation of PURR–PUSS

In discussing the teaching of PURR–PUSS in the last chapter, the operation

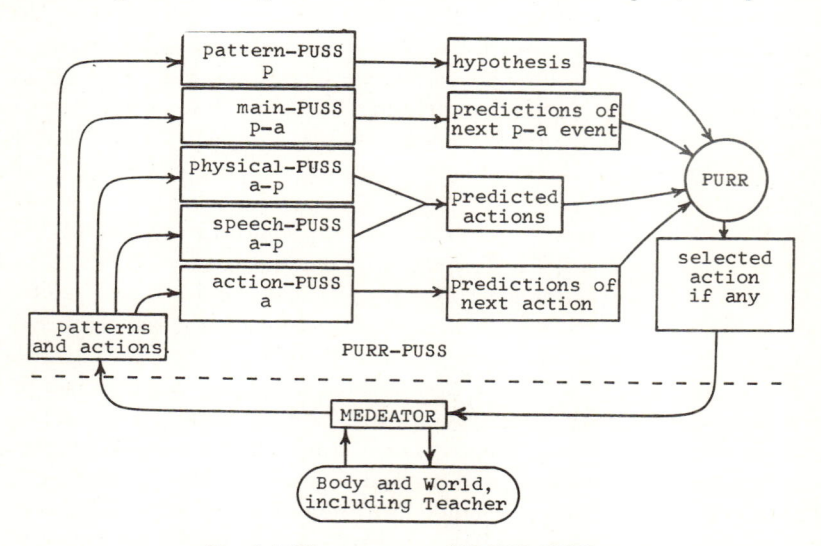

Fig. 5.1. The structure of PURR-PUSS

*The hurried reader may like to go straight on to Chapter 6, using the rest of this chapter for back reference.

```
When an event is stored in a memory location, five pieces
of information are held in that location. These are
written (E,P,p,n,d) where
    E is the number of the event,
    P is the number of the PUSS concerned,
    p is the number of the prime number used,
    n is a novelty marker (1 for novel, 0 for not novel),
and d is a disapproval marker (1 if disapproved, 0 if not).
Step
 1  Set a counter to zero.
    Set p = 1.
    Let PRIME = largest prime not larger than size of memory.
    Let MAXp  = maximum number of prime numbers allowed.
    Code the context of N events in the window into a number C.
 2  Calculate the address of a location in memory.
    This is done by dividing C by PRIME and taking the
    remainder R.
 3  If location R is not empty and does not contain E,P and p,
    go to step 5.
 4  If location R is empty or contains E,P and p,  store
    (E,P,p,n,d) in it and add one to the counter.
 5  If the counter now holds 3, stop.
 6  If p = MAXp, stop.
 7  Add one to p.
    Let PRIME be the next largest prime below what it was.
    Return to step 2.
```

Fig. 5.2. PUSS storage procedure.

of PURR–PUSS was assumed. It was obvious that patterns were being obtained, actions were being selected, PUSSes were being updated, and so on, but details were avoided. A formal prescription of the cycle of operations is given in Fig. 5.4.

```
Step
 1  As for PUSS Storage Procedure (Figure 5-2).
 2  As for PUSS Storage Procedure (Figure 5-2).
 3  If location R is empty, go to step 8.
    If location R does not contain P and p, go to step 6.
 4  Copy the event E, novelty marker n, and disapproval
    marker d from location R onto a list.
 5  If the prediction is being used for the construction
    of an hypothesis, set the novelty marker in location
    R to 0.
 6  If p = MAXp, go to step 8.
 7  As for PUSS Storage Procedure (Figure 5-2).
 8  Predict all those events which occur three times on
    the list (together with their novelty and disapproval
    markers) and stop.
```

Fig. 5.3. PUSS prediction procedure.

88   THINKING WITH THE TEACHABLE MACHINE

> 1. MEDEATOR obtains the next pattern from Teacher, Body or World. (If Teacher is asked and does not respond, the pattern is a null pattern. See Figure 4-6.)
> 2. If the new pattern begins with a letter (speech), speech-PUSS is updated≠ with the new pattern as action and pattern of the new event.
> 3. If the new pattern does not begin with a letter and the last action did begin with [, then physical-PUSS is updated with the last action and the new pattern as its new event.
> 4. Pattern-PUSS is updated with the new pattern as its new event. Apply the hypothesis formation procedure of Figure 5-6 to pattern-PUSS.
> 5. Action-PUSS is updated with the last action as its new event, unless the last action was null and the new pattern is speech, in which case the new event for action-PUSS is the new pattern.
> 6. Select an action with main-PUSS and the PURR action selection procedure of Figure 5-8. If no action is selected, MEDEATOR requests an action from Teacher. The action is null if Teacher does not respond. See Figure 4-6.
> 7. Main-PUSS is updated with the new pattern and the new action as its new event.
>
> The cycle is repeated.
>
> ≠ By "updating a PUSS with a new event", is meant:
> (a) apply the PUSS storage procedure of Figure 5-2;
> (b) shift the new event into the window, pushing out the oldest event;
> (c) apply the PUSS prediction procedure of Figure 5-3.

Fig. 5.4. The operation of PURR–PUSS

It will be noticed that each of the five PUSSes is updated in turn by the PUSS storage and prediction procedures. In addition, there is the formation of an hypothesis with pattern–PUSS[2] and the selection of an action with main–PUSS. The cycle of operations is summarized in Fig. 5.5.

The hypothesis formation procedure[3], presented formally in Fig. 5.6, employs a succession of pattern–PUSS predictions starting from the present context (as illustrated in Fig. 5.7). The current context is saved so that it can be restored after the hypothesis formation is over. At each stage, a random one of the predictions is taken, except that predictions with novelty (marker = 1) are given preference and predictions with disapproval (marker = 1) are disregarded. If a novel event is predicted, the hypothesis is complete and consists of the succession of predictions ending with the novel one. If a novel

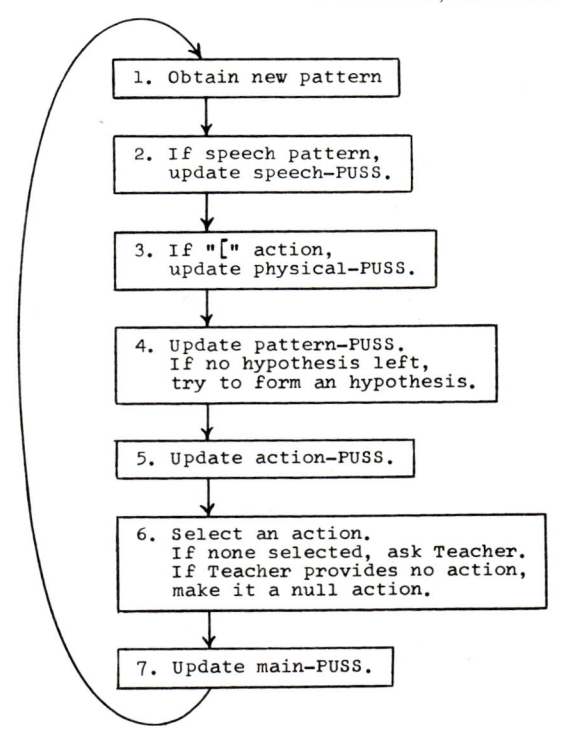

```
┌─────────────────────────────┐
│ 1. Obtain new pattern       │
└─────────────────────────────┘
              ↓
┌─────────────────────────────┐
│ 2. If speech pattern,       │
│    update speech-PUSS.      │
└─────────────────────────────┘
              ↓
┌─────────────────────────────┐
│ 3. If "[" action,           │
│    update physical-PUSS.    │
└─────────────────────────────┘
              ↓
┌─────────────────────────────┐
│ 4. Update pattern-PUSS.     │
│    If no hypothesis left,   │
│    try to form an hypothesis.│
└─────────────────────────────┘
              ↓
┌─────────────────────────────┐
│ 5. Update action-PUSS.      │
└─────────────────────────────┘
              ↓
┌─────────────────────────────┐
│ 6. Select an action.        │
│    If none selected, ask Teacher.│
│    If Teacher provides no action,│
│    make it a null action.   │
└─────────────────────────────┘
              ↓
┌─────────────────────────────┐
│ 7. Update main-PUSS.        │
└─────────────────────────────┘
```

Fig. 5.5. Skeleton diagram of the operation of PURR–PUSS

event is not predicted, then the chosen prediction is taken as a new event, it is shifted into the window and from the new context in the window a further prediction is made. Again, shifting the new prediction into the window as though it had occurred we get a context for a further prediction, and so on. This succession of predictions stops if

(i) only predictions with disapproval are found; any partially formed hypothesis is discarded.

(ii) the window contains a sequence of events which duplicates an earlier section of the hypothesis; in this case, the hypothesis formation is going around in a loop so it is abandoned and the hypothesis is discarded.

(iii) a novel event is predicted, i.e. a successful hypothesis has been formed up to and including this novel event.

The PURR Strategy

The PURR action selection procedure is given in Figs 5.8 and 5.9 so that the reader can refer to them for details. In the last chapter we saw some of

90 THINKING WITH THE TEACHABLE MACHINE

this procedure in operation and in the following chapters the remaining features will be fully illustrated. Here we are more concerned with the strategy behind the procedure.

One of the objectives which one might expect to see as part of the PURR strategy is the objective of satisfying PURR–PUSS's "needs". We can think of the need of a robot to recharge its batteries or the need of a sociable robot to have "company". This objective is *not* included in the current strategy. Needs are not obviously necessary for a system which does not have to survive or compete.[4] Also, it would be very difficult to decide what needs were worth incorporating. However, it must be admitted that without needs PURR–PUSS is unlikely to become ego-centric or emotional. For some, this will come as a disappointment. The advantage of omitting this objective is simplicity. Its omission should be treated as temporary.

```
1. If Teacher is applying disapproval, delete hypothesis
   and exit.
2. Remove the first pattern from the hypothesis list.
   If the list is still not empty, then a new hypothesis
   is not needed so exit with the remainder of the
   hypothesis.
3. Save the current context that is in the window.
4. Make a prediction with the PUSS prediction procedure
   of Figure 5-3, including step 5.
5. If there are any predictions with novelty and without
   disapproval, choose one of them at random. Add the
   pattern of this prediction to the hypothesis list,
   restore the saved context to the window and exit
   with an hypothesis formed.
6. If there are no predictions without disapproval,
   delete any hypothesis formed so far, restore the saved
   context to the window and exit without an hypothesis.
7. Choose at random one of the predictions without
   disapproval and add the pattern of the prediction to
   the end of the hypothesis list. Shift the event of
   the prediction as a new event into the window.
8. If the patterns of the N events in the window are a
   repetition of an earlier sequence of patterns on the
   hypothesis list, delete the list, restore the saved
   context to the window, and exit without an hypothesis.
9. Return to 4.
```

Fig. 5.6. The hypothesis formation procedure (in pattern–PUSS).

```
The window contains the events E_1, E_2 and E_3. These
are saved. The diagram shows a series of predictions
(E_4, E_5, E_6 and E_7), the patterns of which are added
to the hypothesis list.
```

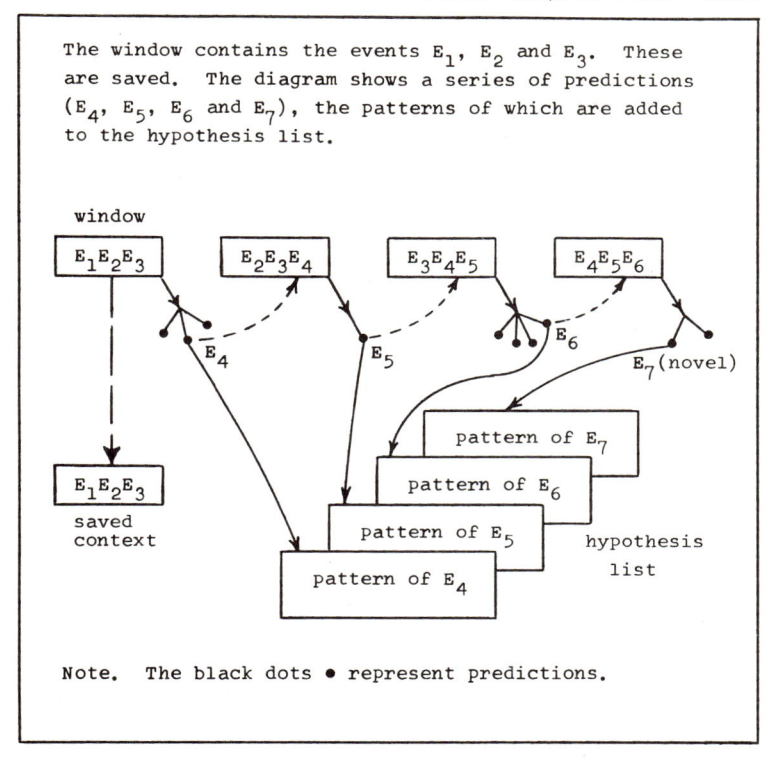

[Diagram showing window with $E_1E_2E_3$, $E_2E_3E_4$, $E_3E_4E_5$, $E_4E_5E_6$ boxes; predictions E_4, E_5, E_6, E_7(novel); saved context $E_1E_2E_3$; and hypothesis list with pattern of E_4, pattern of E_5, pattern of E_6, pattern of E_7.]

Note. The black dots ● represent predictions.

Fig. 5.7. Schematic diagram of hypothesis formation in pattern–PUSS

The primary objective in the strategy of PURR is "teachableness". Nothing matters quite as much as that we should be able to teach PURR–PUSS everything that we wish. At first sight this looks like a clear objective because we think we know what we mean by "teaching" in a human context. In the machine context, the objective is not so clear. The main requirement seems to be "not rigid like present-day computer programming".

The primary objective is reflected in several features of the PURR action selection procedure:

(a) Disapproval allows Teacher to make mistakes and to change his mind.

(b) There is no restriction on what patterns and actions can be used.

(c) Actions are not selected unless there is "good reason" so Teacher is given plenty of opportunity to determine actions.

(d) PURR–PUSS tends to repeat sequences but does not go into endless repetitions.

```
1. If disapproval is being applied, exit without an action.
2. Put all actions in events with disapproval predicted by
   main-, action-, speech- and physical-PUSS onto an
   "Inhibit" list.
3. For each event E predicted by main-PUSS and containing
   an action not on the Inhibit list, we shall say that
   there is
   (a) an "hypothesis match" if a further prediction by
       main-PUSS, assuming the event E to have occurred,
       predicts an event (without disapproval) containing
       the top pattern on the hypothesis list;
   (b) a "pattern match" if the current pattern is in E;
   (c) a "thread match" if the action in E is predicted
       by a threading PUSS (speech- or physical-PUSS).
   Put each action, unless it is the null action, on
     priority 1 list if hypothesis and pattern and thread
       match;
     priority 2 list if hypothesis and pattern match;
     priority 3 list if hypothesis and thread match;
     priority 4 list if pattern and thread match.
4. For each action A predicted by action-PUSS and not on
   the Inhibit list: if A is also predicted by a threading
   PUSS, put A, unless it is the null action, on priority 4
   list. This is called an "action match".
5. If all four priority lists are empty, go to step 8.
6. If priority 1 list is not empty, select an action from
   it at random and exit. If priority 1 list is empty
   but priority 2 list is not, select an action from
   priority 2 list at random and exit. If both priority
   1 and 2 lists are empty, but priority 3 list is not,
   select an action from priority 3 list at random and
   exit.
7. If priority 1,2 and 3 lists are empty, but priority 4
   list is not, then compare the number KORSHN (explained
   in the text) with a random number generated in the
   range 0 to 511. If the random number is larger, select
   an action from priority 4 list at random and exit.
8. Delete the hypothesis, unless a null action was found
   at priority 1,2 or 3, and exit with no action selected.
```

Fig. 5.8. The PURR action selection procedure.

A second objective in the strategy of PURR, which can be seen as a consequence of the primary objective, is "reachableness". If PURR–PUSS learns, then her past experiences stored away in memory must be accessible or they will be of little use. Indeed, it would seem desirable that a stored experience be reachable from many other experiences. Novelty-seeking and novelty-removal, which are an important part of hypothesis formation and the PURR action selection procedure, tend to make stored events in memory occur in "loops". The first time an event occurs it is marked as novel. This novel event becomes a goal for the hypothesis formation procedure until an hypothesis is formed to it or until the event occurs again for some other

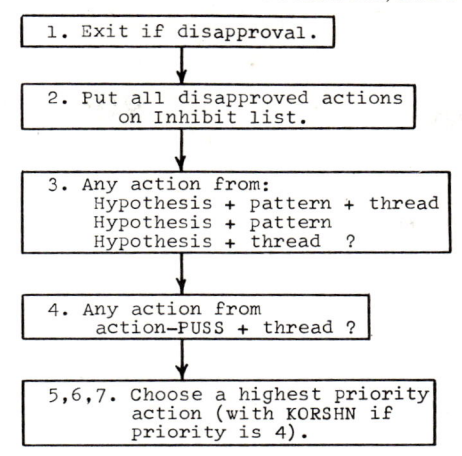

```
┌─────────────────────────────┐
│ 1. Exit if disapproval.     │
└─────────────┬───────────────┘
              ▼
┌─────────────────────────────┐
│ 2. Put all disapproved actions │
│    on Inhibit list.         │
└─────────────┬───────────────┘
              ▼
┌─────────────────────────────┐
│ 3. Any action from:         │
│    Hypothesis + pattern + thread │
│    Hypothesis + pattern     │
│    Hypothesis + thread  ?   │
└─────────────┬───────────────┘
              ▼
┌─────────────────────────────┐
│ 4. Any action from          │
│    action-PUSS + thread ?   │
└─────────────┬───────────────┘
              ▼
┌─────────────────────────────┐
│ 5,6,7. Choose a highest priority │
│    action (with KORSHN if   │
│    priority is 4).          │
└─────────────────────────────┘
```

Fig. 5.9. Main steps of PURR action selection procedure.

reason. In this way, each event becomes connected to itself via a sequence in memory: it is in a loop.[5] A memory which consists of many loops *tends* to have most of its events reachable from each other. Extreme cases of this interconnectedness can be seen in Figs 2.8 and 2.13. In the multiple context situation provided by the five PUSSes of PURR–PUSS, there will be an even greater tendency for events to be reachable from other events because there are more ways in which they can be connected.[6]

Endless Repetitions

In the last section it was stated (see feature (d)) that PURR–PUSS tends to repeat sequences but does not go into endless repetitions.

Suppose that an action is "right" for a particular situation and that the situation does not change when the action is performed. The action must still be right and so it will be repeated, and repeated for ever if the situation does not change. To prevent endless repetitions occurring for this reason, we must ensure that repetition changes the situation even when the environment does not change. We need PURR–PUSS to change even if the situation in the environment does not. Humans get tired of doing the same thing over and over again. In the case of PURR–PUSS repetition causes a parameter called KORSHN to increase. Even when nothing else changes, KORSHN will increase and stop the repetition.

Actions selected at priority levels above 4 cannot go into an endless repetition because hypothesis formation automatically removes the novelty on which it depends.[7] Endless hypotheses are prevented by step 8 of the hypothesis formation procedure (Fig. 5.6). However, at priority level 4 the predictions of action–PUSS, physical–PUSS and speech–PUSS could generate endless repetitions, were it not for KORSHN.

KORSHN is a number which measures the amount of novelty encountered by PURR–PUSS. Every time one of the PUSSes receives an event, KORSHN is incremented by one, but each time one of the PUSSes receives a novel event, KORSHN is halved (the remainder being discarded). A sprinkling of novel events will keep KORSHN low. For instance, if at least one PUSS receives a novel event every 10 steps, then KORSHN cannot stay above 80 because a novel event would halve this number to 40; 10 more steps with each of four PUSSes receiving 10 increments would then be needed to get KORSHN back to 80. Similarly, KORSHN can only stay above 200 if there is no novelty for 25 steps. A high value of KORSHN measures a small amount of novelty.

Because of the way KORSHN is used in the PURR action selection procedure (Fig. 5.8), selection of actions at priority level 4 is probabilistic. If actions are available at priority level 4, but no higher, then the chance of an action being selected is one in 511/(511–KORSHN). There is no chance if KORSHN is 511 or higher, about 50% chance if KORSHN is 256, and about 75% chance of an action being selected if KORSHN is 128. In other words, if PURR–PUSS has been receiving plenty of novelty, then priority level 4 decisions, which tend to be repetitive, are acceptable; if she has not received novelty for some time, the priority level 4 decisions are less acceptable and are less likely to be selected.

Notice that the effect of not selecting an action is to give Teacher a chance to introduce some novelty. If Teacher does not respond and a series of null actions and patterns ensue, then there is reason to expect PURR–PUSS to start selecting actions again at level 4 or lower. This additional possibility has not been included in the PURR action selection procedure yet.

Body and World

Having described PURR–PUSS completely in the first part of this chapter, we now go on to discuss her body and world.[8] In the chapters to follow, an attempt is made to demonstrate the abilities of PURR–PUSS by teaching her a number of tasks. These tasks have been chosen for the way they illustrate the principles that have been discovered to date.[9] The body and world presented to PURR–PUSS are not more elaborate than is necessary for these tasks. The tasks are not more complex than is necessary to expose the principles.

Brief mention will be made of robot bodies (CAESAR and ESAW) which have been used with PURR–PUSS, but for the time being we consider a body and world with the following features;—

Null patterns and actions
Speech, with echo and mimic
HAND
ABACUS
SQUARES

The null patterns and actions and their representation of the passage of time were discussed in Chapter 4. Echo and mimic speech were demonstrated too.

In so far as a part of the environment is under the direct control of PURR–PUSS, it is referred to as part of her body. The speech that she generates and hears is mainly a feature of her body. On the other hand, the speech that comes from Teacher comes from the world. It is characteristic of most of the environments that are given to PURR–PUSS that they have body *and* world aspects, like speech. HAND, however, is intended to be just body. We do not allow Teacher to move a finger of HAND without PURR–PUSS knowing, because it is *her* HAND. HAND provides PURR–PUSS with a useful and important kind of memory[10]. If she raises a finger of HAND, then it stays raised until she lowers it. Most of us use our fingers for counting sometimes and when we do we use them for remembering. In two of the tasks which will be taught to PURR–PUSS, namely COUNTING OBJECTS and COUNTING BEADS, she will use HAND to help with the counting.

The actions that alter HAND and the patterns that result are summarised in Fig. 5.10 for future reference. All these actions are managed for Teacher by MEDEATOR so that the correct patterns will be given to PURR–PUSS[11]. It is suggested that the reader wait until the actions and patterns of HAND appear in a teaching situation before referring to Fig. 5.10.

ABACUS is part of the world of PURR–PUSS. While individual fingers of HAND can be raised and lowered by appropriate actions without affecting the positions of other fingers, the beads of ABACUS are not so independent of each other. When one bead is pushed left or right, it is likely to move or be stopped by a neighbouring bead. What happens to one bead depends upon the positions of the other beads. ABACUS promises to be a good world in which to teach PURR–PUSS a great deal about counting, since the beads can occur singly, in groups or in patterns[12]. The actions and patterns for ABACUS are gathered together in Fig. 5.11, for reference. ABACUS is not restricted to 3 beads and 5 places.

SQUARES enable us to put PURR–PUSS into a 2-dimensional world, a maze in which she moves around between walls. High walls can be seen from afar, but low walls can be seen only if they are adjacent. Each square of a maze is either a floor square, on which PURR–PUSS can stand or turn, or a

96 THINKING WITH THE TEACHABLE MACHINE

Condition of HAND before action	Action	Effect of action	HAND pattern displayed immediately after action
-----	[:	Look at HAND	-----
-1-11	[:	Look at HAND	-1-11
-----	[+1	Raise first finger	1----
111--	[-1	Lower first finger	-11--
-11--	[+34	Raise 3rd & 4th fingers	-111-
11111	[-5	Lower fifth finger	1111-
1-1-1	[-25	Lower 2nd & 5th fingers	1-1--
1-111	[-12345	Close HAND	-----
11111	[-12345	Close HAND	-----
-----	[-12345	Close HAND	-----
-----	[+12345	Raise all fingers	11111

Fig. 5.10. Some actions and patterns of five finger HAND.

The three beads on the five-place ABACUS are shown as O's, the spaces being ='s, e.g. =O=OO. The underline shows the position of PURR-PUSS, so PURR-PUSS is touching the bead in the second place from the left. Patterns following the actions [>, [<, [>> and [<< are 3-digit patterns, with digits indicating (1=yes, 0=no) whether PURR-PUSS is at the left end of ABACUS, is touching a bead, and is at the right end of ABACUS, respectively, or not. The one-digit patterns following the actions [=<, [== and [=> indicate whether PURR-PUSS is at the left end of ABACUS, is touching a bead, or is at the right end of ABACUS, respectively.

ABACUS before action	Action	Effect of action	ABACUS after action	Pattern for PURR-PUSS after action
=O=OO	[>	Move right one place	=O=OO	000
=OO=O	[<	Move left one place	=OO=O	010
=O=OO	[>>	Push right one place	==OOO	010
==OOO	[<<	Push left one place	=OOO=	010
==OOO	[==	Touching bead?	==OOO	1
=O=OO	[=<	At left end?	=O=OO	1
=O=OO	[=>	At right end?	=O=OO	1
=O=OO	[<	Move left one place	=O=OO	100
=O=OO	[>>	Push right one place	=O=OO	011
=OO=O	[==	Touching bead?	=OO=O	0
=OO=O	[=>	At right end?	=OO=O	0
=OO=O	[=<	At left end?	=OO=O	0

Fig. 5.11. Some actions and patterns of ABACUS.

PURR-PUSS, BODY AND WORLD   97

(a)

[Map diagram with rooms labeled SMALL ROOM, SUN ROOM, LONG ROOM, with north arrow. Grid squares contain numbers read across or down:]

SUN ROOM area:
37
1 3
7 4
23

32   7
6 1 1 3
   0   4
   1 20

Other squares:
36   17
1 3 3 3
7 0   4
   3 20

30   2   4   10   2   7
3   3 1 1 2 2   3 1 3 3
6 3 0 1 1 2 2 3 0 3 1 7
17   6   12   14   16   36
              21
              4 4
              21

34   12   6   17
3   2 3 1 3 3 3 3
7   3 2 3 1 3 3 7
17   16   16   36

Note. Read numbers across or down[13].

                                    LONG ROOM

The patterns seen by PURR-PUSS in each possible position in SQUARES following any of the actions [F, [L, [R or [G are shown by the numbers in the squares above[13]. The arrow indicates that PURR-PUSS is in the SUN ROOM facing north. If she does a [G action, which does not move her, the next pattern is "7". A 90° left turn by action [L would then make her face west and see the pattern "1". Now a forward action, [F, would make her move into the neighbouring square to see "6". A 90° right turn with [R would show her "32". This short path is marked by arrows and a dotted line in the diagram (b) below. In addition to [G, PURR-PUSS has the "look" actions [B, [C and [D, which are followed by one-digit patterns (1=yes, 0=no) indicating whether the square to the left, front or right, respectively, is a wall. At the end of the path shown below, the actions [B, [C and [D would give patterns "1", "0" and "0", respectively, because there is a wall on her left, but not in front or to the right.

(b)

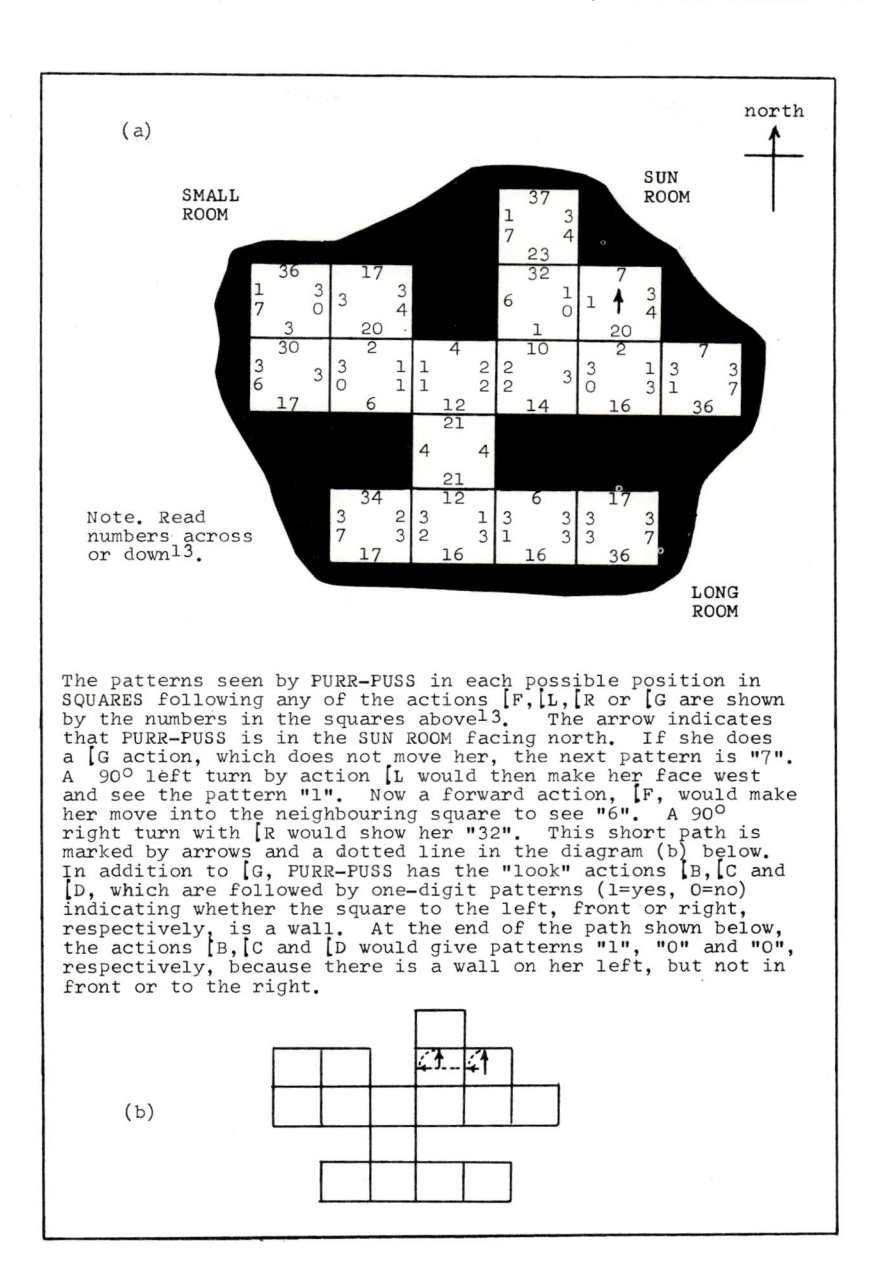

Fig. 5.12. Some actions and patterns of SQUARES.

98 THINKING WITH THE TEACHABLE MACHINE

low wall square, or a high wall square. When floor squares are adjacent PURR–PUSS can move from one to another. The maze will be set up so that there are three connected ROOMS. No high wall will be used. PURR–PUSS will be taught in Chapter 7 to say which room she is in and to go to a specified room. This will illustrate possibilities and difficulties in verbal communication with PURR–PUSS. Figure 5.12 provides a reference for the actions and patterns appropriate to SQUARES.[13]

SQUARES is the last of the body and world features that are determined by MEDEATOR. At times, Teacher will wish to add his own choice of features to the body and world of PURR–PUSS. He is always free to do this. The EYE of Fig. 7.1 is provided in this way. He is also free to instruct MEDEATOR to perform other functions for him. Ideally, we would give PURR–PUSS a real body in a real world so that there would be no need for MEDEATOR to simulate body and world.[14] Unfortunately, robots are difficult to design and expensive to build. We had a robot CAESAR that provided a taste of the advantages of a real body and world, but the behaviour of CAESAR when driven by PURR–PUSS was difficult to describe satisfactorily with the printed word. CAESAR was a self-propelled trolley (Fig. 1.1) fitted with touch sensors. The most recent robot, ESAW, has an eye comprising an array of light sensors inserted in the surface of a table. An arm moves over the table and can be lowered to pick up and transport flat objects. The Eye-Sucker-Arm-World is proving to be a rich environment for PURR–PUSS.

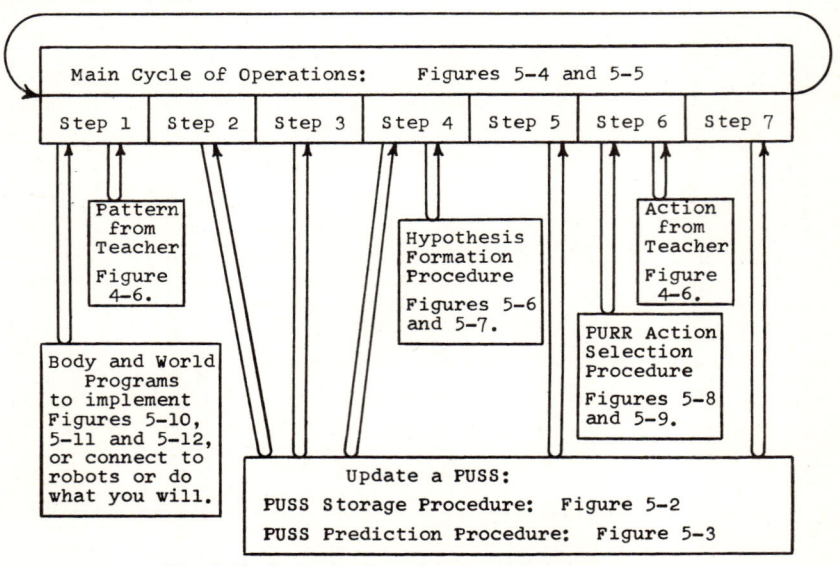

Fig. 5.13. Organization of the complete program.

This chapter has described the detailed operation of PURR–PUSS and of her body and world. To guide the reader who wishes to write his or her own program, Fig. 5.13 brings together the various parts and shows how a complete program should be organized.[15]

Notes on Chapter 5

1. Several PUSSes have been added since the research was thawed out. One PUSS handles the drawing environment used in Chapter 3 for examples. One PUSS handles ESAW, the Eye-Sucker-Arm-World robot. See UC–DES/9 for Alex Palfi's article on teaching with ESAW. The Appendix also represents work carried out since the thaw.

The structure of PURR–PUSS should be seen as but a single example of a "family" of possible structures. We know little as yet about how to channel events from a body and world into a multiple context.

2. Pattern–PUSS provides a "planning space" (Newell and Simon, 1972, p. 433) for hypotheses (i.e. plans) that is smaller than the whole task space (patterns and actions), but is still rather too large. Intuitively, one feels that the planning space should be further limited to, say, external patterns so that PURR–PUSS can look ahead further in time with shorter hypotheses. Perhaps a threading PUSS could be used for hypothesis formation. The patterns of such a threading hypothesis would become a string of subgoals through which a somewhat cleverer PURR would lead PURR–PUSS.

Arguments, like the one above, for reducing the amount of information tend to lead one into further arguments for hierarchical organization and information "chunks" (see Simon and Chase, 1973). A mechanism for generating hierarchical layers of PUSSes was proposed in UC–DSE/3 (p. 26). Higher level PUSSes processed significant events passed up to them from the lower level PUSSes. A significant event was one in which a choice of action occurred. These decision points were the events of the higher PUSSes.

In contrast to this kind of mechanism, it is remarkable how ordinary language copes with a multiplicity of levels in a horizontal fashion. Thus, words in a sentence can operate at different levels without their hierarchical positions being marked in the text. Underlying rules and conventions of syntax and semantics arrange for the hierarchy through features like word order, special words and naming. Often it would be difficult to represent their relative significance even by an hierarchy. Multiple context gives PURR–PUSS this kind of horizontal structure and it is my present opinion that no attempt should be made to impose a hierarchical structure or forced chunking of information until we are sure that it is necessary.

3. In the current program, instead of deleting the hypothesis in step 8 of Fig. 5.8, it is deleted in step 2 of Fig. 5.6 when the first pattern on the hypothesis list does not match the current pattern and pattern–PUSS has predicted (i.e. an alternative hypothesis may be available).

Hypothesis formation to novelty is likely to be the first target of critics of PURR–PUSS. They could point out that, when memory is filled with a great variety of events in a highly interconnected form, the hypothesis formation procedure will be unable to find desirable paths to novelty and will spend a great deal of computation time discovering no path to novelty. For example, suppose that from the present context there are 3 predicted events and from each of these 3 more, and so on. If the only novel event is 4 predictions away, the chance of hypothesising a path to that event is $(1/3)^{4-1}$, or $1/27$, which is very small even for an event so close.

It is not sufficient for me to say that all artificial intelligence systems are up against this problem of complexity, because the hypothesis formation procedure of PURR–PUSS appears to be particularly vulnerable to complexity in the environment. Let me offer a number of answers to such a criticism.

The most honest answer: I don't know.

The design strategy answer: My design strategy (See Note 11 for Chapter 1) has not forced me to face this question yet and, since "as humans" we tend not to be very successful in similar situations (see Gaines, 1976a, "On the Complexity of Causal Models"), it may be some time before I have to face it.

The PUSS net answer: When PUSSes had net memories (UC–DSE/6; Andreae and Cleary, 1976), the problem was much less serious because hypothesis formation started by working backwards through memory from novelty. The mew-gram is quite new and we may yet find better ways to form hypotheses.

The small pattern–PUSS answer: Fast backward processing from novelty could be carried out in a small pattern–PUSS, even if all the other PUSSes were very large.

The mew-Brain answer: A neural net equivalent of the mew, as proposed in the Appendix, might have additional advantages over the serial computer version we are using here. The leak-back of chemical codes provides hypothesis paths to novelty.

The time-sharing answer: It may be possible to arrange for hypothesis formation to be carried out while other processes are continuing in PURR–PUSS or in the environment.

The parallel processing answer: Hypotheses might be generated in parallel by a process akin to Brian Gaines' probability-gates network for action selection in STeLLA (UC–DSE/3, p. 34).

The hypothesis improvement answer: By bringing additional PUSSes into the hypothesis formation procedure, the amount of variety in the forward predictions could be controlled, just as the threading PUSSes control the amount of variety in the forward predictions of main–PUSS and action–PUSS.

The consolidation answer: Although novelty goals were introduced originally to give PURR–PUSS exploratory behaviour, they did not cause her to dash about in a random way. The result was, in fact, much more of a consolidation process in which she "ran around known paths tying up loose ends". The whole of her behaviour is directed to consolidating and making accessible the experience which she has had. To behave intelligently in a world of limitless complexity, this machine tends to organize the ground it knows before letting Teacher lead it farther afield.

4. The provision of "needs" could be related to the battery power supply of the robot CAESAR. We can arrange for the robot to send a "hunger" signal to PURR–PUSS when the voltage of its battery falls below some prescribed value. We can also arrange that at a certain place in the environment ("food store"), the batteries are automatically recharged (by "instinct" or "built-in reflex", if you like).

Now we must organize PURR–PUSS to drive CAESAR to food when she feels hunger. This means *either* that hunger must take precedence over novelty *or* that novelty becomes restricted to food when there is hunger. There will be many different ways of accomplishing these alternatives. An obvious way of achieving the first of the alternatives was implemented in PURR–PUSS in her first design (UC–DSE/5), where she had two kinds of goal, reward and novelty, the former always taking precedence over the latter. A second way, directed to the second alternative, was mentioned in Note 8 of Chapter 1. In a third way, we confuse the alternatives as follows.

First, we distinguish three levels of hunger. When "mildly hungry" (voltage below first hunger level), it is important for long-term survival that PURR–PUSS be more interested in finding new ways to food so novelty should play an important part in her hypothesis formation. When "hungry", she should get food by the most direct way because short-term survival is important. When "desperately hungry" (voltage below third hunger level), she should conserve energy and depend upon outside help unless food becomes "in sight".

However, the above does no more than point out some of the obvious problems. Producing a system that actually works is what matters. The mass of waffly suggestions spewed out by armchair researchers is of little or no use to the constructor of a working system. Many of these Notes should be read as admissions of what my system has *not* achieved, rather than as what it will achieve!

5. The loops of event sequences induced in memory by hypothesis formation are reminiscent of the psychologist's "circular reactions". Consider, for example, how Piaget (1964) defines a circular reaction (p. 11): "Subsequently, it suffices that the infant's random movements fortuitously produce something interesting (interesting because it can be assimilated into a prior schema) for him to repeat these new movements immediately. This 'circular reaction', as it has been called, plays an essential role in sensorimotor development and represents a more advanced form of assimilation".

6. The education of PURR–PUSS will have to provide her with plenty of varied experience and sufficient opportunity to establish the reachableness of her memories by hypothesis-following. "Free expression under guidance" seems to sum up the twofold need of (i) being guided into novel experiences and of (ii) being allowed to consolidate the new experiences by loops.

7. The current version of PURR–PUSS contains an additional option at priority level 3, and not using KORSHN, that allows the action to be selected from the action–pattern predicted by a threading PUSS if the pattern of that action–pattern matches the hypothesis. This additional decision strategy enables speech to be mimicked without the uncertainties (due to KORSHN) of priority 4 decisions.

8. In "The Working Brain" by the Russian neuropsychologist Luria (1973, p. 31), we read " . . . all types of human conscious activity are always formed with the support of external auxiliary tools or aids. . . . The development of any type of complex conscious activity at first is expanded in character and requires a number of external aids for its performance, and not until later does it gradually become condensed and converted into an automatic motor skill."

The importance of the world around us as a vast memory is emphasised by Pribram (1969b, p. 209): "We are little aware of the amount of our memory that is carried 'out there'——not in our brains but in our homes, jobs and libraries. Given these highly structured inputs, the machinery of our brains can restructure——reconstruct——a remembrance from the bits and dabs actually stored in the head."

9. In UC/DSE/7, I have suggested that the main different kinds of body features are represented by echo-speech, fingers, scanning-vision, pauses (i.e. time), mimic-speech and reverberant-sound-images. Another aspect of the importance of the body for thought is what I call "body-coding". It may be illustrated by quoting Norman and Rumelhart (1975, p. 45): "many words must have some underlying primitive

representations, ... " and "we believe the primitives that underlie language are general cognitive building blocks, not just linguistic ones ... " and (p. 56) "In a real sense, a sentence does not exist in memory after it has been interpreted; rather, the sentence is used to provide instructions as to how to modify the structures of memory to convey the deep, underlying components that comprise meaning." I presume that these underlying primitives are represented by internal body functions. We might suspect use of the hundreds of skeletal muscles in the human body. Perhaps, they can be used in a subliminal way to hold information without causing gross distortions of the body. Perhaps, some of this body-coding shows on the surface in facial tensions, grimaces, etc.

Evidence for something like body-coding comes from Furth (1966) who argues strongly for non-linguistic thinking. In summarising his conclusions (p. 228), he says "If then the thinking processes of the deaf can and must be explained without recourse to language, a nonverbal approach to thinking may be a fruitful one for studying thinking in general."

Although body-coding could be used for a few (even up to a hundred) "underlying primitive representations", it is not reasonable for the details of intentions or "current thoughts" to be held in that way. There is a need for an intermediate term memory that will hold a variety of detailed and changing information. This could be provided by a PUSS of limited size that shifted out old information as new information came in (as in the PUSS net memories of UC–DSE/6). Alternatively, (as in the STEMPORE of UC–DSE/5) novelty goals can be restricted to the more recent events. In the current version of PURR–PUSS hypothesis formation has only a small chance of not using the newest prediction associated with a context. In this way, there is an increased accessibility of hypotheses to recent information and PURR–PUSS tends to go on thinking about what she is thinking!

10. The importance of the body, and in particular the hands, for intelligence was neatly stated by Montessori (1949, p. 26) in her fascinating book "The Absorbent Mind": "The hands are the instruments of man's intelligence". I have sometimes thought of PURR–PUSS as being a kind of information-sponge, so the title of Dr. Montessori's book is particularly suggestive for me.

11. The problem of "attention" has been side-stepped in the present design of PURR–PUSS by making an action on her body or world restrict the pattern that follows it. In other words, the choice of action contains the choice of field of attention. In later developments, one can expect (i) simultaneous input of patterns from different parts of the environment to different PUSSes, and (ii) "interrupts" which automatically force the input of patterns (e.g. from large changes in the peripheral field of vision). It is not obvious to me that, even then, the direction of attention need be separated from the choice of action and the dominance of some contexts over others. The central importance often ascribed to the direction of attention (and the associated phenomena of arousal, orientation, etc.) in psychology may be unwarranted. Complex mechanisms are likely to be involved (in the interconnections of brain and body) but I would not go as far as Waddington (in Kenny *et al.* 1972, p. 37) in saying that the direction of attention was "one of the main mysteries in the operations of the mind".

12. Only a few of the actions and patterns of HAND, ABACUS and SQUARES are used in the interactions reported in Chapters 6 and 7. The others are included in Figs 5.10 to 5.12 to provide a better idea of the body and world. For instance, ABACUS becomes much more interesting when PURR–PUSS pushes the beads around.

13. The patterns in the SQUARES world are derived as follows. A 5-bit binary word gives, in order, the presence (1) and absence (0) of a wall in the squares adjacent to PURR–PUSS and lying to the left, half-left, front, half-right, and right of her, respectively. The octal equivalent of this binary word is the pattern given to PURR–PUSS. For example, 37 is octal for 11111 which means that all five of the adjacent squares are walls. This is what PURR–PUSS sees when facing north in the northernmost square of Fig. 5.12 (a).

14. In 1943, Kenneth Craik advanced his well-known hypothesis: "My hypothesis then is that thought models, or parallels, reality——that its essential feature is not 'the mind', 'the self', 'sense-data', nor propositions but symbolism, and that this symbolism is largely of the same kind as that which is familiar to us in mechanical devices which aid thought and calculation . . . Again, there is no doubt that we do use external and mechanical symbolization to assist our own thinking. Provided with a piece of paper we can . . . ". (Pages 57, 59.) Was this the first anticipation of a computer system that incorporates the body and world in its predictive model of that same body and world?

The importance of the body for intelligence is stressed by many other people, but few more strongly than Dreyfus (1972) in his "What Computers Can't Do". (For some obscure reason he does not seem to think that digital computers can be given bodies.) On page 167 he writes "The body contributes three functions not present, and not as yet conceived in digital computer programs: (1) the inner horizon, that is, the partially indeterminate, predelineated anticipation of partially indeterminate data (this does not mean the anticipation of some completely determinate alternatives, or the anticipation of completely unspecified alternatives, which would be the only possible digital implementation); (2) the global character of this anticipation which determines the meaning of the details it assimilates and is determined by them; (3) the transferability of this anticipation from one sense modality and one organ of action to another. All these are included in the general human ability to acquire bodily skills. Thanks to this fundamental ability an embodied agent can dwell in the world in such a way as to avoid the infinite task of formalizing everything." PURR–PUSS demonstrates that digital systems, too, can avoid formalizing everything if they are taught paradigmatically with a body in the real world.

The importance of the body is emphasised in a different way by Eastern cultures. As Ornstein (1972) points out (p. 168): "More consideration is given within these traditions to the interrelatedness of consciousness and 'the body' than is usual in Western psychology."

15. Ian Witten has written an Algol program of PURR–PUSS from the procedures in this chapter. It is given in UC-DSE/11, with an explanation of how to use it.

6. Learning to Count

"... as showing that just the ability to count is itself something rather striking."

A. J. P. Kenny
"The Nature of Mind"

Two Tasks

Counting is a familiar procedure. In our youth we learn to count with our hands. The ability to count is something that we use in many different ways. Its importance is unquestionable.

In teaching PURR–PUSS to count objects with her HAND, we find how easy it is to teach her simple tasks and how she can treat a never-seen-before object as an object, just because it is presented in an appropriate context.

After teaching PURR–PUSS the COUNTING OBJECTS task, we go on to teach her COUNTING BEADS. The second task will use the ability to count with HAND and it will be found that the counting process does not have to be re-taught for the new task. Once the appropriate context is presented, the previous ability is transferred to the new task. This is an example of cumulative learning. However, transfer of learning from an earlier experience to a new experience is not all that is necessary for cumulative learning. We must also be sure that PURR–PUSS retains the ability in the earlier task. With the multiple context provided by the PUSSes, PURR–PUSS can, indeed, use the counting on HAND procedure for either COUNTING OBJECTS or COUNTING BEADS and she learns to "know" which of the two tasks she is engaged in.[1]

In this chapter, the teaching will be carefully planned and executed so the result will appear quite formal. This has been done to ensure that the result is as easy to follow as possible. The teaching will illustrate most of the concepts, like threads and dense events, introduced in Chapter 3. First, we must introduce a more concise method of listing the interaction with PURR–PUSS.

A Short Form Description

The illustrative interactions given in Figs 4.2 and 4.7 were useful for explaining in detail what PURR–PUSS was doing during a short introductory run. In the longer interactions to be described now, a short form of description is

LEARNING TO COUNT 105

employed to emphasise the overall pattern of behaviour, to avoid irrelevant detail and to present a more readable result. A short form equivalent of Figs 4.2 and 4.7 is given in Fig. 6.1.

Predictions, priority levels and hypotheses are omitted from the short form description; they will be mentioned only when needed to clarify particular steps.[2] When Teacher selects an action for PURR–PUSS the action is underlined. Null patterns and actions are shown as "–". Echoed patterns are indicated by "e" in the short form; the actual pattern received by PURR–PUSS in each case can be seen by looking at the preceding speech action.

```
=START   =DOONE      [TWO     [DOTHREE   [4       [DOFIVE    e      SEA
=ONE     =DOTWO      [THREE   [DOFOUR    [5       =ANYTHING  e      SHORE
=TWO     =DOTHREE    [FOUR    [DOFIVE    –        [DOONE     ... 81 ...
=THREE   =DOFOUR     [FIVE    =ANYTHING  ... 56 ...           e      –
=FOUR    =DOFIVE     ... 31 ...          –        –          AND    –
... 6 ...            =START   [DOONE     –        –          THE    –
=FIVE    =ANYTHING   [ONE     [DOTWO     –        –          SHELLS –
=START   =DOONE      [TWO     [DOTHREE   SAY      –          SHE    –
=ONE     =DOTWO      [THREE   [DOFOUR    –        SHE        ... 86 ...
=TWO     =DOTHREE    [FOUR    [DOFIVE    ... 61 ...           SELLS  –
=THREE   =DOFOUR     ... 36 ...          e        SELLS      ARE    –
... 11 ...           [FIVE    =ANYTHING  e        SEA        SEA    –
=FOUR    =DOFIVE     =START   [DOONE     e        SHELLS     SHELLS –
=FIVE    =ANYTHING   [1       [DOTWO     e        ON         I'M    –
=START   =DOONE      [2       [DOTHREE   e        THE        ... 91 ...
=ONE     =DOTWO      [3       [DOFOUR    ... 66 ...           SURE   –
=TWO     =DOTHREE    ... 41 ...          e        SEA        –      –
... 16 ...           [4       [DOFIVE    e        SHORE      –      –
=THREE   =DOFOUR     [5       =ANYTHING  e        –          –      –
=FOUR    =DOFIVE     =START   [DOONE     –        –          –      –
=FIVE    =ANYTHING   [ONE     [DOTWO     –        –          ... 96 ...
=START   [DOONE      [TWO     [DOTHREE   ... 71 ...           SAY    –
[ONE     [DOTWO      ... 46 ...          –        –          e      SHE
... 21 ...           [THREE   [DOFOUR    SAY      –          e      SELLS
[TWO     [DOTHREE    [FOUR    [DOFIVE    –        SHE        e      SEA
[THREE   [DOFOUR     [FIVE    =ANYTHING  e        SELLS      e      SHELLS
[FOUR    [DOFIVE     =X       [DOONE     e        SEA        ... 101 ...
[FIVE    =ANYTHING   [1       [DOTWO     ... 76 ...           e      ON
=START   [DOONE      ... 51 ...          e        SHELLS     e      THE
... 26 ...           [2       [DOTHREE   e        ON         e      SEA
[ONE     [DOTWO      [3       [DOFOUR    e        THE        etc.
```

Fig. 6.1. Short form version of Figs 4.2 and 4.7.

A Schedule for Two Tasks

In Fig. 6.2, the two tasks, COUNTING OBJECTS and COUNTING BEADS, are related to the subtask for finger-raising and numbering. Each of the main tasks uses the subtask. When the subtask is entered from a main task, it must be left by the exit appropriate to that main task. We shall see that the choice of exit is determined by the threading context of speech. In a loose way, we can say that PURR–PUSS keeps track of which task she is engaged in by talking to herself as she goes along.

106   THINKING WITH THE TEACHABLE MACHINE

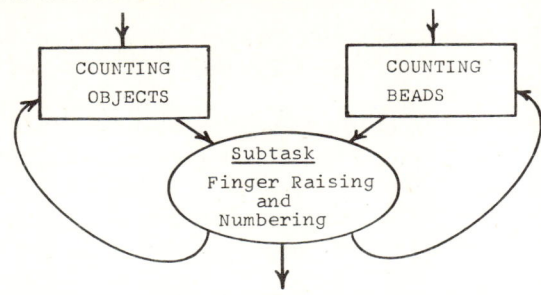

Fig. 6.2. COUNTING OBJECTS and COUNTING BEADS with common subtask.

The subtask comprises two parts, the finger-raising part, which increases the count on the fingers when a new object or bead is encountered, and the numbering part, which reports the number of fingers raised. These two parts are shown to the right and to the left, respectively, in the dotted box in Fig. 6.3. It can be seen from Fig. 6.3 that the relationship between main tasks and

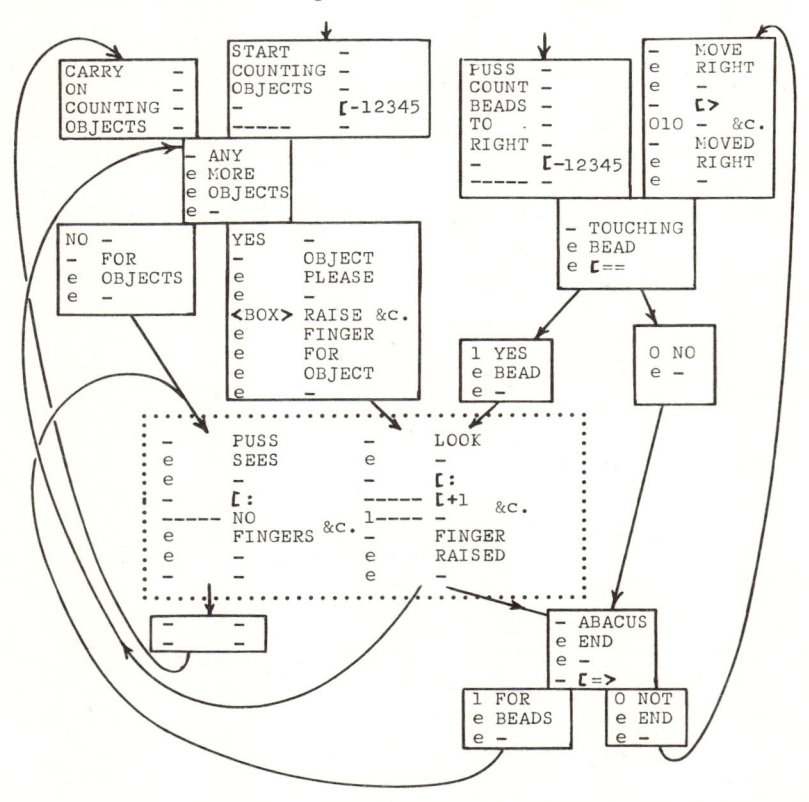

Fig. 6.3. Schedule for COUNTING OBJECTS and COUNTING BEADS.

LEARNING TO COUNT   107

subtask is, in fact, slightly more complicated than suggested by Fig. 6.2, but the choice of exit is a problem only after the finger-raising part of the subtask.

It was not possible to show in full the dense events in Fig. 6.3, so they have been abbreviated there to:

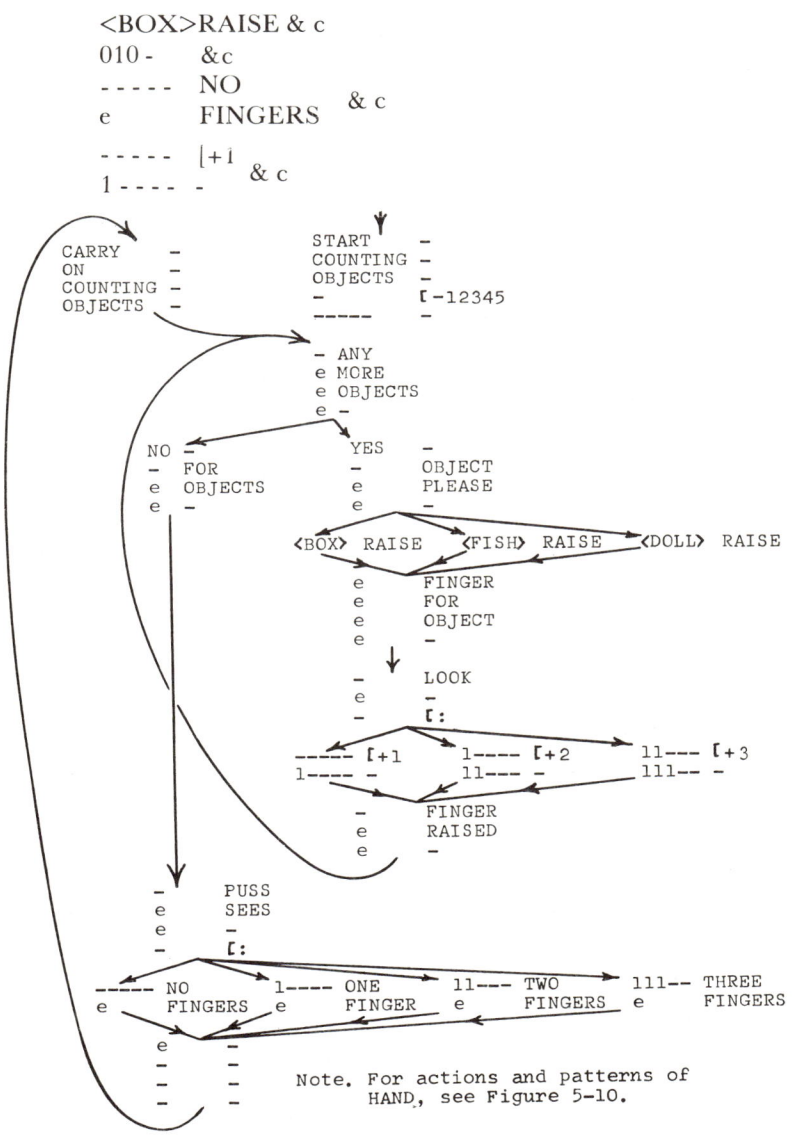

```
         <BOX>RAISE & c
010 -        & c
- - - - -    NO
   e         FINGERS    & c

- - - - -    |+1
1 - - - -  -          & c
```

```
                              ↓
         CARRY      -      START         -
         ON         -      COUNTING      -
         COUNTING   -      OBJECTS       -
         OBJECTS    -         -        [-12345
                              - - - - -

                           -  ANY
                           e  MORE
                           e  OBJECTS
                           e  -

              NO  ←        YES          -
              -   FOR      -         OBJECT
              e   OBJECTS  e         PLEASE
              e   -        e

            <BOX> RAISE    <FISH> RAISE    <DOLL> RAISE

                           e      FINGER
                           e      FOR
                           e      OBJECT
                           e      -

                              ↓   LOOK
                           e      -
                           -      [:

         - - - -  [+1     1 - - -  [+2     11 - - -  [+3
         1 - - -  -       11 - - -  -      111 - -   -

                           -   FINGER
                           e   RAISED
                           e   -

              -      PUSS
              e      SEES
              e      -
              -      [:

         - - - -  NO     1 - - -  ONE     11 - - -  TWO     111 - -  THREE
         e        FINGERS  e      FINGER   e        FINGERS   e      FINGERS
         e        -        -               -                  -
         -        -
         -        -       Note. For actions and patterns of
                                HAND, see Figure 5-10.
```

Fig. 6.4. Schedule for COUNTING OBJECTS

108   THINKING WITH THE TEACHABLE MACHINE

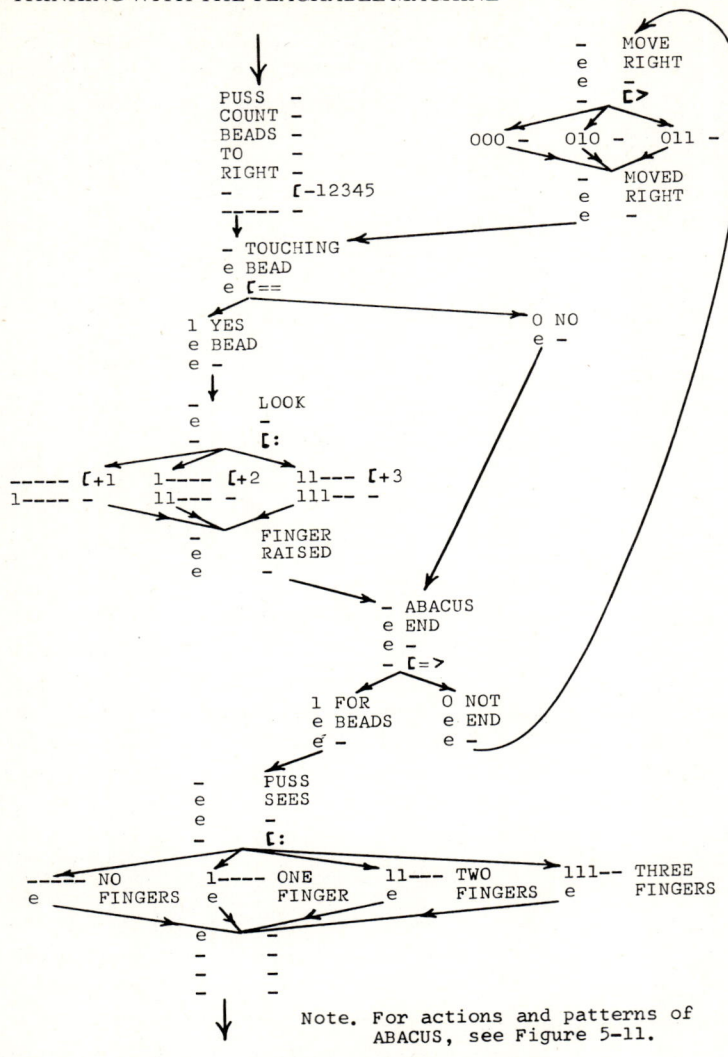

```
                                              -   MOVE
                                              e   RIGHT
                                              e
                    PUSS    -                 -   [>
                    COUNT   -
                    BEADS   -        000 -  010  -   011 -
                    TO      -
                    RIGHT   -
                    -        [-12345          -   MOVED
                    -----  -                  e   RIGHT
                      ↓                       e
                       -  TOUCHING     ←
                       e  BEAD
                       e  [==
                  1 YES                          0 NO
                  e BEAD                         e -
                  e  -
                    ↓     LOOK
                    -      -
                    e      [:
                    -
         ------ [+1    1---- [+2    11---  [+3
         1----  -      11--- -      111--  -
                       -     FINGER
                       e     RAISED
                       e     -

                             -   ABACUS
                             e   END
                             e   -
                             -   [=>

                    1 FOR            0 NOT
                    e BEADS          e END
                    e  -             e  -
                       PUSS
                    -  SEES
                    e  -
                    e  [:
                    -
         ------ NO    1---- ONE    11--- TWO    111-- THREE
         e      FINGERS e    FINGER  e    FINGERS e   FINGERS
                       e     -
                       -
                       e     -
                       -
                       ↓
                    Note. For actions and patterns of
                          ABACUS, see Figure 5-11.
```

Fig. 6.5. Schedule for COUNTING BEADS

With more space available in Figs 6.4 and 6.5, where the schedules of the main tasks are shown separately, the dense events have been given in all of their possible forms.

Two points about the schedules must be emphasised. Teaching PURR–PUSS is not usually preceded by the drawing up of schedules. This is being done to help the reader to see where we are going. Secondly, the reactions of PURR–PUSS will normally determine the course of the teaching as

LEARNING TO COUNT 109

much as will the intentions of Teacher. Even here we shall be unable to follow the schedule exactly and disapproval will have to be used to block unwanted behaviour.

Teaching COUNTING OBJECTS

The main part of the teaching for COUNTING OBJECTS is listed in short form in Fig. 6.6. By comparing this with the schedule for the task given in Fig. 6.4, it will be seen that the first 50 steps take PURR–PUSS around the schedule once. It is all new to PURR–PUSS so she is unable to select an action herself. Teacher provides all actions except the null actions.

On step 57, the context is familiar, being the same as on step 14, so PURR–PUSS starts selecting actions. All goes well until step 64 when the novel pattern 1 - - - - is disregarded and a priority 4 decision NO is disapproved by Teacher. Disapproval is indicated by a ⟨D⟩ just after the action in the listing. From step 66 to 69 Teacher establishes the same context again[3] so as to be able to give PURR–PUSS the desired response ONE on step 70.

The same error arises again on step 85, but here the action YES is selected by a priority 4 decision together with mimic-speech. Disapproval on this occasion and on step 110 for the NO case forces PURR–PUSS to wait for Teacher to say whether it is YES or NO, instead of trying to mimic Teacher's earlier words.

However, priority 4 decisions are not always disapproved, as can be seen from steps 94 to 97 where the actions "RAISE FINGER FOR OBJECT" are all selected at this priority level since main–PUSS and pattern–PUSS have novel contexts from the never-seen-before object <FISH>. (This is an example of the 4th case in Fig. 3.8).

The patterns and actions of HAND occur throughout the listing of Fig. 6.6. On step 7 the action [-12345 closes the HAND and the pattern - - - - - following is intended to represent the five lowered fingers. On step 20, the look action [:shows the HAND to be closed still. On step 46, after the look action [: has shown the HAND to be closed, Teacher provides the raise-first-finger action [+1, which is followed by the first-finger-up pattern 1 - - - -.

On steps 63 and 69 the look action shows the first finger to be still raised. Notice that even the second of these actions is selected[3] by PURR–PUSS (at priority level 2) because main–PUSS and pattern–PUSS have familiar contexts. Finger-raising actions have to be provided by Teacher on steps 102 and 151. To understand why PURR–PUSS does not venture a priority 4 decision here, the reader should note the context of physical–PUSS.

The lack of decision by PURR–PUSS on step 118 deserves an explanation. On step 116, the hypothesis "YES – OBJECT PLEASE <BOX> RAISE" was formed. With the arrival of NO on step 117, the hypothesis becomes "–

110   THINKING WITH THE TEACHABLE MACHINE

```
.. 1 ..               .. 46 ..              .. 91 ..              .. 136 ..
- -                   - [:                  - OBJECT              e MORE
- -                   ----- [+1             e PLEASE              e OBJECTS
- -                   1---- -                e -                  e -
START -               - FINGER              <FISH> RAISE          YES -
COUNTING -            e RAISED              e FINGER              - OBJECT
.. 6 ..               .. 51 ..              .. 96 ..              .. 141 ..
OBJECTS -             e -                   e FOR                 e PLEASE
- [-12345             - ANY                 e OBJECT              e -
----- -               e MORE                e -                   <DOLL> RAISE
- ANY                 e OBJECTS             - LOOK                e FINGER
e MORE                e -                   e -                   e FOR
.. 11 ..              .. 56 ..              .. 101 ..             .. 146 ..
e OBJECTS             NO -                  - [:                  e OBJECT
e -                   - FOR                 1---- [+2             e -
NO -                  e OBJECTS             11---- -              - LOOK
- FOR                 e -                   - FINGER              e -
e OBJECTS             - PUSS                e RAISED              - [:
.. 16 ..              .. 61 ..              .. 106 ..             .. 151 ..
e -                   e SEES                e -                   11---- [+3
- PUSS                e -                   - ANY                 111-- -
e SEES                - [:                  e MORE                - FINGER
e -                   1---- NO(D)           e OBJECTS             e RAISED
- [:                  e -                   e NO(D)               e -
.. 21 ..              .. 66 ..              .. 111                .. 156 ..
----- NO              - PUSS                e -(D)                - ANY
e FINGERS             e SEES                STOP -                e MORE
e -                   e -                   - ANY                 e OBJECTS
- -                   - [:                  e MORE                e -
- -                   1---- ONE             e OBJECTS             NO -
.. 26 ..              .. 71 ..              .. 116 ..             .. 161 ..
- -                   e FINGER              e -                   - FOR
CARRY -               e -                   NO -                  e OBJECTS
ON -                  - -                   - FOR                 e -
COUNTING -            - -                   e OBJECTS             - PUSS
OBJECTS -             - -                   e -                   e SEES
.. 31 ..              .. 76 ..              .. 121 ..             .. 166 ..
- ANY                 CARRY -               - PUSS                e -
e MORE                ON -                  e SEES                - [:
e OBJECTS             COUNTING -            e -                   111-- TWO(D)
e -                   OBJECTS -             - [:                  e -
YES -                 - ANY                 11---- TWO            - PUSS
.. 36 ..              .. 81 ..              .. 126 ..             .. 171 ..
- OBJECT              e MORE                e FINGERS             e SEES
e PLEASE              e OBJECTS             e -                   e -
e -                   e YES(D)              - -                   - [:
<BOX> RAISE           e -(D)                - -                   111-- THREE
e FINGER              STOP -                - -                   e FINGERS
.. 41 ..              .. 86 ..              .. 131 ..             .. 176 ..
e FOR                 - ANY                 CARRY -               e -
e OBJECT              e MORE                ON -                  - -
e -                   e OBJECTS             COUNTING -            - -
- LOOK                e -                   OBJECTS -             PUSS -
e -                   YES -                 - ANY
```

Note. See Figure 5-10 for the actions and patterns of HAND.

Fig. 6.6. Teaching COUNTING OBJECTS.

LEARNING TO COUNT 111

OBJECT PLEASE <BOX> RAISE" and the prediction of main–PUSS is the null pattern "–" in agreement with the hypothesis. However, the further prediction FOR from main–PUSS does not agree with OBJECT which is on the top of hypothesis for step 118. Without an hypothesis match, a decision could only be taken at the fourth priority level, but this is precluded by the unfamiliar context "STOP ANY MORE OBJECTS NO" in speech-PUSS.

Teaching COUNTING BEADS

The teaching of Fig. 6.7 follows the schedule of Fig. 6.5 for COUNTING BEADS. Because the finger-raising and numbering subtask is used in this task as well as in COUNTING OBJECTS, we find that PURR–PUSS begins to respond after a few steps with her previously learned ability. Thus, on step 196, after being given the context "–LOOK e – – [:", she is able to raise the first finger correctly. Similarly, the second and third fingers are raised without help on step 250 and step 279, respectively. *The previously learned finger-raising is transferred to the new task as soon as the appropriate context is invoked.*

Disapproval has to be given on step 201, to show that the finger-raising is not to be followed by a return to the COUNTING OBJECTS task, and on step 288 when PURR–PUSS reaches the end of the ABACUS for the first time.

By step 303, most of the COUNTING BEADS task has been learned, but there is still confusion with the COUNTING OBJECTS task because of the common finger-raising procedure. PURR–PUSS has yet to learn to remember which task she is engaged in while doing the finger-raising. On step 201 she was shown that, if she enters the finger-raising (steps 193 to 200) from the COUNTING BEADS task, then she must not try to return to the COUNTING OBJECTS task with "ANY MORE OBJECTS". From steps 306 to 341, we take her into the COUNTING OBJECTS task again and on step 333 disapprove of her attempt to go back to the COUNTING BEADS task.

Now PURR–PUSS has the two tasks distinguished while she does the finger-raising. It is true that a few other minor confusions remain, but, before removing them, let us see how the separation of the tasks has been accomplished so effortlessly. After all, Teacher had to do no more than press the disapproval button on the two occasions that PURR–PUSS made a mistake.

Task-Distinguishing Threads

Figure 6.8(a) shows the two speech threads that pass through the finger-raising procedure according to whether PURR–PUSS is COUNTING OBJECTS or COUNTING BEADS. Since the window of speech–PUSS is of length 5, as PURR–PUSS leaves the finger-raising sequence, the window of

112   THINKING WITH THE TEACHABLE MACHINE

```
  .. 181 ..        .. 221 ..        .. 261 ..        .. 301 ..
COUNT  -         - TOUCHING       e -              111-- THREE
BEADS  -         e BEAD           - MOVE           e FINGERS
TO     -         e [==            e RIGHT          e -
RIGHT  -         0 NO             e -              - -
- [-12345        e -              - [>             - -
  .. 186 ..        .. 226 ..        .. 266 ..        .. 306 ..
-----            - ABACUS         011 -            - -
- TOUCHING       e END            - MOVED          START -
e BEAD           e -              e RIGHT          COUNTING -
e [==            - [=>            e -              OBJECTS -
1 YES            0 NOT             =0=00           - [-12345
 =0=00             .. 231 ..       - TOUCHING       .. 311 ..
  .. 191 ..      e END              .. 271 ..      -----
e BEAD           e -              e BEAD           - ANY
e -              - MOVE           e [==            e MORE
- LOOK           e RIGHT          1 YES            e OBJECTS
e -              e -              e BEAD           e -
- [:               .. 236 ..      e -                .. 316 ..
  .. 196 ..      - [>               .. 276 ..      YES -
----- [+1        010 -            - LOOK           - OBJECT
1---- -          - MOVED          e -              e PLEASE
- FINGER         e RIGHT          - [:             e -
e RAISED         e -              11---- [+3       <CAKE> RAISE
e -               =0=00           111-- -            .. 321 ..
  .. 201 ..        .. 241 ..        .. 281 ..      e FINGER
- ANY (D)        - TOUCHING       - FINGER         e FOR
e -              e BEAD           e RAISED         e OBJECT
- FINGER         e [==            e -              e -
e RAISED         1 YES            - ABACUS         - LOOK
e -              e BEAD           e END              .. 326 ..
  .. 206 ..        .. 246 ..        .. 286 ..      e -
- ABACUS         e -              e -              - [:
e END            - LOOK           - [=>            ----- [+1
e -              e -              1 NOT (D)        1---- -
- [=>            - [:             e -              - FINGER
0 NOT            1---- [+2        - ABACUS           .. 331 ..
  .. 211 ..        .. 251 ..        .. 291 ..      e RAISED
e END            11---- -         e END            e -
e -              - FINGER         e -              - ABACUS (D)
- MOVE           e RAISED         - [=>            e -
e RIGHT          e -              1 FOR            - FINGER
e -              - ABACUS         e BEADS            .. 336 ..
  .. 216 ..        .. 256 ..        .. 296 ..      e RAISED
- [>             e END            e -              e -
000 -            e -              - PUSS           - ANY
- MOVED          - [=>            e SEES           e MORE
e RIGHT          0 NOT            e -              e OBJECTS
e -              e END            - [:               .. 341 ..
 =0=00                                              e -
                                                   - -
```

Note. The position of PURR-PUSS on the ABACUS is shown within the ellipses. Refer to Figure 5-11 for the actions and patterns of ABACUS.

Fig. 6.7. Teaching COUNTING BEADS.

LEARNING TO COUNT 113

speech–PUSS will contain "FOR OBJECT LOOK FINGER RAISED" if she is COUNTING OBJECTS and will contain "YES BEAD LOOK FINGER RAISED" if she is COUNTING BEADS. In (b) and (c) of Fig. 6.8 are given the predictions from these contexts, without and with disapproval marks, respectively. It can be seen that speech–PUSS will prevent PURR–PUSS from giving the wrong action on exit from the finger-raising sequence.

(a) Threads extracted from Figure 6-3.

```
        Speech Thread                              Speech Thread
             for                                        for
      COUNTING OBJECTS                           COUNTING BEADS

                                                       MOVE
    YES                                                RIGHT
    OBJECT                                             MOVED
    PLEASE                                             RIGHT
    RAISE                                              TOUCHING
    FINGER                                             BEAD
    FOR                                                YES
    OBJECT                                             BEAD

       LOOK           }     common      {      LOOK
       FINGER            finger-raising         FINGER
       RAISED              sequence             RAISED

    ANY        ←──── task-distinguishing action ────→   ABACUS
    MORE              on exit from finger-raising       END
    OBJECTS                                             NOT
                                                        END
```

(b) Predictions from speech–PUSS giving correct action for exit from finger-raising.

window of speech–PUSS	prediction	task
FOR OBJECT LOOK FINGER RAISED	ANY	in COUNTING OBJECTS
YES BEAD LOOK FINGER RAISED	ABACUS	in COUNTING BEADS

(c) Predictions from speech–PUSS with disapproval mark preventing incorrect action on exit from finger-raising.

window of speech–PUSS	prediction	disapproval given
FOR OBJECT LOOK FINGER RAISED	ABACUS ⬡D	step 333
YES BEAD LOOK FINGER RAISED	ANY ⬡D	step 201

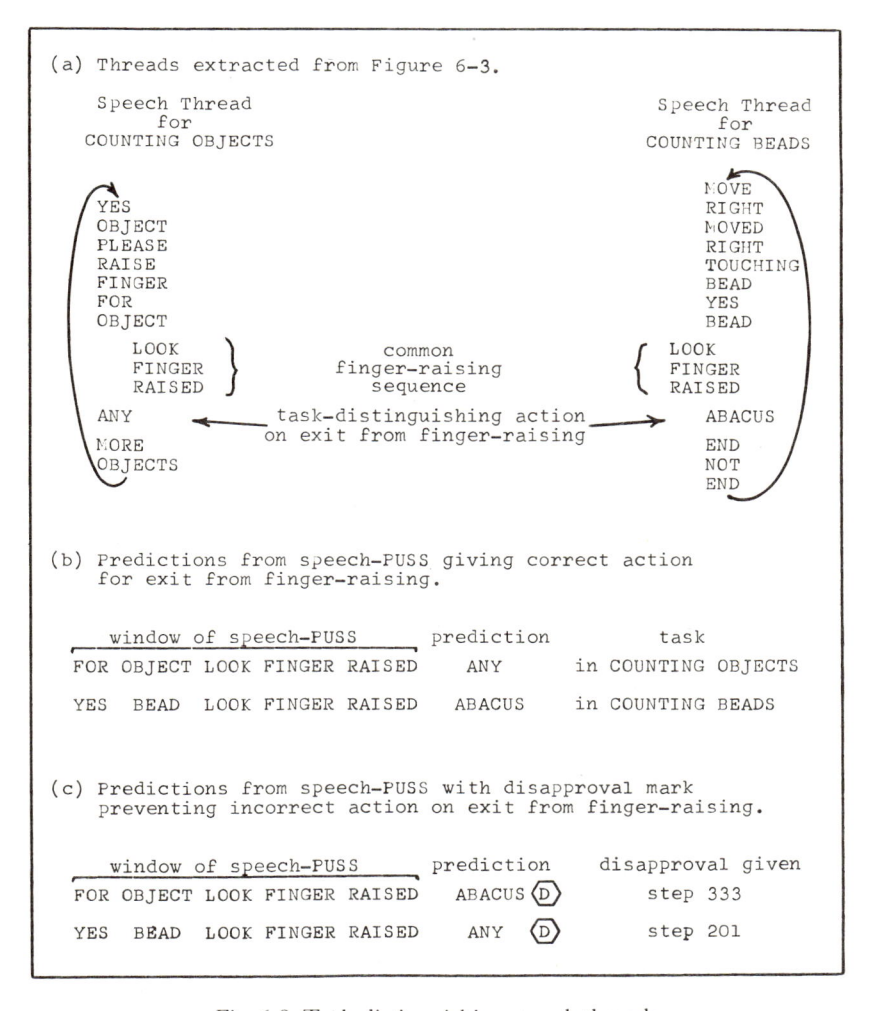

Fig. 6.8. Task-distinguishing speech threads.

114   THINKING WITH THE TEACHABLE MACHINE

However, this does not mean that PURR–PUSS will necessarily choose the correct action. Because of the dense event in the middle of the finger-raising sequence, it will be some time before action–PUSS will have both exit actions (ANY and ABACUS) for all forms of the dense event. On the other hand, main–PUSS with its window of only 3 events is quite clear of the dense event and always has "– FINGER e RAISED e–" in its window on exit from the finger-raising. Indeed, main–PUSS has the correct exit actions from their first occurrences on steps 52 (Fig. 6.6) and 206 (Fig. 6.7). This is still not the whole story, because on step 201 the first action (ANY) was disapproved. Main–PUSS has the disapproval mark finally removed from ANY on step 338 and from ABACUS on step 364 (Fig. 6.9). Disapproval must be established on the longer context of speech–PUSS before it can be removed from the shorter context of main–PUSS.

```
PUSS  –              .. 356 ..          1 FOR              – [=>
COUNT –              – LOOK             e BEADS            1 FOR
BEADS –              e –                e –                .. 381 ..
.. 346 ..            – [:                                  e BEADS
TO –                 ----- [+1          =0=OO              e –
RIGHT                1---- –            .. 371 ..          – PUSS
– [–12345            .. 361 ..          – PUSS             e SEES
----- –              – FINGER           e SEES             e –
– TOUCHING           e RAISED           e –                .. 386 ..
.. 351 ..            e –                – [:               – [:
e BEAD               – ABACUS           1---- THREE (D)    1---- ONE
e [ ==               e END              .. 376 ..          e FINGER
1 YES                .. 366 ..          e –                e –
e BEAD               e –                – END              – –
e –                  – [=>              e –                – –
```

Fig. 6.9. Continuation from Fig. 6.7.

The numbering part of the subtask also has its difficulties, as seen on step 375. Here the pattern 1---- did not induce an hypothesis and a priority 4 decision gave the wrong answer. Disapproval soon prescribes the appropriate context for the situation.[4]

Summary

In this chapter, PURR–PUSS has been shown capable of cumulative learning, earlier learned abilities (like finger-raising) becoming available in their entirety to a new situation as soon as the appropriate context is presented.[5] Her "original" actions have enabled her to count never-seen-before objects and, even when we have disapproved of these low priority actions, they have given us a chance to clarify the appropriateness of various contexts to the task in hand.

Teaching has not required a knowledge of how PURR–PUSS was working but only a certain swiftness in pressing the disapproval button when she did something wrong. It is too difficult to work out ahead what one should do to teach a particular task because PURR–PUSS's actions are so often unexpected. As with teaching humans, when we do not seem to be making progress with teaching PURR–PUSS, the best solution is to try another approach with different contexts. We usually get some idea of the reasons for unsuccessful teaching from the behaviour of PURR–PUSS. In a rather simple way her actions reflect her "thinking".

Notes on Chapter 6

1. As Piaget and Inhelder (1966) say, "One must not think that a young child understands number simply because he can count verbally". The concept of number lies far beyond the simple tasks taught in Chapter 6 and I have no idea what lies between.

The two counting tasks illustrate basic abilities of PURR–PUSS, in so far as we have discovered them to date. The reader should not conclude that, because the tasks appear to be formal ones, that PURR–PUSS is being taught within a formal system. The paradigmatic learning of PURR–PUSS avoids the trap of formal systems and escapes the chains of paradox, as explained in Chapter 1. When the philosopher Lucas (1961, page 44) says "Gödel's theorem must apply to cybernetical machines, because it is of the essence of being a machine, that it should be a concrete instantiation of a formal system", he is forgetting that the formality of an isolated machine disappears in an open system, like PURR–PUSS, interacting with her body and the world.

In looking for tasks to give PURR–PUSS, naturally we considered the experiments used by psychologists for testing such theoretical ideas as the conditioned reflex, habituation, short-term memory and paired-associate learning. Although these concepts appear, at first sight, to be basic and straightforward, they become vague and meaningless when applied to as simple a real system as PURR–PUSS. For example, the person who wants to show that PURR–PUSS does exhibit a conditioned reflex (response) will find no difficulty in constructing illustrative sequences, while the person who wants to show that PURR–PUSS does *not* exhibit a conditioned reflex will find many reasons for discrediting the examples. This concept, like the others, is too vague to be tested.

2. For the reader requiring more details than are given of the interaction with PURR–PUSS in Figs 6.6, 6.7, 6.9 and its continuation in Chapter 7, I have assembled a compact mass of carefully checked data in Figs 6.10 and 6.11. These tables, taken with the data in the text, are designed to enable the determined reader to work out the reasons for each and every one of PURR–PUSS's decisions.

3. The decision of PURR–PUSS to do a [: on step 69 of Fig. 6.6 was made possible by Teacher's delayed disapproval on step 64. It can be seen from Fig. 5.5 that if Teacher

116   THINKING WITH THE TEACHABLE MACHINE

```
         1   2   3   4   5   6   7   8   9  10  11  12  13  14  15  16  17  18  19  20
   0     -   -   -   -   -   -   -   -   -   -   -  KN   -  KN   -   -   -   -   -   -
  20     -   -   -   -   -   -   -   -   -   -   -   -   -   -   -   -   -   -   -   -
  40     -   -   -   -   -   -   -   -   -   -   -   -   -   -   -   -  P2  P1   -  P1
  60    P1   -  P2  P4   D   -   -   -  P2   -   -   -   -   -   -   -   -   -   -  P2
  80    P1  P1  P4   D   D   -   -   -   -   -   -  P1   -  P4  P4  P4  P4   -  P1   -
 100    P2   -   -   -   -   -  P1  P1  P1  P4   D   D   -  P2   -   -   -  P1   -   -
 120    P1  P1   -  P2   -   -   -   -   -   -   -   -   -   -  P1  P1  P1   -   -  P4
 140    P1   -  P3  P4  P4  P4   -  P1   -  P2   -   -   -   -   -  P1  P1  P1   -   -
 160    P1  P1   -  P1  P1   -  P2  P4   D   -   -   -   -   -   -   -   -   -   -   -
 180     -   -   -   -   -   -   -   -   -   -   -   -   -   -   -  P2   -  P2  P2   -
 200    P2   D   -   -   -   -   -   -   -   -   -   -   -   -   -   -   -   -   -   -
 220     -   -   -   -   -   -   -  P2  P2  P2   -  P2  P1   -  P2   -   -  P4  P4   -
 240    P1  P1  P2  P2  P2   -  P1   -  P2  P2   -  P1  P1   -  P2  P2   -  P2  P2  P1
 260     -  P1  P1   -  P2   -  P4  P4   -  P1  P1  P2  P1  P1   -  P1   -  P2  P2   -
 280    P1  P1   -  P1  P1   -  P2  P3   D   -   -   -   -   -   -   -   -   -   -  P2
 300    P2  P2   -   -   -   -   -   -  P2   -  P2  P2  P1   -   -  P4  P1   -   -  P4
 320    P4  P4  P4   -  P1   -  P2  P2   -  P1  P1   -  P2   D   -   -   -   -   -  P2
 340     -   -   -   -   -   -  P2   -  P1  P1  P2  P1  P1   -  P1   -  P2  P1   -   -
 360    P1  P1   -   -  P4   -  P1   -  P2   -  P2  P1   -  P2  P4   D   -   -   -   -
 380    P2   -  P2  P2   -  P2   -  P2  KN   -   -   -   -   -   -   -   -   -   -   -
 400     -  P2  P2   -   -   -   -   -   -   -  P2  P2   -   -   -   -   -   -   -   -
 420     -   -   -   -   -   -   -   -   -   -   -   -   -  P1  P1   -   -   -   -   -
 440     -   -   -   -   -   -   -   -  P2  P2  P2  P1   -  P2  P1  P1  P1  P1  P1  P4
 460    P4  P4   -  P4  P4  P4  P4   -  P4  P4   -   -   -   -   -   -   -   -   -  P2
 480    P2  P2  P2  P1  P1  P1  P1   -  P1  P1   -  P1   -   -   -   -   -   -   -   -
 500     -   -   -  P1  P1  P2  P1  P1  P1  P1  P1   -  P2  P1  P1  P1  KN  P4  P4   -
 520    P4  P4  P1  P1   -   -  P1  P1   D   -   -  P4  P4  P4  P4   -  KN   -   -   -
 540     -   -   -   -   -   -   -   -   -   -   -   -   -  P2   -   -  P4  P4  P4  P4
 560     -   -  P4  P4  P4  P4   -   -  P4  P4  P4  P4  P4   -   -   -   -   -   -   -
 580     -   -   -   -   -   -   -   -   -   -   -   -   -   -   -   -   -   -   -   -
 600     -   -  KN   -   -   -   -   -   -   -   -   -   -   -   -   -   -   -   -   -
 620    P2   -   -   -   -   -   -   -   -   -   -   -   -   -   -   -   -   -   -  P1
 640    P1  P1   -   -   -  P4  P4   -   -  P4  P1  P1  P1   -  P4  P4  P1  P1  P1  P1
 660    P4  P4  P1  P1  P1  P4  P4  P4  P4  P4   -   -  P4  P1  P1  P1  P1  P1  P4  KN
 680    P4  P4  P4  P4  P4  P4  P4   -   -  P4  P4  P4  P4   -  P1  P1  P1  P1  P2  P2   -
 700     -   -  P1   -   -   -   -   -  P4   -   -  P4  P1  P1  P1  P1  P1  P4  P4  P1
 720    P1  P1  P1  P1  P1  P1   -   -  P1  P1  P1  P1   -  P1  P1  P1  P1  P1  P1  P1
 740    P1  P4  P4  P4  P4  P4  KN  P4   -  P4  P1  P1  P1  P1  P1  P1  P1  P1  P1  P1
 760    P1  P1  P1  P1  P1   -  KN  P3   D  P4  P4   -  P1  P1  P1  P1  P1  P1  P1  P1
 780    P1  P1  P1  P1  P1  P1   -   -  P1  P1  P1  P1  P1  P1   -  P1  P1  P1  P1  P1
 800    P1  P1  P1  P1   -   -   -   -   -   -   -   -   -   -   -   -   -   -   -   -
 820     -  P2  P2  P1   -  P2  P1  P1  P1  P1  P4  P1  P1  P1  P1  P1  P1  P1  P4  KN
 840     -   -  P4  P1  P1  P1  P1  P1  P1  P1  P1  P1  P1  P1  P1  P1   -   -  P3
 860    P4  P4  P4  P4   -   -   -   -   -   -   -   -  P4   -   -  P4  P4  P1   -   -
 880    P1  P1  P1  P1  P1  P1  P1  P1  P1  P1  P1  P1  P1  P1  P1  P1  P4  P4   -  P4
```

P1 = priority 1, P2 = priority 2, P3 = priority 3,
P4 = priority 4, D = disapproval, KN = KORSHIN exit.

To obtain step number add row number to column number.
Disapproval is indicated in the step following the
   disapproved action.

Fig. 6.10. Priority at which actions were selected.

LEARNING TO COUNT 117

```
        1   2   3   4   5   6   7   8   9  10  11  12  13  14  15  16  17  18  19  20
   0    -   -   -   -   -   -   -   -   -   -   -   -   -   -   -   -   -   -   -   -
  20    -   -   -   -   -   W-  -   -   -   -   -   -   U-  W1  -   -   -   -   -   -
  40    -   -   -   -   -   -.  .   -   -   -   -   -   -   U-  C1  U1  U1  U1  U1  U1
  60    U1  U1  W1  -   -   -   U-  C1  -   -   -   -   -   C-  U1  U1  U1  U1  U1  U1
  80    U1  U1  -2  -   -   -   -   U-  CL  Uh  U-  U1  W1  -   -   U-  U1  U1  U1  U1
 100    W1  -   -   -   -   U-  U1  U1  U1  -5  -   -   -   U-  U1  C6  Uh  U-  U8  Uh
 120    Uh  Uh  Uh  Wh  -   -   -   -   U-  C1  UL  Uh  Uh  Uh  Uh  Uh  Uh  Ch  Uh  U-
 140    U4  Wh  -h  -   -   U-  U4  Uh  Uh  Wh  -   -   -   -   U-  UL  Uh  Uh  Ch  Uh
 160    Uh  Uh  Uh  Uh  Uh  Uh  Wh  -   -   -   -   U-  C-  -   -   -   -   U-  WL  -
 180    -   -   -   -   -   -   -   -   -   -   -   -   -   C-  U1  U1  U1  U1  U1  U1
 200    UL  -   -   -   U-  -   -   -   -   -   -   -   -   -   -   -   -   -   -   -
 220    -   -   W-  -   -   -   -   U-  U1  U1  U1  U1  U1  U1  U1  W1  -   -   -   U-
 240    U1  U1  C1  U1  U1  U1  U1  U1  U1  U1  U1  U1  U1  U1  U1  U1  U1  U3  Uh  Uh
 260    Uh  Uh  Uh  Uh  Wh  -   -   -   U-  U3  Uh  Ch  U6  Uh  Uh  Uh  Uh  Ch  U1  U1
 280    U1  U1  U1  UL  Uh  Uh  Wh  -h  -   -   -   U-  C-  -   -   -   -   -   U-  C2
 300    U1  U1  U1  U1  U1  C1  U1  U1  U1  U1  U1  U1  U1  U1  CL  Uh  U-  U2  Wh  -
 320    -   -   U-  U4  Uh  Uh  Ch  UL  Uh  Uh  Uh  Uh  -   -   -   U-  U-  U1  UL
 340    Wh  -   -   U-  U1  U1  U1  U1  U1  U1  U1  C1  U6  Uh  Uh  Uh  Uh  Ch  U8  Uh
 360    Uh  Uh  Uh  U-  UL  Ch  U-  U1  U1  U1  U1  U1  U1  C3  -   -   -   -   -   U-
 380    UL  Uh  Uh  Uh  Uh  Ch  U-  U1  U1  U1  U1  C1  -   -   -   -   -   -   -   -
 400    C-  U1  W1  -   -   -   -   C-  U2  Wh  -   -   -   -   -   -   -   -   -   -
 420    -   -   -   -   -   -   -   -   -   -   -   -   U-  U1  U1  W1  -   -   -   -
 440    -   -   -   -   -   -   -   U-  U1  U1  U1  U1  U1  U1  U1  U1  U1  U3  Uh  -h
 460    -   -   -   -   -   -   -   -   W-  -   -   -   -   W-  -   U-  U1  U1  U1  U1
 480    U1  U1  U1  U1  UL  Uh  Uh  Uh  Uh  Wh  U-  U1  W1  -   -   -   -   U-  U6  -
 500    Uh  Uh  Uh  Ch  Uh  U1  U1  U7  Uh  Uh  Uh  Uh  Ch  U1  U2  -h  -   -   -   -
 520    -   U-  U7  Uh  Uh  Uh  Ch  Uh  U-  U1  U1  -1  -   -   -   -   -   C-  W1
 540    -   -   -   -   -   U-  U1  -   -   -   -   U-  C1  U1  U1  U1  -1  -   -   -
 560    -   -   -   -   -   -   -   -   U-  U-  U-  W-  -   -   -   C-  W9  -
 580    -   -   -   -   -   -   -   -   -   -   -   -   -   -   -   -   -   -   -   -
 600    -   -   -   -   -   -   W-  -   -   -   W-  -   -   -   -   -   U-  UL  Ch
 620    Uh  -h  -   -   -   -   -   -   W-  -   -   -   W-  -   -   -   -   -   U-  U1
 640    U1  U1  U1  U1  U1  U1  -1  -   -   C-  U1  U1  U1  U1  -1  U-  U4  Uh  Uh
 660    -   U-  U1  U1  -1  -   -   -   -   -   C-  U1  U1  U1  U1  U-  U-
 680    U-  -   -   U-  -   C-  U-  -   U-  U-  U-  U9  Uh  Uh  Wh  -
 700    -   U-  U1  U1  U1  U1  C1  -1  -   C-  U1  U1  U1  U-  U-  UL
 720    Uh  Uh  Uh  Uh  Uh  Uh  Uh  Ch  Uh  Uh  Uh  Uh  Uh  Uh  Ch  U1  U1
 740    U1  U-  -L  -   -   -   U-  U-  C-  UL  Uh  Uh  Uh  Uh  Uh  Uh  Uh
 760    Uh  Uh  Uh  Uh  Uh  Uh  Wh  -h  -   -   U-  UL  Uh  Uh  Uh  Uh  Uh  Uh  Uh
 780    Uh  Uh  Uh  Uh  Uh  Uh  Uh  Ch  Uh  Uh  Uh  Uh  Uh  Uh  Uh  Uh  Uh  Uh
 800    Uh  Uh  Uh  Uh  Uh  C-  -   -   -   U-  W-  -   -   -   -   -   U-  U3  U-
 820    C-  UL  Uh  Uh  Uh  Uh  Uh  Uh  Ch  U-  UL  Uh  Uh  Uh  Uh  Uh  Uh  -h  -
 840    -   U-  C-  UL  Uh  Uh  Uh  Uh  Uh  Uh  Uh  Uh  Uh  Uh  Uh  Uh  Uh  Ch  -h
 860    -   -   U-  -   -   -   -   -   U-  U1  U1  -1  -   C-  C-  U-  U-  UL  Uh
 880    Uh  Uh  Uh  Uh  Uh  Uh  Uh  Uh  Uh  Uh  Uh  Uh  Uh  Uh  Uh  Uh  -h  -   -   -
```

W = wrong prediction, U = unique correct prediction
C = correct prediction amongst two or more,
1,2,..9 = hypothesis of length 1,2,..9 patterns formed,
L = hypothesis longer than 9 patterns formed,
h = formed hypothesis being followed.
To obtain step number add row number to column number.

Fig. 6.11. Hypotheses and main–PUSS predictions.

does not disapprove an action selected (box 6 of the figure) immediately, the update of main–PUSS (box 7) will take place without disapproval. This is what happened on step 64, so the main–PUSS event "1 - - - - NO" was stored without disapproval. If Teacher had been prompt, this event would have been stored with disapproval and hypothesis match would not have been possible on step 69. It is normal for disapproval to be delayed because the actions to be disapproved are usually unexpected.

4. Newell and Simon (1972) make a number of predictions about the human information processing system (IPS). In particular, on page 803 they "confess to a strong premonition that the actual organization of human programs closely resembles the production system organization, . . .". Their production systems are somewhat more sophisticated than the simple context → event productions of my PUSSes, but their "features of productions and production systems that point to their being an appropriate theoretical construct" are equally applicable to PUSSes:—

"1. A production system is capable of arbitrary calculations. . . . 2. . . encodes homogeneously . . . 3. . . each production is independent of the others . . 4. . . strong stimulus-response flavour . . 5. The productions themselves seem to represent meaningful components . . . 6. The dynamic working memory for a production system is the STM (i.e. the memory on which its productions are contingent . . .) . . 7. . . the LTM *is* just a very large production system. . . 8. . . the overly focused non-distractable character of programming models . . . is not a structural feature of a production organization . . .".

According to number 6, the windows of the PUSSes would provide STM (short term memory), while the PUSSes themselves are, according to 7, the long term memory (LTM). Newell and Simon go on to list "the important characteristics of the human IPS" on page 808. It can be read as a specification for a PURR–PUSS with about seven PUSSes and a faster processing speed than at present! A point in their specification that seems particularly relevant to the distinguishing of two tasks is "3. Its STM holds about five to seven symbols, but only about two can be retained for one task while another unrelated task is performed. All the symbols in STM are available to the processes (i.e. there is no accessing or search of STM)". Interpreting a "symbol" as a PUSS window-length context, this suggests a system of at least seven PUSSes (to provide seven contexts) of which four are threading PUSSes so that two can hold contexts for one task while the other two are helping with the task in hand. If they are right and *if* this kind of interpretation is valid, the present complexity of PURR–PUSS is not too far below what is needed for human competence in problem-solving.

5. The immediate learning of PURR–PUSS may be contrasted with the gradual learning of those systems which depend upon weight-changing and probability estimation. In PURR–PUSS, the strength with which some memory trace is learned may be seen as the density of memory sequences leading to that trace. A much-learned situation will be characterized by a high density of sequences leading to the recall of that situation. We can also imagine a well-learned topic characterized by many sequences leading out of the topic and back into it again. I call this "thicket" learning to emphasise the ability of the re-entrant memory sequences to hold thinking within the thicket and thus provide a short-term memory of the topic being thought about. This is highly speculative.

Several proposals have been made (see, for example, Gaines, 1976c) for softening the hard dichotomies of mathematical logic (true or false, 0 or 1, black or white, etc) so that human reasoning can be represented in a realistic manner. In PURR–PUSS, we avoid the numerical measures of probability and fuzzy sets (the main contenders for fuzzy reasoning) by storing, for each context, those alternatives which actually occur. The overall effect of this nondeterministic arrangement may still be probabilistic and fuzzy because of the variety of sequences associated with particular situations, but there is no accumulation of numbers based on unlikely statistical or fuzzy assumptions. At a higher level, PURR–PUSS would be able to use the inherent fuzziness of natural language, as we do. (See the editorial to UC-DSE/9.)

7. Into the Unknown

"Would you tell me, please, which way I ought to walk from here?"
"That depends a good deal on where you want to get to," said the Cat.
"I don't care where——" said Alice.
"Then it doesn't matter which way you walk," said the Cat.

Lewis Carroll
"Alice's Adventures in Wonderland"

Choosing a Task

What should we try to teach PURR–PUSS next? My choice of the HELLO task and the ROOMS task was made because they represented, for me, two classes of problems that might be beyond PURR–PUSS. I am unable to say how well the results discussed in this chapter provide satisfactory solutions to the two tasks. How we assess the performance of PURR–PUSS is likely to depend strongly on how we think we carry out such tasks ourselves.

The HELLO task is typical of question and answer tasks, in that something has to be *said* as a result of something being *heard*[1]. Without mimic-speech PURR–PUSS would not be able to say what she heard. With a better form of mimic-speech she might become easier to teach.[2] This is a good example of the importance of her "body" functions.

In teaching PURR–PUSS the HELLO task, we take a first tentative step into a very difficult area: coping with the unfamiliar.

In asking someone to do something for us we do not usually command them to carry out a certain procedure through which they have been taken before,[3] as we did to PURR–PUSS with COUNTING OBJECTS and COUNTING BEADS. Instead, we indicate in one of many ways what we want to be achieved. "Fetch me a . . .". We expect the person to use his experience to achieve the objective which we set. Also, unless we are applying explicitly or implicitly some threat of punishment or discomfort, we avoid making our request sound like a dull or repetitive chore. The trick used to "persuade" PURR–PUSS to go to a particular room in the ROOMS task has a little of this flavour. The reader who accepts my treatment of the ROOMS task may also be tolerant of a speculation that this is the direction

120

in which we must advance to enable the machine to set its own goals. (In a simple way, PURR–PUSS already sets her own goals by forming hypotheses.)

The HELLO Task

"Hello Reader, Hello Reader."
"Hello Stranger. What's your name?"
"John Brown".
"Glad to meet you, John Brown".

A simple conversation like the above conceals an elaborate process involving vision, speech and memory. We could analyse it as follows:—

1. Is there a face with that voice?
   (a) Check that there is a face.
   (b) Check that it is looking at you.
   (c) Identify the face in some way.
2. Say "Hello Stranger. What's your name?".
3. Get set to hear Stranger's reply.
4. Hear and hold Stranger's reply.
5. Make your reply.
   (a) Formulate a reply "Glad to meet you, – – –".
   (b) Substitute the heard Stranger's name in the reply.
   (c) Say it.

Even if this scheme is inaccurate and inadequate, we can be sure that the Stranger's name has to be remembered for the final reply and that it has to be substituted in that reply. To ease our burden in teaching this task, the process of substitution will be simplified to straightforward copying. The format of the conversation with PURR–PUSS becomes:—

Stranger	"HELLO PUSS HELLO PUSS"
PURR–PUSS	"HELLO"
Stranger	"MISTER SQUARE FACE HOW DO YOU DO"
PURR–PUSS	"HELLO MISTER SQUARE FACE HOW DO YOU DO"

To enable PURR–PUSS to see the Stranger's face, she is given an imaginary EYE with the special actions explained in Fig. 7.1. The [LOOKFACE action distinguishes a face looking at PURR–PUSS from anything else. The remaining actions enable her to identify the face by scanning around it and finding different kinds of corner (square, wedge, hat, vee or none at all).[4]

122 THINKING WITH THE TEACHABLE MACHINE

(a) Face looking at PURR-PUSS.

with ☺ the action [LOOKFACE results in the pattern <FACING>

with ☹ , ☹ etc. [LOOKFACE results in the pattern <GONE>.

(b) Three heads with a face looking at PURR-PUSS.

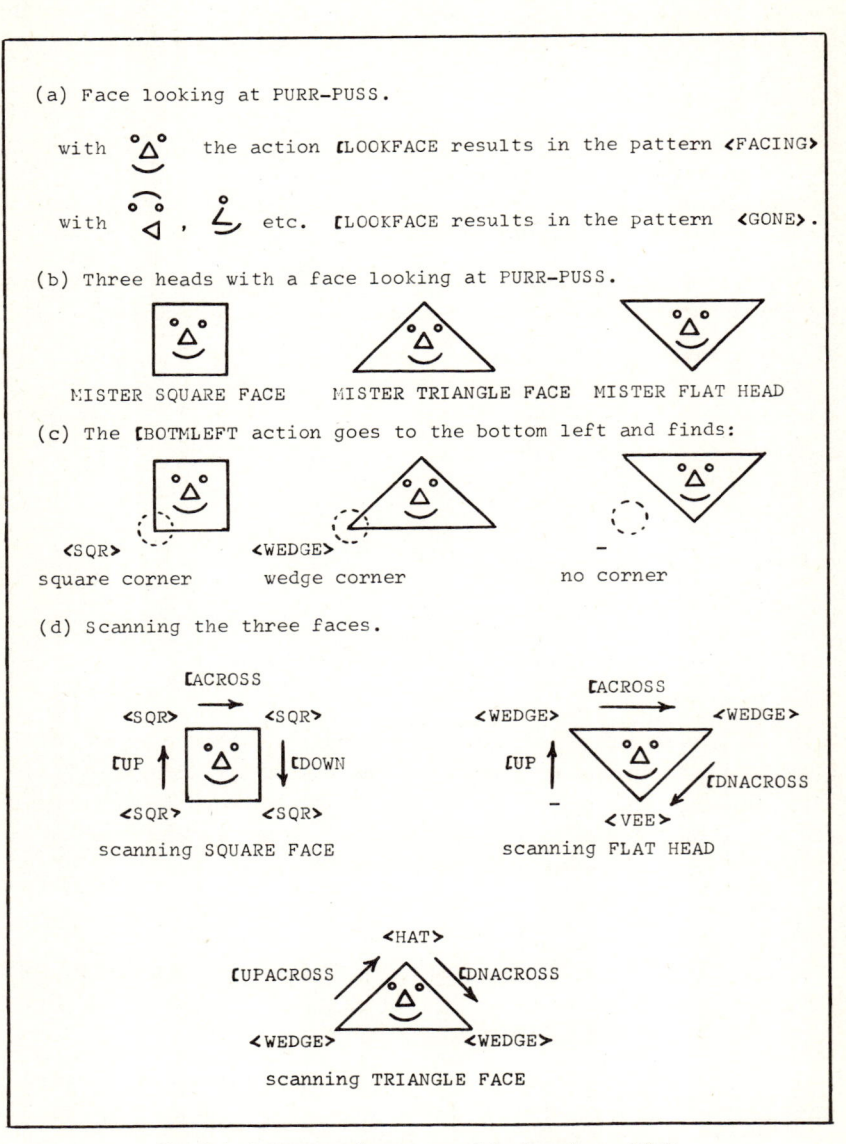

    MISTER SQUARE FACE   MISTER TRIANGLE FACE   MISTER FLAT HEAD

(c) The [BOTMLEFT action goes to the bottom left and finds:

    <SQR>   <WEDGE>   —
    square corner   wedge corner   no corner

(d) Scanning the three faces.

    [ACROSS   [ACROSS
<SQR> → <SQR>   <WEDGE> → <WEDGE>
[UP ↑ ☺ ↓ [DOWN   [UP ↑ ☺ ↘ [DNACROSS
<SQR> <SQR>   <VEE>
scanning SQUARE FACE   scanning FLAT HEAD

    <HAT>
[UPACROSS ↗ ☺ ↘ [DNACROSS
<WEDGE> <WEDGE>
scanning TRIANGLE FACE

Fig. 7.1. Actions and patterns of the imaginary EYE.

INTO THE UNKNOWN   123

```
      ↓
      - -
      - -
      -       [LOOKFACE
  <FACING>   [BOTMLEFT
  <SQR>  [UP         <WEDGE> [UPACROSS      -         [UP
  <SQR>  [ACROSS     <HAT>   [DNACROSS    <WEDGE>    [ACROSS
  <SQR>  [DOWN       <WEDGE> -            <WEDGE>    [DNACROSS
  <SQR>  -                                <VEE>      -
  - -
  HELLO  -
  PUSS   -
  HELLO  -
  PUSS   -
  -          [RAISEBROWS
  <FEELBROWS> [LOOKFACE
  <FACING>    HELLO
  e           [TOSELF
  <INNERFEEL> I
  e           MUST
  e           REMEMBER
  e           HIS
  e           NAME
  e           -
  -           [LOOKFACE
  <FACING>    [BOTMLEFT
  <SQR>  [UP         <WEDGE> [UPACROSS     -          [UP
  <SQR>  [ACROSS     <HAT>   [DNACROSS   <WEDGE>    [ACROSS
  <SQR>  [DOWN       <WEDGE> -           <WEDGE>    [DNACROSS
  <SQR>  -                               <VEE>
  -
  MISTER -                              MISTER
  SQUARE - TRIANGLE - FLAT -          e SQUARE  e TRIANGLE  e FLAT
  FACE   -  FACE    - HEAD -          e FACE    e FACE      e HEAD
  -                                     e         e           e
  -                                     -
  HOW  -
  DO   -                              - HOW
  YOU  -                              e DO
  DO   -                              e YOU
  -                                   e DO
  -                                   e -
  -    [LOOKFACE                        -
                                        - -
                                        ↓
```

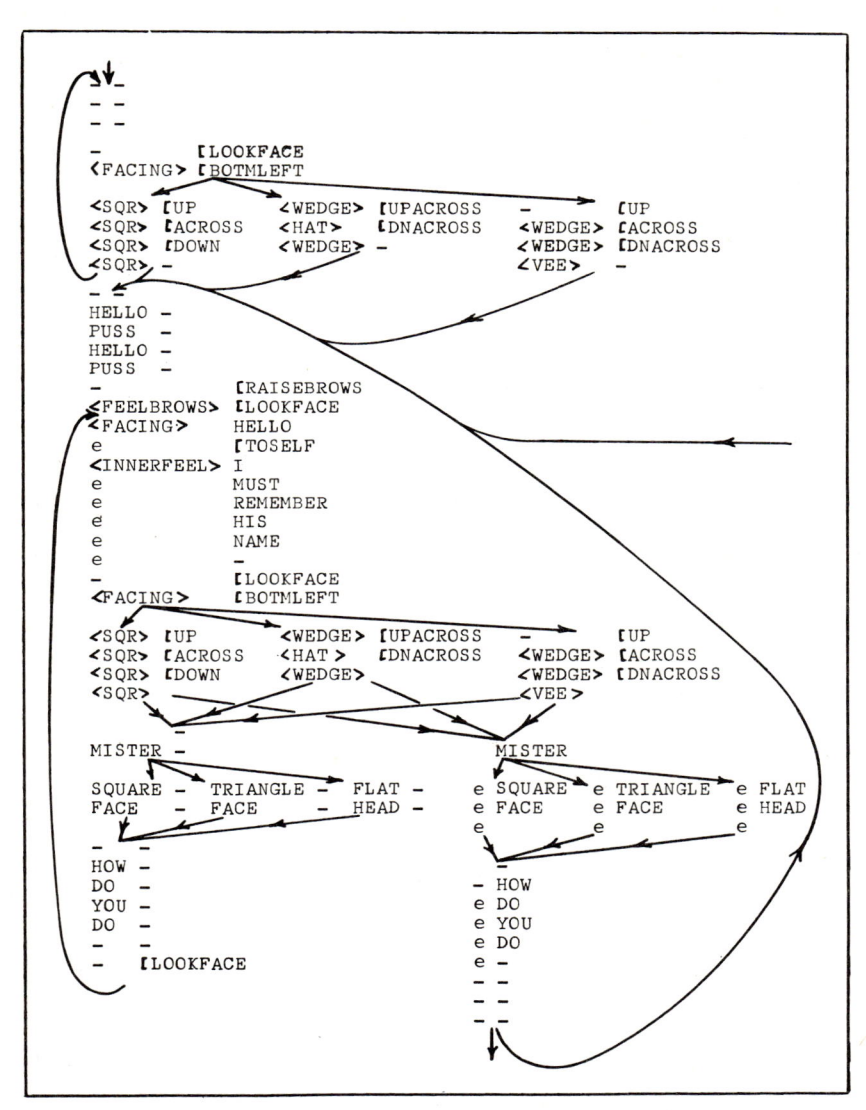

Fig. 7.2. Schedule for HELLO task.

124   THINKING WITH THE TEACHABLE MACHINE

```
.. 391 ..
- -
- -
- [LOOKFACE
<FACING> [BOTMLEFT
<SQR> [UP                    learning to
.. 396 ..                    look at
<SQR> [ACROSS
<SQR> [DOWN                  SQUARE FACE
<SQR> -
- -
- -
.. 401 ..
- -
- [LOOKFACE
<FACING> [BOTMLEFT
<WEDGE> [UPACROSS            learning to
<HAT>    [DNACROSS           look at
.. 406 ..
<WEDGE> -                    TRIANGLE FACE
- -
- -
- -
- [LOOKFACE
.. 411 ..
<FACING> [BOTMLEFT
- [UP                        learning to
<WEDGE> [ACROSS              look at
<WEDGE> [DNACROSS
<VEE>   -                    FLAT HEAD
.. 416 ..
- -
HELLO -
PUSS -
HELLO -                      Stranger calling
PUSS -
.. 421 ..
- [RAISEBROWS                set physical-PUSS context and
<FEELBROWS> [LOOKFACE        check that face is looking at
<FACING> HELLO               PURR-PUSS;  say HELLO.
e [TOSELF
<INNERFEEL> I
.. 426 ..                    critical sequence
e MUST
e REMEMBER                   muttered to herself
e HIS
e NAME                       sets context for speech-PUSS
e -
.. 431 ..
- [LOOKFACE                  check that face is still there
<FACING> [BOTMLEFT
<SQR> [UP                    scan face to set up contexts
<SQR> [ACROSS
<SQR> [DOWN                  for action-PUSS and physical-PUSS
.. 436 ..
<SQR> -                      prepared for hearing Stranger's
MISTER -                     name
```

Fig. 7.3. Teaching the HELLO task.

```
SQUARE -                                          e MUST
FACE -                                            .. 486 ..
- -                  hears Stranger's name        e REMEMBER
.. 441 ..                                         e HIS
HOW -                                             e NAME
DO -                 this how-do-you-do           e -
YOU -                ending is a                  - [LOOKFACE
DO -                 convenient "cheat"           .. 491 ..
- -                                               <FACING> [BOTMLEFT
.. 446 ..            set context                  <WEDGE> [UPACROSS
- [LOOKFACE          and check face               <HAT>   [DNACROSS
<FACING> HELLO                                    <WEDGE> MISTER -
e [TOSELF                                         .. 496 ..
<INNERFEEL> I                                     TRIANGLE -
e MUST               set speech                   FACE -
.. 451 ..            context for                  - -
e REMEMBER           reply                        HOW -
e HIS                                             DO -
e NAME                                            .. 501 ..
e -                                               YOU -
- [LOOKFACE                                       DO -
.. 456 ..                                         - -
<FACING> [BOTMLEFT                                - [LOOKFACE
<SQR> [UP            scan face to                 <FACING> HELLO
<SQR> [ACROSS        set context                  .. 506 ..
<SQR> [DOWN                                       e [TOSELF
<SQR> MISTER         this reply goes with         <INNERFEEL> I
.. 461 ..            the HELLO on step 447        e MUST
e SQUARE                                          e REMEMBER
e FACE                                            e HIS
e -                                               .. 511 ..
- HOW                                             e NAME
e DO                                              e -
.. 466 ..                                         - [LOOKFACE
e YOU                                             <FACING> [BOTMLEFT
e DO                                              <WEDGE> [UPACROSS
e -                                               .. 516 ..
- -                                               <HAT> [DNACROSS
- [LOOKFACE          clumsy termination           <WEDGE> MISTER ≠
.. 471 ..                                         e TRIANGLE
<GONE> HELLO                                      e FACE
e -                                               e -
- -                                               .. 521 ..
- -                                               - HOW
.. 476 ..                                         e DO
HELLO -                                           e YOU
PUSS -               another Stranger             e DO
HELLO -              arrives                      e -
PUSS -                                            .. 526 ..
- [RAISEBROWS                                     - -
.. 481 ..
<FEELBROWS> [LOOKFACE          ≠  KORSHN>random number
<FACING> HELLO                    in step 7 of Figure 5-8.
e [TOSELF
<INNERFEEL> I
```

126   THINKING WITH THE TEACHABLE MACHINE

The schedule for the HELLO task, given in Fig. 7.2, is not easy to follow, so the reader is recommended to turn to the annotated interaction shown in Fig. 7.3, where the "conversation" can be followed step by step.

In Fig. 7.3, steps 391 to 416 take PURR–PUSS through a sequence for learning how to scan faces. This is only suggestive of what could be a very difficult task on its own. At the end of the period, PURR–PUSS can scan faces in a way that suffices for what follows.

The "[RAISEBROWS <FEELBROWS>]" on steps 421 and 422 distinguish the sequence 421–444 from the sequence 446–467. It represents the initial "surprise" of PURR–PUSS on hearing the caller. This "surprise" is not, of course, present when PURR–PUSS prepares to reply on step 446.

The "[LOOKFACE <FACING>]" on steps 422 and 423 checks that the caller has a face looking towards PURR–PUSS. The same action-pattern provides a sparse event entry into the face-scanning procedures on steps 393, 402, 410, 431, 455, 490 and 513.

The HELLO on step 423 is said "aloud". Then we imagine an action-pattern "[TOSELF <INNERFEEL>]" to set PURR–PUSS in a speaking-to-herself mode so that the speech context (425-30) "I MUST REMEMBER HIS NAME" can be established without becoming part of the message to the Stranger.[5] This speech context becomes joined in speech–PUSS to the Stranger's reply "MISTER SQUARE FACE" so that, when the context is introduced again on steps 447-53, speech–PUSS is predicting the Stranger's name. However, between the context and the reply we have the face-scanning (431–6) that prepares action–PUSS for either a familiar or, as in this case, an unfamiliar reply.

The face-scanning on steps 455–60 has already been followed by a Stranger's reply in the sequence 431 to 444, so PURR–PUSS, under the guidance of action–PUSS and speech–PUSS, launches straight into the Stranger's name (460–7). Notice that, if the same Stranger calls again, PURR–PUSS would address him correctly straight away and not wait (as with the null action of step 436) for him to give his name.

With the second Stranger, PURR–PUSS carries out the whole operation smoothly except for the action on step 492 (there is a simple reason for this which can be left as an exercise for the reader to work out) and the KORSHN failure on step 517.

Teaching the HELLO task has been difficult to organize and many different ways have been tried. Most of the trouble has been due to our having only two threading PUSSes for three concurrent jobs:—
1. Hearing and holding Stranger's reply for mimicking;
2. Checking and scanning the face of Stranger;
3. Connecting across the unfamiliar reply of Stranger to PURR–PUSS's reply.

The first job was tackled with speech–PUSS, the second by physical–PUSS and the third was circumvented by making Stranger provide the "HOW DO YOU DO" context. With a third threading PUSS this last trick could have been avoided.

The ROOMS Task

The only way to get the "feel" of an interacting system is to interact with it. To obtain the teaching interactions for the COUNTING OBJECTS, COUNTING BEADS and HELLO tasks, I made several attempts during which I simplified the teaching according to what I had learned about PURR–PUSS's reactions. In this way I was able to provide interactions that were easier to understand than my first attempts would have been.

With the ROOMS task I hope to meet the requirements of the enthusiast, who feels that he or she has not been given details to sufficient depth, and of the critic, who is looking for a crack in which to stick his knife.[6] The less demanding reader may prefer to skim lightly over the sections in which the behaviour of PURR–PUSS is analysed.

The first time I attempted to teach PURR–PUSS the ROOMS task, I chose ROOMS that were too large. Also I led PURR–PUSS through the ROOMS along paths that were too long, so that I spent a long time watching her plod along these paths without reaching the stage at which I could show her what I really wanted. After 1200 steps I gave up, made the ROOMS smaller and designed a schedule for teaching the task. With this schedule, I started a second interaction in which I got very much the worst of a battle in which PURR–PUSS showed me that I was not at all clear as to what I wanted her to do!

After more thought, I designed the schedule of Fig. 7.4 and set off again with great confidence. It is this interaction which will be described and discussed, even though she did not do quite what I expected.

Before going any farther, explanation is due to the reader of how the teaching of PURR–PUSS has been presented in one continuous sequence from a completely empty memory at the beginning of Fig. 6.6, through the interactions of Figs 6.7, 6.9 and 7.3 to where we are now and from here on to the end. After each task has been taught, the whole of PURR–PUSS with all her PUSSes (memories) and her body and her world are "dumped" (stored away) on a magnetic tape memory. Any time that we "load" the magnetic tape back into the computer, we put the whole system back to the exact state in which it was when we dumped it. This means that we can try teaching PURR–PUSS a new task and, if we do not like the result, we can go back to the point at which we last dumped everything. This is possible because all of the system (except Teacher) is in the computer. This cannot be done when

PURR–PUSS is driving the laboratory robot CAESAR (or ESAW), because real physical things like the robot cannot be dumped and re-loaded. In other words, we cannot take the robot and put it back in exactly the same position on the laboratory floor as it was at some earlier time. We cannot record exactly what the robot is doing since every movement is affected by unpredictable variations in friction, torque, voltage, temperature and so on. These very features that make the robot a realistic body for PURR–PUSS in a realistic world, also make it unsuitable for description by the printed word.

Planning the Interaction

PURR–PUSS is in the LONG ROOM of the SQUARES environment (Fig. 5.12). I am Teacher. Teacher is going to introduce novelty into her memory of either the SMALL ROOM or the SUN ROOM, according to which of these two rooms Teacher wants PURR–PUSS to go to. Teacher will introduce novelty into her memory of the desired room by talking about that room in a way Teacher has not talked about it before.[7]

By the way, Teacher will not put any words "into the mouth" of PURR–PUSS in teaching this task. All speech *to* PURR–PUSS will be typed in as patterns, none as actions.

Looking at the schedule of Fig. 7.4, notice the "interruption" sequence at the bottom right of the diagram. "<CATCHEYE> [LOOKFACE <FACING> –" interrupts the behaviour in the rest of the schedule to enable Teacher to say "PUSS IN SMALL ROOM PLEASE" or "PUSS IN SUN ROOM PLEASE". This introduces novelty with the word PLEASE which will not have followed "IN SMALL ROOM" or "IN SUN ROOM" before, so when this interruption is made pattern–PUSS will remember PLEASE with a novelty mark. Then Teacher goes on to say "NOW PUSS IN LONG ROOM" to bring her back to where she was before the interruption (at least, this will be true for the contexts in the windows of main–PUSS, pattern–PUSS and action–PUSS).

A test of this injection of novelty can be made by trying it first with "PUSS IN SMALL ROOM PLEASE" and then with "PUSS IN SUN ROOM PLEASE". If PURR–PUSS goes to the SMALL ROOM in the first case and to the SUN ROOM in the second case, we shall be able to say that the method works.

The main part of the schedule of Fig. 7.4 is concerned with teaching PURR–PUSS the way from the LONG ROOM to the SMALL ROOM and SUN ROOM so that the choice of route can be made between them. The critical sequence is "–PUSS NOW MOVE" followed by "LEFT [L" or "RIGHT [R". It is taught first in the training cycle at the top of the schedule and it is then incorporated below into the main "walk around the rooms". To

INTO THE UNKNOWN   129

get PURR–PUSS to recognize alternatives is not easy unless they are forced on her from outside. She "prefers" to stick to an established habit. In this case we want her to choose to move LEFT or RIGHT (at the bottom of Fig. 7.4) as *she* wishes. This is to be an open choice, not dependent upon the past as in the alternative actions of Fig. 6.8 which were specifically ANY for COUNTING OBJECTS and ABACUS for COUNTING BEADS. In the training cycle at the top of Fig. 7.4, we make sure that the MOVE LEFT option does not become established before the MOVE RIGHT option is presented. How can one get her to MOVE RIGHT if she has already learned to MOVE LEFT? Each time PURR–PUSS comes to the choice point, you will have to watch her MOVE LEFT! Disapproval only causes confusion because if you disapprove of MOVE LEFT, she will happily MOVE RIGHT for you the next time, but then you will not be able to get her to MOVE LEFT. You have only switched her choice from MOVE LEFT to MOVE RIGHT. Disapproval must not be given for something that is not wrong. Of course, you could wait until the novelty wears off and a KORSHN exit (step 7 of Fig. 5.8) conveniently allows you to type LEFT or RIGHT to set up the alternatives. This solution is not to be recommended because KORSHN exits rarely occur when they are wanted.

In case the training cycle appears arbitrary, it should be emphasised that, by presenting the choice sequence "– PUSS NOW MOVE" in the training cycle without any prior context associated with the rooms, we establish the choice independently of prior context. The sequence is long enough to fill the windows of main–PUSS and pattern–PUSS so that a priority 2 decision based upon an hypothesis from pattern–PUSS can be taken without confirmation by speech–PUSS. As a general rule in teaching, we have to remember that PURR–PUSS "hangs onto" any context that is within her grasp. If we want to teach her something, then we must try to avoid the implied relevance of extraneous contexts.

Having discussed the interruption and training cycle, we must now see how they are placed in the main part of the schedule of Fig. 7.4. From the LONG ROOM the routes to the SMALL ROOM and to the SUN ROOM diverge at a crucial "LEFT [L" or "RIGHT [R" decision, so the choice sequence "–PUSS NOW MOVE" is placed before this. The routes have been carefully chosen so that the SMALL ROOM can be reached from the LONG ROOM without going through the SUN ROOM, and the SUN ROOM can be reached from the LONG ROOM without going through the SMALL ROOM. The reader may like to check the patterns and actions of the routes in the schedule against the patterns and actions of the SQUARES environment in Fig. 5.12. We shall be following these routes with PURR–PUSS, shortly.

Two uncertainties remain in the schedule of Fig. 7.4. It is not known at

130 THINKING WITH THE TEACHABLE MACHINE

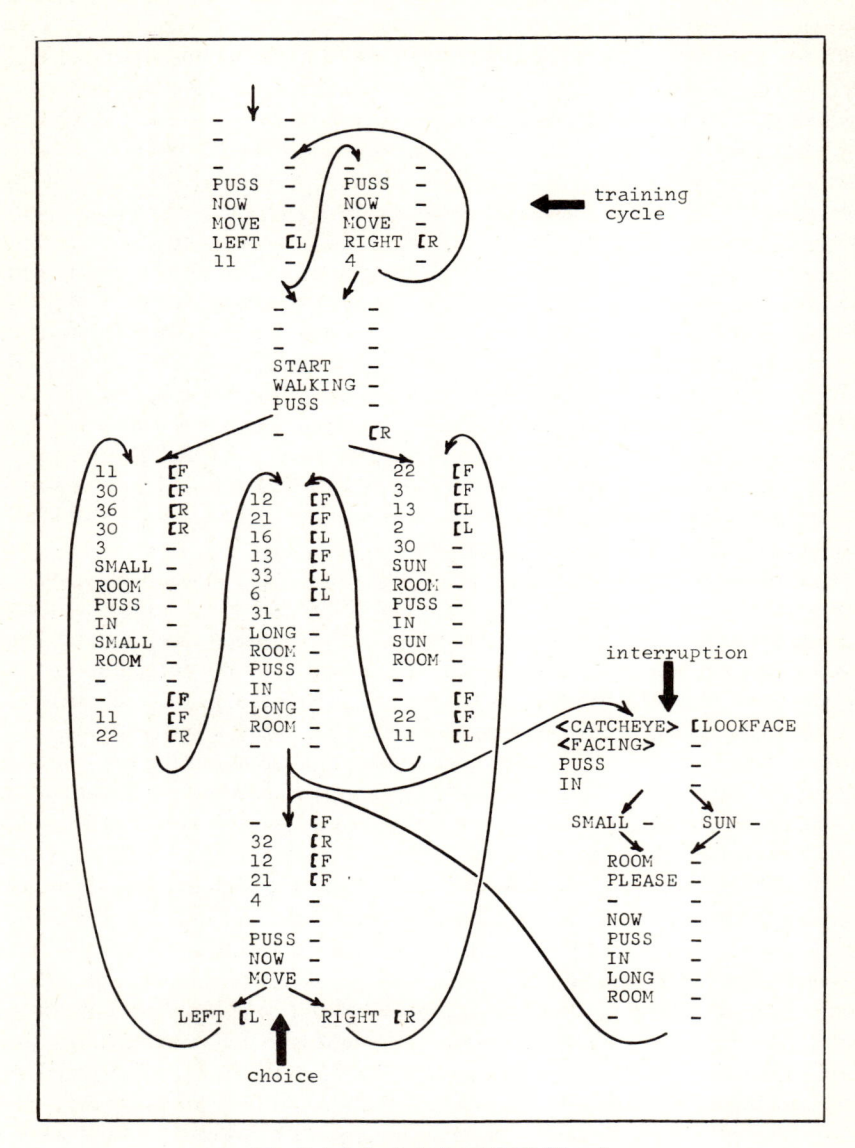

```
                    ↓
                    -
                    -
                    -
                 PUSS  -      PUSS  -
                 NOW   -      NOW   -          ← training
                 MOVE  -      MOVE  -            cycle
                 LEFT  [L     RIGHT [R
                 11           4
                    -
                    -
                    -
                 START    -
                 WALKING  -
                 PUSS     -
                    -         [R
    11    [F                 22    [F
    30    [F      12   [F    3     [F
    36    [R      21   [F    13    [L
    30    [R      16   [L    2     [L
    3     -       13   [F    30    -
    SMALL -       33   [L    SUN   -
    ROOM  -       6    [L    ROOM  -
    PUSS  -       31   -     PUSS  -
    IN    -       LONG -     IN    -
    SMALL -       ROOM -     SUN   -
    ROOM  -       PUSS -     ROOM  -
    -     [F      IN   -       -    [F         interruption
    11    [F      LONG -     22    [F             ↓
    22    [R      ROOM -     11    [L    <CATCHEYE>  [LOOKFACE
                                         <FACING>    -
                                         PUSS        -
                                         IN          -
                    -    [F              SMALL   -   SUN   -
                    32   [R
                    12   [F               ROOM    -
                    21   [F               PLEASE  -
                    4    -
                    -                     NOW     -
                    PUSS -                 PUSS    -
                    NOW  -                 IN      -
                    MOVE -                 LONG    -
                 LEFT [L   RIGHT [R        ROOM    -
                                             -
                       ↑
                     choice
```

Fig. 7.4. Schedule for ROOMS task.

what point in the training cycle Teacher will manage to terminate the exercise. Therefore we do not know whether the "START WALKING PUSS" will come after a "LEFT [L" or a "RIGHT [R". This is of small consequence so long as the appropriate one of the two arrows below "START WALKING PUSS" is followed.

A second and major uncertainty is attached to the interrupting pattern <CATCHEYE> as it will introduce novelty itself. However, I argued that, because LONG ROOM cannot be reached from LONG ROOM except via SMALL ROOM or SUN ROOM, the novelty intentionally attached to one of the rooms would be more likely to determine the hypotheses of PURR–PUSS than would the novelty of <CATCHEYE>. Anyway, I was accustomed to the way PURR–PUSS responded to teaching by schedule and there did not seem much point in trying to work out exactly how she would treat <CATCHEYE>. With the schedule of Fig. 7.4, Teacher launched optimistically into the teaching of the ROOMS task.

The Training Cycle

Figure 7.5 shows what happened when Teacher continued the interaction from the end of Fig. 7.3 to go through the training cycle shown at the top of Fig. 7.4. The reader will have no difficulty in interpreting the not-so-short form of listing which is intermediate between the forms of listing used in Figs 4.7 and 6.1. On step 471 of Fig. 7.3 it would have been reasonable to disapprove of PURR–PUSS's HELLO after the stranger had <GONE>, but that was not done so it is done now on step 528 of Fig. 7.5. This does not, however, put an end to the HELLO task which induces PURR–PUSS to mimic a stranger on steps 532 to 535. We allow that to pass.

Steps 537 to 539 form a sequence of null patterns and actions, and on step 539 there are 5 predictions by main–PUSS: START, CARRY, PUSS, HELLO and null (–). Because we start tasks from a null sequence (long pause), the null sequence predicts all of the beginnings of tasks and appears at the end of all tasks. The null sequence can be looked upon as a "thinking focus" from which and to which all activity flows. By having a thinking focus, we ensure that any task can begin naturally from the end of any other task. The thinking focus is a natural pause between tasks. Perhaps the most important property of the thinking focus is that it will tend to be a situation in which novelty is created by new tasks for the benefit (for instance, for their recall) of all old tasks. Notice how a null sequence of length 3 fills the window of main–PUSS, but does not quite fill the window of pattern–PUSS. An hypothesis can extend across a null sequence of length 3 (as in step 743 of Fig. 7.9), but not one of length 4 or more. However, threading PUSSes can predict across thinking focuses and influence the beginnings of new tasks.

132 THINKING WITH THE TEACHABLE MACHINE

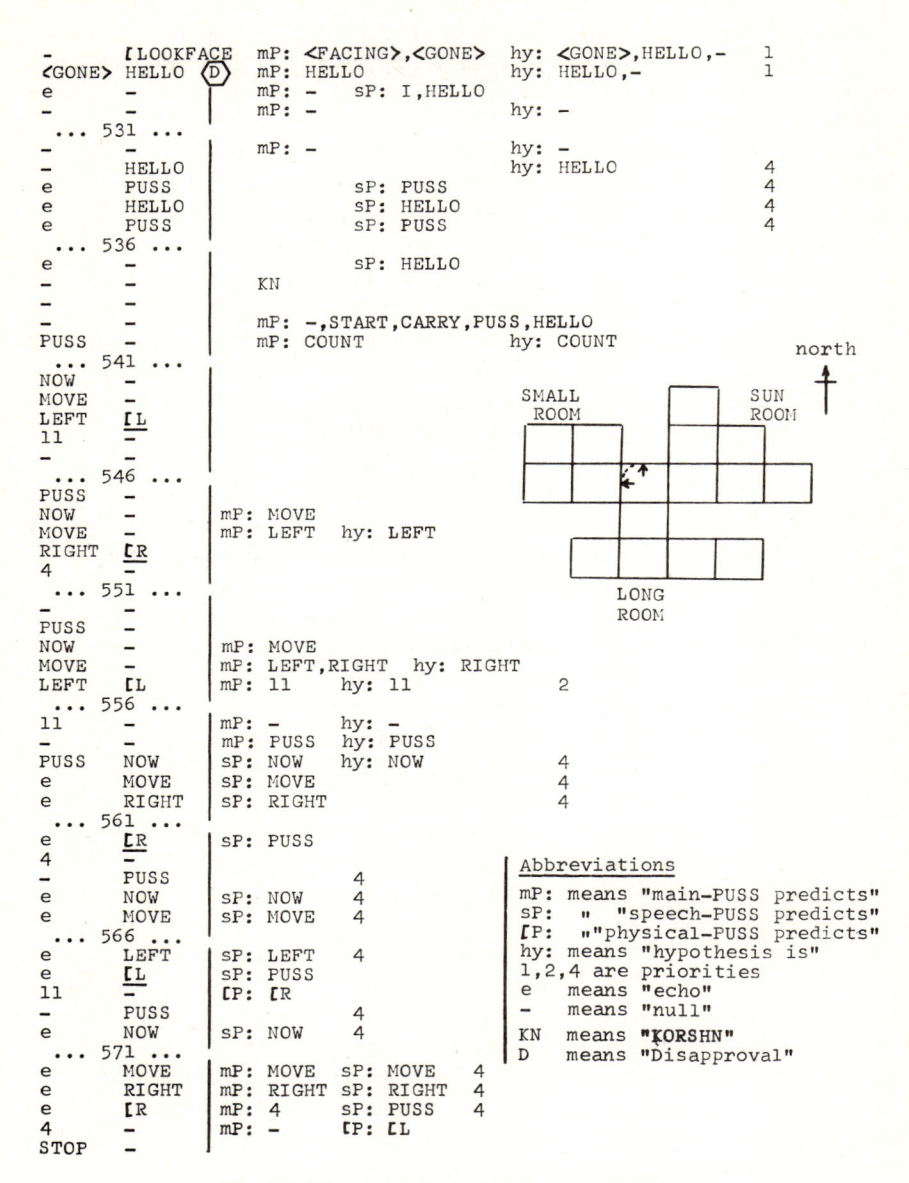

```
-           [LOOKFACE    mP: <FACING>,<GONE>    hy: <GONE>,HELLO,-    1
<GONE>   HELLO    (D)    mP: HELLO              hy: HELLO,-           1
e           -            mP: -    sP: I,HELLO
-           -            mP: -                  hy: -
   ... 531 ...
-           -            mP: -                  hy: -
-           HELLO                                hy: HELLO            4
e           PUSS                  sP: PUSS                            4
e           HELLO                 sP: HELLO                           4
e           PUSS                  sP: PUSS                            4
   ... 536 ...
                                  sP: HELLO
-           -            KN
-           -
-           -            mP: -,START,CARRY,PUSS,HELLO
PUSS        -            mP: COUNT              hy: COUNT
   ... 541 ...
NOW         -
MOVE        -
LEFT       [L
11           -
-            -
   ... 546 ...
PUSS         -
NOW          -           mP: MOVE
MOVE         -           mP: LEFT    hy: LEFT
RIGHT      [R
4            -
   ... 551 ...
-            -
PUSS         -
NOW          -           mP: MOVE
MOVE         -           mP: LEFT,RIGHT  hy: RIGHT
LEFT       [L            mP: 11      hy: 11                           2
   ... 556 ...
11           -           mP: -       hy: -
-            -           mP: PUSS    hy: PUSS
PUSS        NOW          sP: NOW     hy: NOW                          4
e           MOVE         sP: MOVE                                     4
e           RIGHT        sP: RIGHT                                    4
   ... 561 ...
e          [R            sP: PUSS
4            -
-           PUSS                        4
e           NOW          sP: NOW        4
e           MOVE         sP: MOVE       4
   ... 566 ...
e           LEFT         sP: LEFT       4
e          [L            sP: PUSS
11           -           [P: [R
-           PUSS                        4
e           NOW          sP: NOW        4
   ... 571 ...
e           MOVE         mP: MOVE    sP: MOVE    4
e           RIGHT        mP: RIGHT   sP: RIGHT   4
4          [R            mP: 4       sP: PUSS    4
4            -           mP: -       [P: [L
STOP         -
```

```
                                              north
                                                ↑
                   SMALL              SUN
                   ROOM               ROOM

                         ↖↑

                   LONG
                   ROOM
```

Abbreviations
mP: means "main-PUSS predicts"
sP: " "speech-PUSS predicts"
[P: " "physical-PUSS predicts"
hy: means "hypothesis is"
1,2,4 are priorities
e   means "echo"
-   means "null"
KN means "KORSHN"
D   means "Disapproval"

Fig. 7.5. The training cycle of the ROOMS task.

INTO THE UNKNOWN   133

For the training cycle, PURR–PUSS is started in a square between the SMALL ROOM and the SUN ROOM facing "north" so that the [L and [R actions of the cycle take her back and forth between the two positions indicated in the diagram of SQUARES inset in Fig. 7.5. (As a matter of interest, while teaching PURR–PUSS in the SQUARES environment, MEDEATOR helps Teacher by displaying the position of PURR–PUSS in the environment on a storage oscilloscope screen).

The remainder of the training cycle can be discussed in terms of a series of questions. The answers to these questions are straightforward and will be left to the reader as an exercise. The reader is urged to spend a moment on each question before reading the hint.

How do the following come about?

1. Main–PUSS predicts COUNT on step 540.
2. Main–PUSS predicts MOVE on step 547.
3. PURR–PUSS hypothesises LEFT on step 548.
4. PURR–PUSS selects [L on step 555, but fails to do so on step 567.
5. The decision on step 555 is at priority 2, not 1.
6. PURR–PUSS fails to say PUSS on step 557, but does say NOW on step 558.
7. PURR–PUSS fails to say PUSS on step 575.

The following hints are provided for each of the above questions:—
  Hint for 1. Step 181.
  Hint for 2. Draw the main–PUSS net for steps 539 to 547.
  Hint for 3. Draw the pattern–PUSS net for steps 539 to 548.
  Hint for 4. What is in the window of main–PUSS in each case?
  Hint for 5. The window of physical–PUSS.
  Hint for 6. The window of speech–PUSS.
  Hint for 7. Check carefully what is in the windows of speech–PUSS and
      action–PUSS, remembering 2 and 5 of Fig 5.4.

Walking Around The Rooms

Figures 7.6 to 7.9 show 192 steps during which Teacher shows PURR–PUSS how to go from room to room by a reasonably short route. Details of predictions, priorities and hypotheses are provided to enable the reader to work out the reason for each action of PURR–PUSS. There is no particular difficulty in this part of the task so it will be sufficient to point out a few occurrences which might otherwise go un-noticed.

On step 579 (Fig. 7.6), the pattern START triggers an hypothesis through past memory associated with the COUNTING OBJECTS task. The next pattern WALKING is new and the hypothesis is deleted. The KORSHN exit

134   THINKING WITH THE TEACHABLE MACHINE

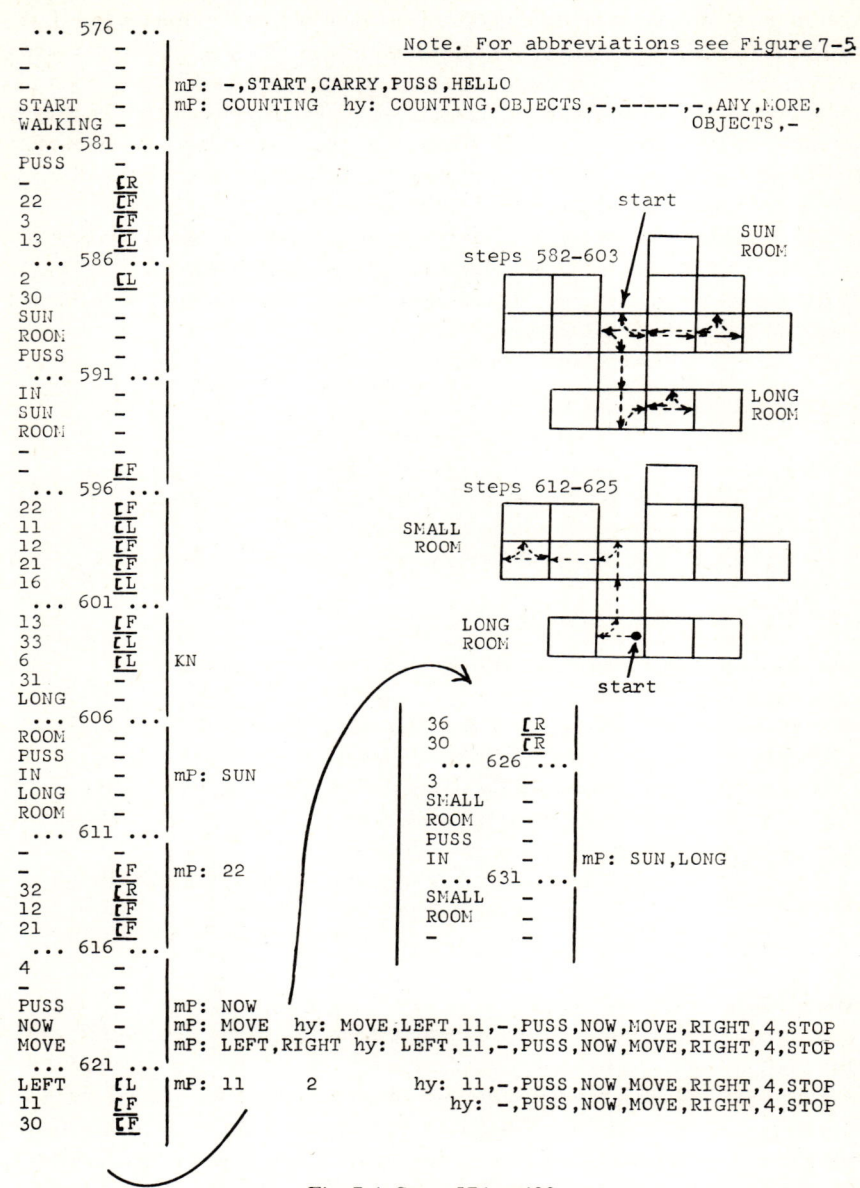

```
   ... 576 ...
   -        -                Note. For abbreviations see Figure 7-5
   -        -       mP: -,START,CARRY,PUSS,HELLO
START    -          mP: COUNTING    hy: COUNTING,OBJECTS,-,-----,-,ANY,MORE,
WALKING  -                                                          OBJECTS,-
   ... 581 ...
PUSS     -
-       [R
22      [F
3       [F
13      [L
   ... 586 ...
2       [L
30       -
SUN      -
ROOM     -
PUSS     -
   ... 591 ...
IN       -
SUN      -
ROOM     -
-        -
-       [F
   ... 596 ...
22      [F
11      [L
12      [F
21      [F
16      [L
   ... 601 ...
13      [F
33      [L
6       [L       KN
31       -
LONG     -
   ... 606 ...
ROOM     -
PUSS     -
IN       -       mP: SUN
LONG     -
ROOM     -
   ... 611 ...
-        -
-       [F       mP: 22
32      [R
12      [F
21      [F
   ... 616 ...
4        -
-        -
PUSS     -       mP: NOW
NOW      -       mP: MOVE    hy: MOVE,LEFT,11,-,PUSS,NOW,MOVE,RIGHT,4,STOP
MOVE     -       mP: LEFT,RIGHT hy: LEFT,11,-,PUSS,NOW,MOVE,RIGHT,4,STOP
   ... 621 ...
LEFT    [L       mP: 11      2        hy: 11,-,PUSS,NOW,MOVE,RIGHT,4,STOP
11      [F                            hy: -,PUSS,NOW,MOVE,RIGHT,4,STOP
30      [F
```

```
36      [R
30      [R
   ... 626 ...
3        -
SMALL    -
ROOM     -
PUSS     -
IN       -       mP: SUN,LONG
   ... 631 ...
SMALL    -
ROOM     -
-        -
```

steps 582-603   SUN ROOM   LONG ROOM

steps 612-625   SMALL ROOM   LONG ROOM

Fig. 7.6. Steps 576 to 633.

(KN) on step 603 has no effect there, but is recorded for completeness. The main–PUSS predictions on steps 608, 612, 618 and 630 are readily accounted for.

The hypothesis formed on step 619 is followed for 3 patterns and it enables PURR–PUSS to provide the [L action on step 621 at priority 2. Because the hypothesis was constructed from the pattern–PUSS memory of the training cycle it disagrees with the pattern "30" on step 623. The reader should notice that the hypothesis was formed up to the pattern STOP that was novel on step 575, but will now have lost its novelty (recall step 5 of the PUSS prediction procedure of Fig. 5.3).

Figures 7.7 to 7.9 introduce more activity on the part of PURR–PUSS. Teacher only has to perform four actions for her between steps 639 and 767. One is due to the KORSHN exit on step 680. A considerable number of steps are occupied in converting Teacher's words to PURR–PUSS into actions by PURR–PUSS through mimic-speech. If Teacher had not "put words into PURR–PUSS's mouth" in the earlier tasks, the lengths of the interactions would have been much longer and less easy to follow.

A short hypothesis is followed on steps 658 to 660, a longer one on steps 695 to 699, and a 19-pattern hypothesis is followed from step 720 to step 739. The hypothesis on steps 695 to 699 is interesting in that it causes PURR–PUSS to turn right into the SUN ROOM on her own initiative. This is made possible by the turn right option learned during the training cycle (Fig. 7.5) and by the fact that the hypothesis has a greater influence on the selection of an action than a threading PUSS (speech–PUSS is recommending LEFT).

The hypothesis formed on step 752 takes PURR–PUSS to the end of Fig. 7.9 and would take her farther if we did not have something else in store for her.

Boomerang!
On step 768 (Fig. 7.10), as Teacher, I typed in the pattern <CATCHEYE> to commence the interruption sequence shown in Fig. 7.4 and discussed earlier. PURR–PUSS tried to carry on with the hypothesis she was following by selecting the action [F (step 768) at priority 3. I press the disapproval button.

Now, I was in trouble. Having made the mistake of trying to interrupt PURR–PUSS while she was following an hypothesis, I had not started the interruption as planned and she was already one step on her way from the LONG ROOM. So as not to introduce any more confusion, I gave her a turn right action and watched her move forward two steps (770 and 771) on her own. Then she constructed an hypothesis all the way to the SMALL ROOM and back to get <CATCHEYE> again!

136 THINKING WITH THE TEACHABLE MACHINE

```
   -    [F     mP: 22,32
  11    [F
  ... 636 ...                                      SMALL
  22    [R                                         ROOM
  12    [F
  21    [L
  16    [L    mP: 13
  13    [F    mP: 33  [P:[F  hy: 33    1
  ... 641 ...
  33    [L    mP: 6   [P:[L  hy: 6     1
   6    [L    mP: 31  [P:[L  hy: 31    1
  31     -    mP: LONG [P: [F hy: LONG
  LONG   -    mP: ROOM        hy: ROOM
  ROOM   -    mP: PUSS        hy: PUSS
  ... 646 ...
  PUSS   -    mP: IN         hy: IN
  IN    LONG  sP: LONG  hy: LONG   4
   e    ROOM  sP: ROOM              4
   e     -    sP: PUSS
   -     -
  ... 651 ...
   -    [F    mP: 22,32,11                4
  32    [R    mP: 12  [P: [R  hy: 12    1
  12    [F    mP: 21  [P: [F  hy: 21    1
  21    [F    mP: 4   [P: [F  hy: 4     1
   4     -    mP: -   [P: [L  hy: -
  ... 656 ...
   -    PUSS             hy: PUSS   4
   e    NOW   mP: NOW   sP: NOW             4
   e    MOVE  mP: MOVE  sP: MOVE   hy: MOVE,LEFT,11,30   1
   e    LEFT  mP: LEFT  sP: LEFT   hy: LEFT,11,30        1
   e    [L    mP: 11    sP: SMALL  hy: 11,30             1
  ... 661 ...
  11    [F    [P: [F                  4
  30    [F    mP: 36    [P: [F                  4
  36    [R    mP: 30    [P: [R   hy: 30     1
  30    [R    mP: 3     [P: [R   hy: 3      1
   3    SMALL           [P: [F   hy: SMALL  4
  ... 666 ...
   e    ROOM            sP: ROOM            4
   e    PUSS            sP: PUSS            4
   e    IN              sP: IN              4
   e    SMALL           sP: SMALL           4
   e    ROOM            sP: ROOM            4
  ... 671 ...
   e     -              sP: LONG
   -    [F    mP: 22,32,11                 4
  11    [F    mP: 22    [P: [F   hy: 22     1
  22    [R    mP: 12    [P: [R   hy: 12     1
  ... 676 ...
  12    [F    mP: 21    [P: [F   hy: 21     1
  21    [F    mP: 16    [P: [F   hy: 16     1
  16    [L    mP: 13    [P: [L   hy: 13     1
  13    [F    mP: 33    [P: [F              4
  33    [L    mP: 6     [P: [L             KN
  ... 681 ...
   6    [L    mP: 31    [P: [L              4
```

steps 634–642

SMALL ROOM

start

LONG ROOM

SMALL ROOM

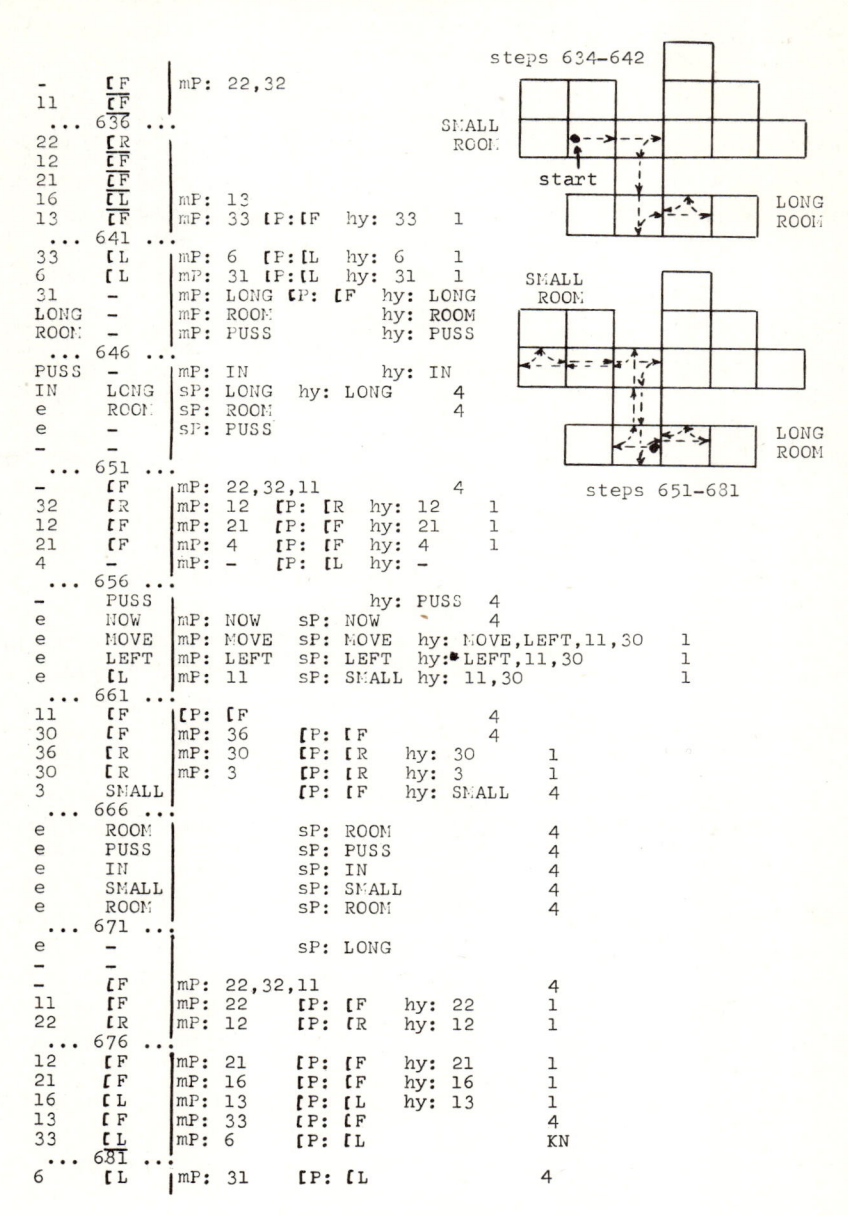

steps 651–681

LONG ROOM

Fig. 7.7. Steps 634 to 681

INTO THE UNKNOWN   137

```
31    LONG    [P:  [F      4              steps 690-720        SUN
e     ROOM    sP:  ROOM    4                                   ROOM
e     PUSS    sP:  PUSS    4
e     IN      sP:  IN      4
   ... 686 ...
e     LONG    sP:  LONG    4
e     ROOM    sP:  ROOM    4
e     -       mP:  -    sP: PUSS
-     -       mP:  -                                           LONG
-     [F      mP:  22,32,11          4                         ROOM
   ... 691 ...
32    [R      mP: 12     [P:  [R     4
12    [F      mP: 21     [P:  [F     4
21    [F      mP: 4      [P:  [F     4
4     -       mP: -      [P:  [L
-     PUSS    mP: PUSS   hy:  PUSS,NOW,MOVE,RIGHT,4,STOP,-,-,-    1
   ... 696 ...
e     NOW     mP:  NOW    sP: NOW    hy: NOW,MOVE,...,STOP,-,-,-    1
e     MOVE    mP:  MOVE   sP: MOVE   hy: MOVE,RIGHT,......,-,-,-    1
e     RIGHT   mP:  RIGHT  sP: LEFT   hy: RIGHT,4,STOP,-,-,-         2
e     [R      mP:  4                 hy: 4,STOP,-,-,-               2
22    [F
   ... 701 ...
3     [F
13    [L      mP:  2     [P:  [L
2     [L      mP:  30    [P:  [L     hy:  30                   1
30    -       mP:  SUN   [P:  [F     hy:  SUN
SUN   -       mP:  ROOM              hy:  ROOM
   ... 706 ...
ROOM  -       mP:  PUSS              hy:  PUSS
PUSS  -       mP:  IN                hy:  IN
IN    -       mP:  SUN,LONG,SMALL    hy:  SUN
SUN   ROOM                 sP:  ROOM hy:  ROOM                 4
e     -                    sP:  LONG
   ... 711 ...
-     -
-     [F      mP:  22,32,11                                    4
22    [F      mP:  11    [P:  [F     hy:  11                   1
11    [L      mP:  12    [P:  [L     hy:  12                   1
12    [F      mP:  21    [P:  [F     hy:  21                   1
   ... 716 ...
21    [F      mP:  16    [P:  [F     hy:  16                   1
16    [L      mP:  13    [P:  [L     hy:  13                   1
13    [F      mP:  33    [P:  [F                               4
33    [L      mP:  6     [P:  [L                               4
6     [L      mP:  31    [P:  [L     hy:  31,LONG,ROOM,PUSS,IN,LONG,ROOM,
     -,-,32,12,21,4,-,PUSS,NOW,MOVE,RIGHT,22       1
   ... 721 ...
31    LONG    mP:  LONG  [P:  [F     hy:  LONG,..              1
e     ROOM    mP:  ROOM    sP: ROOM  hy:  ROOM,..              1
e     PUSS    mP:  PUSS    sP: PUSS  hy:  PUSS,..              1
e     IN      mP:  IN      sP: IN    hy:  IN,..                1
e     LONG    mP:  LONG    sP: LONG  hy:  LONG,..              1
   ... 726 ...
e     ROOM    mP:  ROOM    sP: ROOM  hy:  ROOM,..              1
e     -       mP:  -       sP: PUSS  hy:  -,-,..
-     -       mP:  -                 hy:  -,32,..
```

Fig. 7.8. Steps 682 to 728.

138   THINKING WITH THE TEACHABLE MACHINE

```
 -    [F     |mP: 22,32,11           hy: 32,12,..    1
 32   [R     |mP: 12      [P: [R     hy: 12,21,..    1
   ... 731 ...
 12   [F     |mP: 21      [P: [F     hy: 21,4,..     1
 21   [F     |mP: 4       [P: [F     hy: 4,-,..      1
 4    -      |mP: -       [P: [L,[R  hy: -,PUSS,..
 -    PUSS   |mP: PUSS                hy: PUSS,..     1
 e    NOW    |mP: NOW     sP: NOW    hy: NOW,..      1
   ... 736 ...
 e    MOVE   |mP: MOVE    sP: MOVE   hy: MOVE,..     1
 e    RIGHT  |mP: RIGHT   sP: LEFT,RIGHT  hy: RIGHT,22   1
 e    [R     |mP: 4,22    sP: SUN    hy: 22          1
 22   [F     |mP: 3       [P: [F     hy: 3           1
 3    [F     |mP: 13      [P: [F     hy: 13          1
   ... 741 ...
 13   [L     |mP: 2       [P: [L     hy: 2           1
 2    [L     |mP: 30      [P: [L                     4
 30   SUN                 [P: [F     hy: SUN,ROOM,PUSS,IN,SUN,ROOM,-,-,22,
    11,12,21,16,13,33,6,31,LONG,ROOM,PUSS,IN,LONG,ROOM,-,-,32,12,21,4,
    PUSS,NOW,MOVE,RIGHT,4,STOP,-,-,-,START        4
 e    ROOM   sP: ROOM                              4
 e    PUSS   sP: PUSS                              4
   ... 746 ...
 e    IN     sP: IN                                4
 e    -      sP: SUN                               KN
 SUN  ROOM   sP: ROOM                              4
 e    -      |mP: -       sP: LONG
 -    -      |mP: -
   ... 751 ...
 -    [F     |mP: 22,32,11                          4
 22   [F     |mP: 11      [P: [F     hy: 11,12,21,16,13,33,6,31,LONG,ROOM,
    PUSS,IN,LONG,ROOM,-,-,32,12,21,4,-,PUSS,NOW,MOVE,RIGHT,4,STOP,-,-,
    -,START,WALKING,PUSS                           1
 11   [L     |mP: 12      [P: [L     hy: 12,21,..    1
 12   [F     |mP: 21      [P: [F     hy: 21,16,..    1
 21   [F     |mP: 16      [P: [F     hy: 16,13,..    1
   ... 756 ...
 16   [L     |mP: 13      [P: [L     hy: 13,33,..    1
 13   [F     |mP: 33      [P: [F     hy: 33,6,..     1
 33   [L     |mP: 6       [P: [L     hy: 6,31,..     1
 6    [L     |mP: 31      [P: [L     hy: 31,LONG,.   1
 31   LONG   |mP: LONG    [P: [F     hy: LONG,..     1
   ... 761 ...
 e    ROOM   |mP: ROOM    sP: ROOM   hy: ROOM,..     1
 e    PUSS   |mP: PUSS    sP: PUSS   hy: PUSS,..     1
 e    IN     |mP: IN      sP: IN     hy: IN,LONG,.   1
 e    LONG   |mP: LONG    sP: LONG   hy: LONG,..     1
 e    ROOM   |mP: ROOM    sP: ROOM   hy: ROOM,-,..   1
   ... 766 ...
 e    -      |mP: -       sP: PUSS   hy: -,-,32,..
 -    -      |mP: -                  hy: -,32,..     KN
```

Fig. 7.9. Steps 729 to 767.

Instead of setting up a novelty goal for PURR–PUSS in one of the other rooms, all I had managed to do was to set up a novelty goal where she was, so she proceeded (steps 768 to 806) to take a boomerang route all the way to SMALL ROOM and back to where I had introduced the novel pattern <CATCHEYE>. Though not planned, this turned out quite well, because now I could give <CATCHEYE> without it being treated as novel. My second attempt at the interruption would be more under my control.

On step 807 in Fig. 7.11, after being given the pattern <CATCHEYE>, PURR–PUSS waits (because of the previous disapproval) for me to give her the action [LOOKFACE and the pattern <FACING> according to the schedule of Fig. 7.4. I continue with "PUSS IN SMALL ROOM PLEASE -NOW PUSS IN LONG ROOM-" and then help her with one [F action on step 821 before she takes over.

For her first hypothesis, she goes back to an earlier memory of <CAKE>, which she has not had since! This also causes her to turn right for the SUN ROOM instead of left for the SMALL ROOM. The SMALL ROOM is where I wanted her to go and to which I had attached novelty by typing "PUSS IN SMALL ROOM PLEASE". On turning right, PURR–PUSS finds that she is not on a route to <CAKE> and constructs a new hypothesis back through SUN ROOM to LONG ROOM again. On step 840 a KORSHN exit puts an end to that, but I help her with ROOM on step 841 and she reconstructs a similar hypothesis back to LONG ROOM. Indeed, she goes back to LONG ROOM to collect the novelty I attached to SMALL ROOM back in LONG ROOM where I gave it. Notice that this is due to the novel contexts produced by <FACING>. Just as the novelty of <CATCHEYE> caused a boomerang route, so now is the novelty of <FACING> doing the same. The second attempt to send PURR–PUSS off to the SMALL ROOM has not been under my control.

The hypothesis to "<FACING>, PUSS, IN, SMALL" runs out on step 861 in Fig. 7.12 and I am now given a third chance to send PURR–PUSS off to a room. Choosing SMALL ROOM again, after PURR–PUSS types "PUSS IN SMALL ROOM PLEASE", I type in "YES PLEASE". The response is as desired. She forms an appropriate hypothesis and goes straight to the SMALL ROOM, where she repeats my words.

It was only chance that gave her the <CAKE> hypothesis before the one that we wanted her to make. On another occasion, with different random numbers, she might go straight off to the desired room the first time. In this teaching interaction I have shown you what *did* happen.

140 THINKING WITH THE TEACHABLE MACHINE

```
<CATCHEYE>  [F  (D)   hy: 32,12,21,4,-,PUSS,NOW,MOVE,RIGHT,4,STOP,-,-,-,
 32    [R          [P: [R                START,WALKING,PUSS   3
 12    [F          [P: [F     4
    ... 771 ...
 21    [F    |mP:  4       [P: [F     4
  4    -     |mP:  -       [P: [L,[R hy: -,PUSS,NOW,MOVE,LEFT,11,30,36,30,
       3,SMALL,ROOM,PUSS,IN,SMALL,ROOM,-,-,11,22,12,21,16,13,33,6,31,
       LONG,ROOM,PUSS,IN,LONG,ROOM,-,<CATCHEYE>
  -    PUSS  |mP: PUSS                hy: PUSS,NOW,..     1
  e    NOW   |mP: NOW     sP: NOW     hy: NOW,MOVE,..     1
  e    MOVE  |mP: MOVE    sP: MOVE    hy: MOVE,LEFT,..    1
    ... 776 ...
  e    LEFT  |mP: LEFT    sP: LEFT,RIGHT   hy: LEFT,...   1
  e    [L    |mP: 11      sP: SMALL   hy: 11,30,36,..     1
 11    [F    |mP: 30      [P: [F      hy: 30,36,30,..     1
 30    [F    |mP: 36      [P: [F      hy: 36,30,3,..      1
 36    [R    |mP: 30                  hy: 30,3,..         1
    ... 781 ...
 30    [R    |mP: 3       [P: [R      hy: 3,SMALL,..      1
  3    SMALL |mP: SMALL   [P: [F      hy: SMALL,ROOM,..   1
  e    ROOM  |mP: ROOM    sP: ROOM    hy: ROOM,PUSS,..    1
  e    PUSS  |mP: PUSS    sP: PUSS    hy: PUSS,IN,..      1
  e    IN    |mP: IN      sP: IN      hy: IN,SMALL,..     1
    ... 786 ...
  e    SMALL |mP: SMALL   sP: SMALL   hy: SMALL,ROOM,..   1
  e    ROOM  |mP: ROOM    sP: ROOM    hy: ROOM,-,-,..     1
  e    -     |mP: -       sP: LONG    hy: -,-,11,22,..
  -    -     |mP: -                   hy: -,11,22,12,..
  -    [F    |mP: 22,32,11            hy: 11,22,12,..
    ... 791 ...
 11    [F    |mP: 22      [P: [F      hy: 22,12,21,..     1 (See Figure 1-2)
 22    [R    |mP: 12      [P: [R      hy: 12,21,16,..     1
 12    [F    |mP: 21      [P: [F      hy: 21,16,13,..     1
 21    [F    |mP: 16      [P: [F      hy: 16,13,33,..     1
 16    [L    |mP: 13      [P: [L      hy: 13,33,6,..      1
    ... 796 ...
 13    [F    |mP: 33      [P: [F      hy: 33,6,31,..      1
 33    [L    |mP: 6       [P: [L      hy: 6,31,LONG,..    1
  6    [L    |mP: 31      [P: [L      hy: 31,LONG,..      1
 31    LONG  |mP: LONG    [P: [F      hy: LONG,ROOM,..    1
  e    ROOM  |mP: ROOM    sP: ROOM    hy: ROOM,PUSS,..    1
    ... 801 ...
  e    PUSS  |mP: PUSS    sP: PUSS    hy: PUSS,IN,..      1
  e    IN    |mP: IN      sP: IN      hy: IN,LONG,..      1
  e    LONG  |mP: LONG    sP: LONG    hy: LONG,ROOM,..    1
  e    ROOM  |mP: ROOM    sP: ROOM    hy: ROOM,-,..       1
  e    -     |mP: -       sP: PUSS    hy: -,<CATCHEYE>
    ... 806 ...
  -    -     |mP: -,<CATCHEYE>
```

steps 768-798

SMALL ROOM

LONG ROOM

Fig. 7.10. Steps 768 to 806

```
<CATCHEYE>  [LOOKFACE                              SUN
<FACING>     -                                     ROOM
PUSS    -      sP: NOW
IN      -
... 311 ...
SMALL          mP: ROOM
ROOM    -      mP: -         sP: LONG
PLEASE  -
-       -
NOW     -
... 816 ...                          steps 821-851
PUSS    -
IN      -
LONG    -      mP: ROOM
ROOM    -      mP: -                hy: -,<CATCHEYE>,<FACING>
-       -      mP: -
... 821 ...
-       [F     mP: 22,32,11
32      [R     mP: 12              hy: 12,21,4,-,PUSS,NOW,MOVE,
   RIGHT,4,STOP,-,-,-,START,COUNTING,OBJECTS,-,-----,-,ANY,MORE,
   OBJECTS,YES,-,OBJECT,PLEASE,<CAKE>                          2
12      [F     mP: 21              hy: 21,4,-,PUSS,...         2
21      [F     mP: 4      [P: [F   hy: 4,-,PUSS,NOW,...        1
4       -      mP: -      [P: [L,[R hy: -,PUSS,NOW,..
... 826 ...
-       PUSS   mP: PUSS            hy: PUSS,NOW,...            2
e       NOW    mP: NOW     sP: NOW,IN hy: NOW,MOVE,...         1
e       MOVE   mP: MOVE    sP: MOVE   hy: MOVE,RIGHT,..        1
e       RIGHT  mP: RIGHT   sP: LEFT,RIGHT hy: RIGHT,4,...      1 (See
e       [R     mP: 4,22    sP: SUN    hy: 4,STOP,-,-,-,..      1  Figure 0)
... 831 ...
22      [F     mP: 3       [P: [F                              4
3       [F     mP: 13      [P: [F   hy: 13,2,30,SUN,ROOM,PUSS,IN,
   SUN,ROOM,-,-,22,11,12,21,16,13,33,6,31,LONG,ROOM,PUSS,IN,LONG,
   ROOM,-,<CATCHEYE>,<FACING>,PUSS
13      [L     mP: 2       [P: [L   hy: 2,30,SUN,...           1
2       [L     mP: 30      [P: [L   hy: 30,SUN,ROOM,..         1
30      SUN    mP: SUN     [P: [F   hy: SUN,ROOM,..            1
... 836 ...
e       ROOM   mP: ROOM    sP: ROOM hy: ROOM,PUSS,IN,..        1
e       PUSS   mP: PUSS    sP: PUSS hy: PUSS,IN,SUN,..         1
e       IN     mP: IN      sP: IN   hy: IN,SUN,ROOM,..         1
e       SUN                sP: SUN  hy: SUN,ROOM,-,-,..        4
e       -                  sP: ROOM                            KN
... 841 ...
ROOM    -                  sP: LONG
-       -      mP: -
-       [F     mP: 22,32,11                                    4
22      [F     mP: 11      [P: [F   hy: 11,12,21,16,13,33,6,31,
   LONG,ROOM,PUSS,IN,LONG,ROOM,-,<CATCHEYE>,<FACING>,PUSS,IN,SMALL  1
11      [L     mP: 12      [P: [L   hy: 12,21,16,13,..         1
... 846 ...
12      [F     mP: 21      [P: [F   hy: 21,16,13,33,..         1
21      [F     mP: 16      [P: [F   hy: 16,13,33,6,..          1
16      [L     mP: 13      [P: [L   hy: 13,33,6,31,..          1
13      [F     mP: 33      [P: [F   hy: 33,6,31,LONG,..        1
33      [L     mP: 6       [P: [L   hy: 6,31,LONG,..           1
... 851 ...
6       [L     mP: 31      [P: [L   hy: 31,LONG,ROOM,..        1
```

Fig. 7.11. Steps 807 to 851.

142   THINKING WITH THE TEACHABLE MACHINE

```
31      LONG      mP: LONG       [P: [F,[LOOKFACE hy: LONG,ROOM,..  1
e       ROOM      mP: ROOM       sP: ROOM         hy: ROOM,PUSS,IN,.. 1
e       PUSS      mP: PUSS       sP: PUSS         hy: PUSS,IN,LONG,.. 1
e       IN        mP: IN         sP: IN           hy: IN,LONG,ROOM,.. 1
   ... 856 ...
e       LONG      mP: LONG       sP: LONG         hy: LONG,ROOM,-,..  1
e       ROOM      mP: ROOM       sP: ROOM         hy: ROOM,-,..       1
e       -         mP: -          sP: PUSS         hy: -,<CATCHEYE>,..
-       -         mP: -,<CATCHEYE>                hy: <CATCHEYE>,..
-       -         [LOOKFACE                       hy: <FACING>,PUSS,.. 3
   ... 861 ...
<FACING> PUSS               [P: [F           4
e       IN                  sP: NOW,IN       4
e       SMALL               sP: SMALL        4
e       ROOM      mP: ROOM  sP: ROOM         4
e       PLEASE              sP: LONG,PLEASE  4
   ... 866 ...
e       -                   sP: NOW
YES     -
PLEASE  -
-       -
NOW     -         mP: PUSS
   ... 871 ...
PUSS    -         mP: IN                     hy: IN
IN      -         mP: LONG                   hy: LONG
LONG    ROOM                sP: ROOM         hy: ROOM                  4
e       -                   sP: PUSS
-       -         mP: -,<CATCHEYE>
-       [F        mP: 22,32,11
32      [R        mP: 12         [P: [R           4
12      [F        mP: 21         [P: [F           4
21      [F        mP: 4          [P: [F     hy: 4,-,PUSS,NOW,MOVE,LEFT,11,
       30,36,30,3,SMALL,ROOM,PUSS,IN,SMALL,ROOM,PLEASE,YES,PLEASE     1
4       -         mP: -          [P: [L,[R  hy: -,PUSS,NOW,..
   ... 881 ...
-       PUSS      mP: PUSS                   hy: PUSS,NOW,MOVE,..     1
e       NOW       mP: NOW        sP: NOW,IN  hy: NOW,MOVE,LEFT,..     1
e       MOVE      mP: MOVE       sP: MOVE    hy: MOVE,LEFT,11,..      1
e       LEFT      mP: LEFT       sP: LEFT,RIGHT hy: LEFT,11,..        1
e       [L        mP: 11         sP: SMALL   hy: 11,30,36,30,..       1
   ... 886 ...
11      [F        mP: 30         [P: [F     hy: 30,36,30,3,..         1
30      [F        mP: 36         [P: [F     hy: 36,30,3,SMALL,..      1
36      [R        mP: 30         [P: [R     hy: 30,3,SMALL,..         1
30      [R        mP: 3          [P: [R     hy: 3,SMALL,ROOM,..       1
3       SMALL     mP: SMALL      [P: [F     hy: SMALL,ROOM,..         1
   ... 891 ...
e       ROOM      mP: ROOM       sP: ROOM    hy: ROOM,PUSS,IN,..      1
e       PUSS      mP: PUSS       sP: PUSS    hy: PUSS,IN,SMALL,..     1
e       IN        mP: IN         sP: IN      hy: IN,SMALL,ROOM,..     1
e       SMALL     mP: SMALL      sP: SMALL   hy: SMALL,ROOM,..        1
e       ROOM      mP: ROOM       sP: ROOM    hy: ROOM,PLEASE,..       1
   ... 896 ...
e       PLEASE    mP: PLEASE sP: PLEASE,LONG  hy: PLEASE,..           1
e       YES                  sP: NOW,YES hy: YES,PLEASE,              4
e       PLEASE               sP: PLEASE       4
       &c.                                               29NOV1975
```

steps 876-889

SMALL ROOM

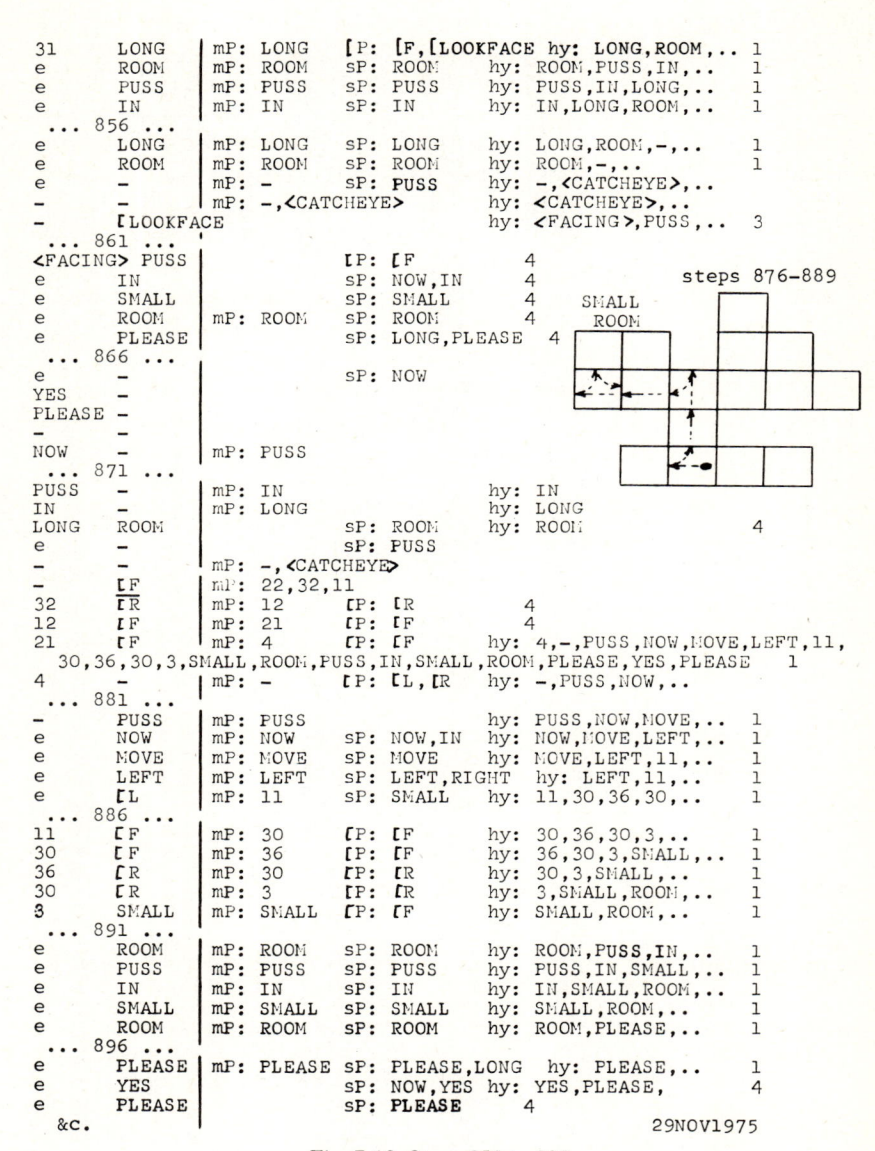

Fig. 7.12. Steps 852 to 898.

Man and Machine

In the ROOMS task, we have seen that PURR–PUSS can set her own goals in a simple way and that we can set goals for her. The possibility of conversational behaviour was explored briefly with the HELLO task. Before that, COUNTING OBJECTS and COUNTING BEADS demonstrated straightforward teaching and the transfer of learned experience to new problems. Her multiple context enabled PURR–PUSS to react appropriately to new situations and to choose actions on her own initiative. PURR–PUSS starts with her PUSS memories quite empty. The PUSS memories are all together in a single mew–gram which can be as large as we can afford. The speed of PURR–PUSS is not affected by the size of her memory.

PURR–PUSS is a developing system.[8] There are many directions in which she can be improved. She can be given new bodies and new worlds. We can change the organization and number of PUSSes. There may be better decision strategies for PURR. Much progress has been made already by the discovery of new teaching methods.

PURR–PUSS seems to have some of the qualities that people have said machines could not have.[9] This book will have been worth writing if it only sheds new light on the behaviour of machines. [10] My hope, however, is that those studying and tending the minds of men and women will be helped in their tasks by thinking with PURR–PUSS.[11]

Notes on Chapter 7

1. Uhr (1973) summarises the situation as follows (page 283): "An extremely interesting situation, one that we all engage in all the time, is conversation, both through words with other people and through acts with our day-to-day environment. What is a statement that calls for a response, at what level, in what detail? How can we evoke a pertinent response in another? These are very ill-formed problems with which all of us cope every day of our lives; yet we are not even aware of what we mean by a conversation, how we choose our responses, or how or even whether we judge their pertinence".

2. A penetrating discussion of the subtle ways in which we use words is given by Austin (1962) in "How to do things with Words".

3. In connection with the special problems of question and answer, Norman (1973) asks "How do people answer questions? At first, the process appears reasonably simple. A person is asked a question, he retrieves the relevant information from his memory, and then he responds with the appropriate answer . . . there is much more to answering questions than simply retrieving something from memory". With PURR–PUSS we have to approach the problem at an even lower level where "retrieving something from memory" is no longer simple in itself.

4. The face-scanning routine for the HELLO task was inspired by the well-known article by Noton and Stark (1971) entitled "Eye Movements and Visual Perception". An interesting re-interpretation of their results is provided by Didday and Arbib (1975).

5. The silent monologue "I MUST REMEMBER HIS NAME" taught to PURR–PUSS is a crude version of something much more difficult in practice. To quote Ryle (1949, page 28): "Much of our ordinary thinking is conducted in internal monologue or silent soliloquy, usually accompanied by an internal cinematograph-show of visual imagery. This trick of talking to oneself in silence is acquired neither quickly nor without effort; and it is a necessary condition of our acquiring it that we should have previously learned to talk intelligently aloud and have heard and understood other people doing so".

6. One of the reasons for attempting the ROOMS task was the importance given in "The Nature of Mind" (Kenny et al, 1972) to the inability of computers to set their own goals. I can also point to a remark by Longuet-Higgins in the same book (page 100): "Even computing languages are only *understood* by computers, not actually *talked* by them, . .". The reverse is true of the words that PURR–PUSS uses at present! I am not suggesting that PURR–PUSS suddenly reveals the nature of the mind, but just that some established ideas on the nature of computers need revising. The argument that I find most convincing in favour of man's superior intelligence at the present time is that we know that we know. Anything comparable in a machine looks a very long way off. On the other hand, I fear that PURR–PUSS will have to begin to know that she knows before she can engage in genuine conversation or really set her own goals.

7. Watanabe (1974) has quoted himself as saying "the robot has goals but the man has values". He goes on to argue "Our contention is that human intelligence functions mainly in terms of paradigmatic symbols, while mechanical intelligence functions uniquely in terms of abstract symbols, resulting in a qualitative difference between natural and artificial intelligence". This echoes the earlier argument of Narasimhan (1969) that "Since I am saying that the paradigmatic mode is the more primitive mode of behaviour, it must be clear that children when they start out must necessarily function predominantly, I would say almost totally, in the paradigmatic mode". This is the way we have been teaching PURR–PUSS.

8. Of recent research being carried out on systems to perform intelligent functions, I should like to make special mention of Winograd's (1972) "Understanding Natural Language", Winston's (1975) "Psychology of Computer Vision", Norman and Rumelhart's (1975) "Explorations in Cognition", and Ambler et al's (1975) computer-controlled assembly.

Uhr (1973) claimed of his program: "No program that I know of does this amount of learning, and it is not clear that so much is needed. . . . And it is relatively powerful in comparison with other learning and pattern recognition programs". (Pages 430, 431) Unfortunately, he gives no results.

An essay of Minsky (1974) is partly reproduced in the book edited by Winston (1975), but without the following important (for my PURR–PUSS) quotation: "I cannot state strongly enough my conviction that the preoccupation with Consistency, so valuable for Mathematical Logic, has been incredibly destructive to those working on models of mind. . . . thinking begins first with suggestive but defective plans and images, that are slowly (if ever) refined and replaced by better ones".

9. In Andreae and Cleary (1976), we offered an alternative hypothesis to Simon's (1968) well-known one: "A man, viewed as a behaving system, is quite simple. The apparent complexity of his behaviour over time is largely a reflection of the complexity of the environment in which he finds himself". Our alternative hypothesis was: "A man, viewed as a behaving system, is complex. His complexity is due to a simple mechanism which aggregates in him a reflection of his past behaviour in the complex environment in which he finds himself". We suggested that PUSS was the kind of simple mechanism needed for our hypothesis to be true. It enables PURR–PUSS to *become* her experience.

10. Some will find the "river-like" PURR–PUSS a retrograde step in artificial intelligence. Not only does it represent a return to the beginning, but it also promises a very long journey ahead even to catch up with the "pipe" programs of today. Others will be reassured by the thought that, to produce an intelligence comparable with our own, we may have to provide a machine with a body and an education like our own.

11. For me, PURR–PUSS is all of the following:—
— an improvement on the conditioned reflex
— a machine that can learn from scratch
— a step towards the abolition of programming
— a teachable and slightly intelligent robot
— a better brain model
— the divorce of machines from formal systems
— a paradigmatic pupil
— a new avenue for research
— an aid to thinking about human behaviour.

Epilogue

You now have learned enough to see
That Cats are much like you and me
And other people whom we find
Possessed of various types of mind.

T. S. Eliot
"Old Possum's Book of Practical Cats"

The magician demonstrates illusions of the impossible. His feats are not only good entertainment, but they also sharpen our perception and make us less gullible. Having seen the conjuror manipulate cards, rabbits, rings and the like, we are less likely to fall for the charlatan who claims supernatural powers.

A good magician chooses his feats to shake our firmest beliefs. He makes something from nothing, a whole from the shattered, the alive from the dead. He will never prove the non-existence of real magic, but he does show how far we can go without it.

For many, the mind is magic.

In this book, I have tried to show you what can be done with a simple system called PURR–PUSS. You have been shown exactly how she works. You have watched each step as she has learned from scratch to perform simple tasks, as she has responded appropriately to novel situations, as she has applied earlier experience to new problems, as she has carried out simple commands and, above all, as she has been taught. These are things which can be done without a mind of magic.

There may be magic in the mind, but there is certainly no magic in PURR–PUSS.

What is man, that thou are mindful of him?

Psalm 8,4.

Appendix

" . . . age-old instincts working away deep down,
mincing up little bits of experience for future use,
watching me carefully like a little sharp-eyed, blonde kitten."

Noel Coward
"Private Lives"

A.1 A Neurochemical Version of PURR–PUSS

Could the operation of PURR–PUSS be similar to the working of the brain? How could we tell? The brain is a neurochemical network of vast complexity[1] and, physically, it is quite different from the digital computer in which PURR–PUSS is programmed. If we designed a neurochemical version of PURR–PUSS, would it be a model of the brain? That is the possibility that I discuss in this Appendix.

Mew-Brain is a neurochemical network designed to be as similar to PURR–PUSS as possible. Unlike the mew-gram version of PURR–PUSS described in Chapters 1 to 7, mew-Brain has not been properly tested. This is one reason why this section has not been given the status of a chapter. Another reason is that the current state of neurophysiology does not permit a detailed comparison of the neural processes proposed for mew-Brain with neural processes in the human brain. Nevertheless, the reader will find a carefully worked out system with some intriguing implications.

Mew-Brain offers certain advantages over the mew-gram version of PURR–PUSS and also suggests improvements to the latter. Thus, hypothesis formation in mew-Brain is more effective than hypothesis formation in either the mew-gram or the PUSS net versions of PURR–PUSS. In the PUSS net version[2] hypothesis formation begins with a "working back" from the novelty goals through the network to guide the forward generation of hypotheses. In mew-Brain there is a similar "chemical leak-back" to mark out forward paths to novelty, but, being a neurochemical network, mew-Brain is not limited to the slow serial operation of the PUSS net version. The mew-gram version of PURR–PUSS would be as fast as mew-Brain with comparable "hardware", but, lacking the possibility of a fast working back process, the random forward generation of hypotheses in the mew-gram suffers from the disadvantages elaborated in Note 3 of Chapter 5.

Multiple context is another feature of PURR–PUSS that receives a somewhat different treatment in mew-Brain because of the different constraints encountered in designing a neurochemical network. The "cortical–PUSSes" into which mew-Brain is divided have been made partly sequential and partly spatial (see Note 1, Chapter 3) to avoid using composite events like pattern-actions and action-patterns. To include such composite events in mew-Brain would have made excessive demands on the chemical aspects of the neurochemical network. However, the mew-Brain contexts have virtues of their own and we plan to study them by introducing them into PURR–PUSS.

Mew-Brain is a physical system with all its parts working at the same time. Only a very small mew-Brain could be simulated in real time on a serial digital computer. PURR–PUSS is a similar, but not identical, structure which operates efficiently in a digital computer. PURR–PUSS may enable us to get a reasonably reliable idea of how a large mew-Brain would behave in complex environments. If there is some correspondence between this behaviour and the behaviour observed of humans, then we may be able to modify mew-Brain and PURR–PUSS to achieve a better correspondence. Even if this psychological approach proves unfeasible, the mechanisms proposed in mew-Brain may provide a working hypothesis for neurophysiologists studying the neurochemistry of the brain.[3]

A.2 Neurons and Connections in Mew-Brain

We start with a number of definitions.

Every neuron has a "firing potential", which determines its readiness to fire.[4] An "integrating neuron" also has a "firing count". Each neuron has at least one "connection" joining it, the "source" neuron, to a "destination" neuron. Each connection has a source, a destination and a "strength". A connection with zero strength is a "potential connection".

A connection is joined to a destination neuron by a "synapse" that may be excitatory (positive strength) or inhibitory (negative strength), as shown in Fig. A.1.

An "input connection" has no specified source neuron, while an "output connection" has no specified destination neuron.

When the source neuron of a connection fires, the firing potential of the destination neuron is increased by an amount equal to the strength of the connection. Subject to certain chemical conditions to be prescribed later, when the source and destination neurons of a potential connection fire simultaneously, the connection becomes established with a non-zero strength.

A.2.1 The Cycle of Operations

Changes are made to neurons and connections in each of four stages of the operation cycle:

    S1. Input stage, during which inputs are transferred to the neural network.
    S2. Increment stage, during which the effects of the previous firing of source neurons are transferred to the destination neurons.
    S3. Firing stage, during which neurons are fired.
    S4. Chemical stage, during which forward propagation and leak-back of chemical codes (MOLs) is carried out.

During the input stage S1, any input connection from an input that is ON causes the firing potential of its destination neuron to be incremented by an amount equal to the strength of the connection.

During the increment stage S2, the firing potentials of all destination neurons of connections from neurons that fired in the last cycle are incremented by the strengths of their connections.

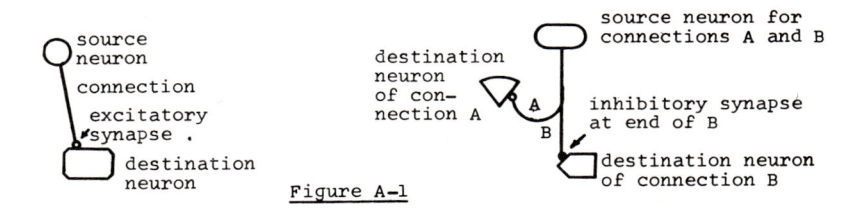

Figure A-1

Fig. A.1.

A.2.2 The Firing Stage, S3

Non-integrating neurons, whose firing potentials exceed the "firing threshold", are fired and then their firing potential is reduced to zero. (The fact that a neuron is fired is recorded for one cycle of the operations.)

    An integrating neuron is fired if its firing count exceeds zero and then its firing count is reduced by one.

    An integrating neuron, whose firing count is zero, will be fired if its firing potential exceeds the firing threshold. Its firing count is then set to an "initial count" and its firing potential is set to zero.

    Every integrating neuron's firing potential is decreased by an amount called the "die-away" in each operation cycle.

A.3 Chemical Coding

The synthesis and movement of chemical codes through mew-Brain perform two functions: the maintenance of locally unique contexts and the formation of hypothesis paths.

A chemical code will be referred to here as a "MOL" to avoid any implication that it is a particular kind of molecule, such as RNA or protein, while bearing such a possibility in mind. A MOL carrying a particular code, such as "XYZ", will be written MOL–XYZ.

MOLs will be used to identify inputs and contexts. Input MOLs are synthesised in "input neurons". Context MOLs are synthesised in "context neurons".

There will always be a plentiful supply of input MOLs in input neurons and these will travel down the connections of the input neurons through both integrating neurons and "prediction neurons" to "output neurons" and context neurons. Input MOLs do not pass through context neurons, but they may contribute to the synthesis of context MOLs in those neurons.

The source neuron of a connection C_U to a context neuron is in the upper layer of integrating neurons (Fig. A.2), the source of a connection C_M is in the middle layer, and the source of a connection C_L is in the lower layer of integrating neurons. Three connections, C_U, C_M and C_L, to a context neuron "fire a context" if their source neurons fire simultaneously. Now, each context neuron has an associated prediction neuron to which it has a potential connection. If the context is fired at the same time as the prediction neuron fires, the potential connection becomes an "established connection" with non-zero strength and a large excess of MOL–MLUP is synthesised in the context neuron "to record the novel event". Here M, L and U are the input codes travelling down connections C_M, C_L and C_U to the context neuron, while P is the input code from the prediction neuron.

Once a context MOL–MLUP has been fired in a context neuron, that MOL is assigned to that neuron and any other context that is fired into that neuron has no effect. Also, to maintain locally unique contexts, an inhibitory message is conveyed by the prediction neuron to all other context neurons having potential connections with it. This message prevents more than one potential connection from being established with the same context.

The second role of context MOLs is in the formation of hypothesis paths. Context MOLs leak-back from the context neurons through integrating neurons to the "body" of an input neuron from which they move out through other connections to other context neurons. Figure A.3. shows the leak-back path from the context neuron synthesising MOL-41R3 back to the context neuron synthesising MOL-24Q1. The coding "match" between "41" in "41R3" and in "24Q1" causes an increased synthesis of MOL-24Q1 which leaks back still farther. The first MOL-41R3 does not proceed beyond the context neuron.[5]

APPENDIX 151

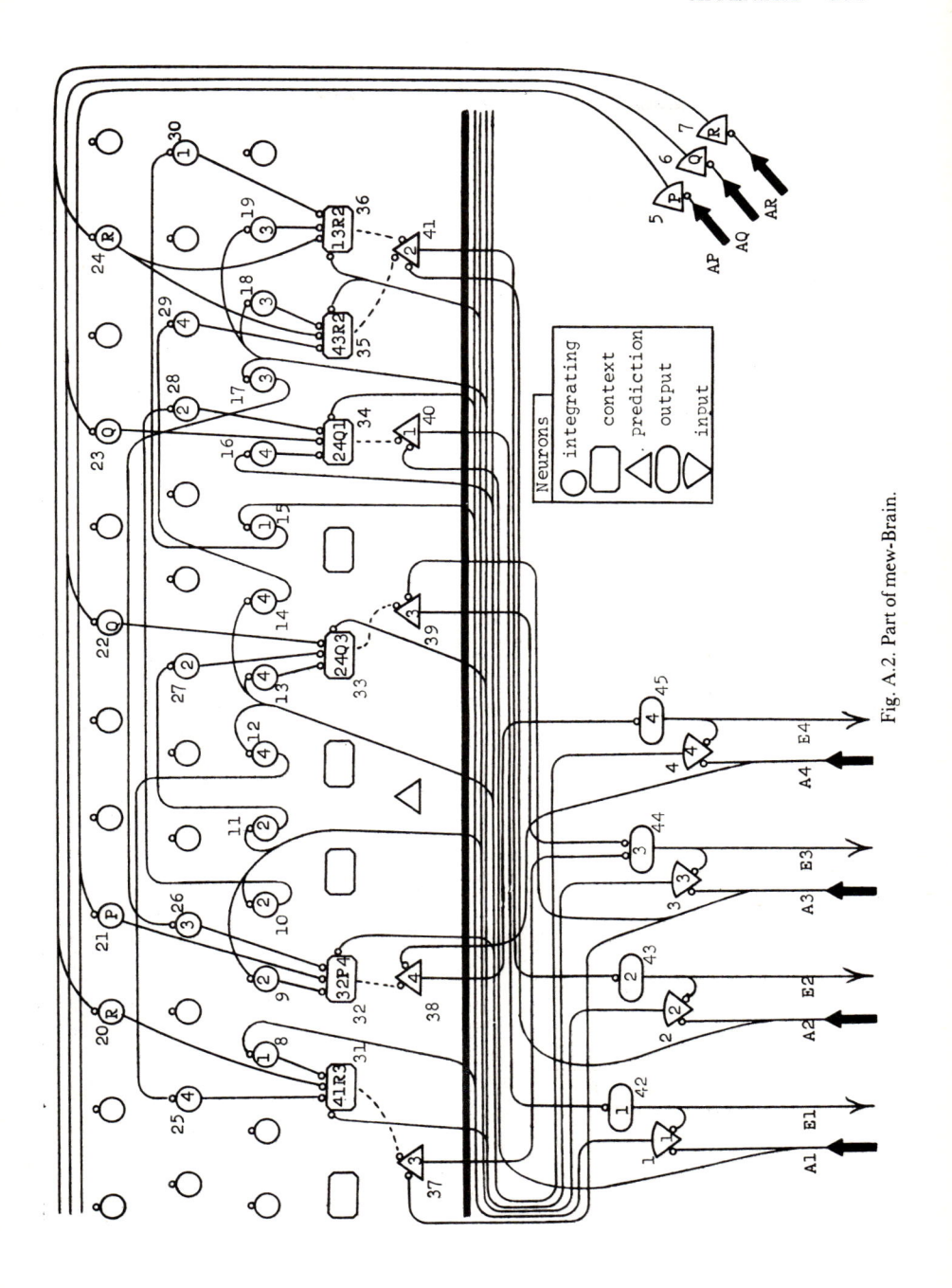

Fig. A.2. Part of mew-Brain.

152   THINKING WITH THE TEACHABLE MACHINE

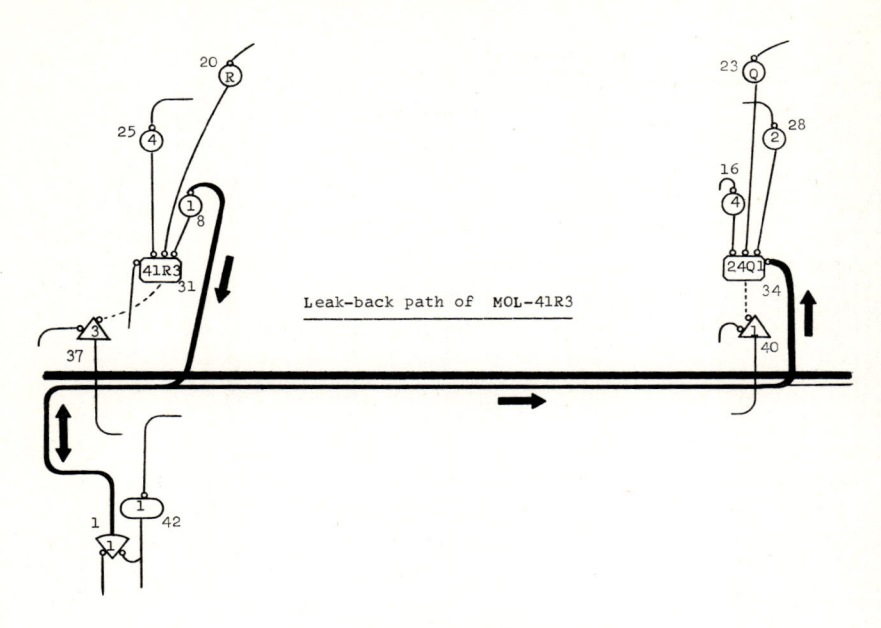

Fig. A.3. Chemical leak-back.

The leaking-back of context MOLs starts from the excess of MOLs in those neurons that record a novel event. The paths of leaked-back MOLs continue through matching context neurons throughout mew-Brain with a gradually decreasing concentration of context MOLs down to the "ambient concentration" which is maintained by all context neurons to record their contexts.

The hypothesis paths influence the activity of mew-Brain through the increased concentrations of context MOLs. The strength of an established connection from a context neuron to a prediction neuron is an increasing function of the concentration of context MOLs in the context neuron. When a context is fired into the context neuron, the strength of the connection to the prediction neuron determines the rate of firing of the latter. Any increased rate of firing of the prediction neuron is passed on to the output neuron. In this way, the hypothesis paths laid down by the leaking-back context MOLs bias the output of mew-Brain.

A.4 A Simulated Network

The neuron properties defined in sections A.2 and A.3 become clearer when the simple network of Fig. A.2 is seen in action. Fig. A.4 shows the neuron firings over a 130 cycle period, while Fig. A.5 displays the corresponding variations in concentration of six MOLs up to the 120th cycle.

APPENDIX 153

During the first 9 cycles (t=1 to t=9), inputs A2 and AP are applied simultaneously. The "impulses" arriving on A2 and AP are shown as rows of dots at the top of Fig. A.4. These input impulses cause the firing of neurons 2, 5 and 41 in the same nine cycles, because the inputs are directly connected to these neurons. The triangle representing the prediction neuron 41 in Fig. A.2 contains a "2" to indicate that it is driven by input A2. In this way, the reader is saved the chore of frequently tracing connections on the diagram.

Careful examination of Fig. A.4 reveals that neuron 43, which is the destination of a connection from neuron 41, fires from t=2 to t=10. The nine firings of neuron 43 occur one cycle later than the nine firings of neuron 41. This is because neuron 41 has to fire before neuron 43 can receive an increment to its firing potential.

The next thing to notice is that neuron 2 fires eleven times. The two firings after input A2 has ceased are due to the firing of neuron 43 being communicated to neuron 2 via the connection between them.

Three neurons, to which the firing of neuron 2 is communicated, are neurons 9, 10 and 11. Since these are integrating neurons, they accept nine impulses before firing themselves. Having an initial count of 9, they then fire for nine cycles. It can be seen in Fig. A.4 how this integrating property of neurons 9, 10 and 11 causes them to delay by nine cycles the input to them from neuron 2. In the same way, neurons 10 and 11 in the lower layer of the top three layers of integrating neurons are connected to neurons 28 and 27 of the middle layer, these latter two neurons firing after a further delay of nine cycles. This can be seen in Fig. A.2 from t=19 to t=27.

Following the nine input impulses from A2 and AP we have nine input impulses from A4 and AQ, and then nine from A3 and AR. During cycle t=19, neurons 13, 22 and 27 fire a context into context neuron 33. Even without the extra (leak-back) connection from neuron 3, this is sufficient to fire neuron 33 during t=20. However, neuron 39 fires at the same time so the potential connection (zero strength) from neuron 33 to neuron 39 is established and the concentration of MOL-24Q3 starts at 0·99. The strength of the connection is made equal to the concentration of the MOL so, as the latter leaks away (see Fig. A.5 from t=21), the strength of the connection decreases. The context is fired into neuron 33 until t=27 so it fires until t=28. During t=28 the strength of the connection from neuron 33 to neuron 39 is down to 0·923, which is just above the firing threshold (0·91) so neuron 39 fires in t=29 causing neuron 44 to fire in t=30 and neuron 3 to fire in t=31. Thus, neuron 3 has fired from t=19 to t=31 as shown by the computer simulation results of Fig. A.4.

The pattern of inputs (A2+AP for nine cycles, A4+AQ for nine cycles and A3+AR for nine cycles) is repeated from t=28 to t=54. MOL-43R2 is generated from t=30 and MOL-32P4 from t=38, as shown in Fig. A.5.

154 THINKING WITH THE TEACHABLE MACHINE

```
Inputs
A1:                                  ..........
A2: ..........          ..........          ..........          ..........
A3:          ..........          ..........          ..........          ..........
A4: ....|....|....|....|....|....|....|....|....|....|....|....|....|
         10   20   30   40   50   60   70   80   90  100  110  120  130
AP: ..........          ..........          ..........          ..........
AQ:          ..........          ..........          ..........          ..........
AR:                   ..........          ..........          ....................
Input Neurons ....|....|....|....|....|....|....|....|....|....|....|....|....|
  1:                                       ...............             ....
  2:  ..........          ..........   .          ... ..............             ....
  3:           ..............           ..............   .          ..............   .
  4:  ..............           ..............           ..............           ..............
  5:  ..........                   ..........                   ..........
  6:           ..........                   ..........                   ..........
  7:                    ..........                   ..........                   ....................
Integrating Neurons – lower layer ....|....|....|....|....|....|....|....|....|....|
  8:                                       ..........
  9:  ..........          ..........          ..........          ..........
 10:           ..........          ..........          ..........          ..........
 11:  ..........          ..........          ..........          ..........
 12:           ..........          ..........          ..........          ..........
 13:           ..........          ..........          ..........          ..........
 14:           ..........          ..........          ..........          ..........
 15:                                       ..........
 16:           ..........          ..........          ..........          ..........
 17:                    ..........          ..........          ..........
 18:                    ..........          ..........          ..........
 19:                    ..........          ..........          ..........
    – upper layer ....|....|....|....|....|....|....|....|....|....|....|....|....|
 20:                             ..........                   ....................
 21:  ..........          ..........          ..........          ..........
 22:           ..........          ..........          ..........          ..........
 23:           ..........          ..........          ..........          ..........
 24:                    ..........          ..........          ..........
    – middle layer ....|....|....|....|....|....|....|....|....|....|....|....|....|
 25:                                                                      ..........
 26:           ..........          ..........          ..........          ..........
 27:           ..........          ..........          ..........          ..........
 28:           ..........          ..........          ..........          ..........
 29:                    ..........          ..........          ..........
 30:                                                ..........
Context Neurons ....|....|....|....|....|....|....|....|....|....|....|....|....|
 31:                                       ..........
 32:           ..........          ..........          ..........
 33:           ..........          ..........          ..........          ..........
 34:           ..........          ..........          ..........
 35:                    ..........          ..........
 36:                                                ..........
Prediction Neurons ....|....|....|....|....|....|....|....|....|....|....|....|....|
 37:           ..........          ..........          ..........
 38:  ..........          ..........          ..........          ..........
 39:           ..............           ..............   .          ..............   .          ....
 40:                                       ..............                     ....
 41:  ..........          ..........          ..........          ..........
Output Neurons ....|....|....|....|....|....|....|....|....|....|....|....|....|
 42:                                       ..............                     ....
 43:  ..........          ..........          ..........          ..........
 44:           ..............           ..............   .          ..............   .          ....
 45:           ..........          ..............           ..............           ..........  .
                                                                                    9oct76
```

Fig. A.4. Neuron firings.

APPENDIX 155

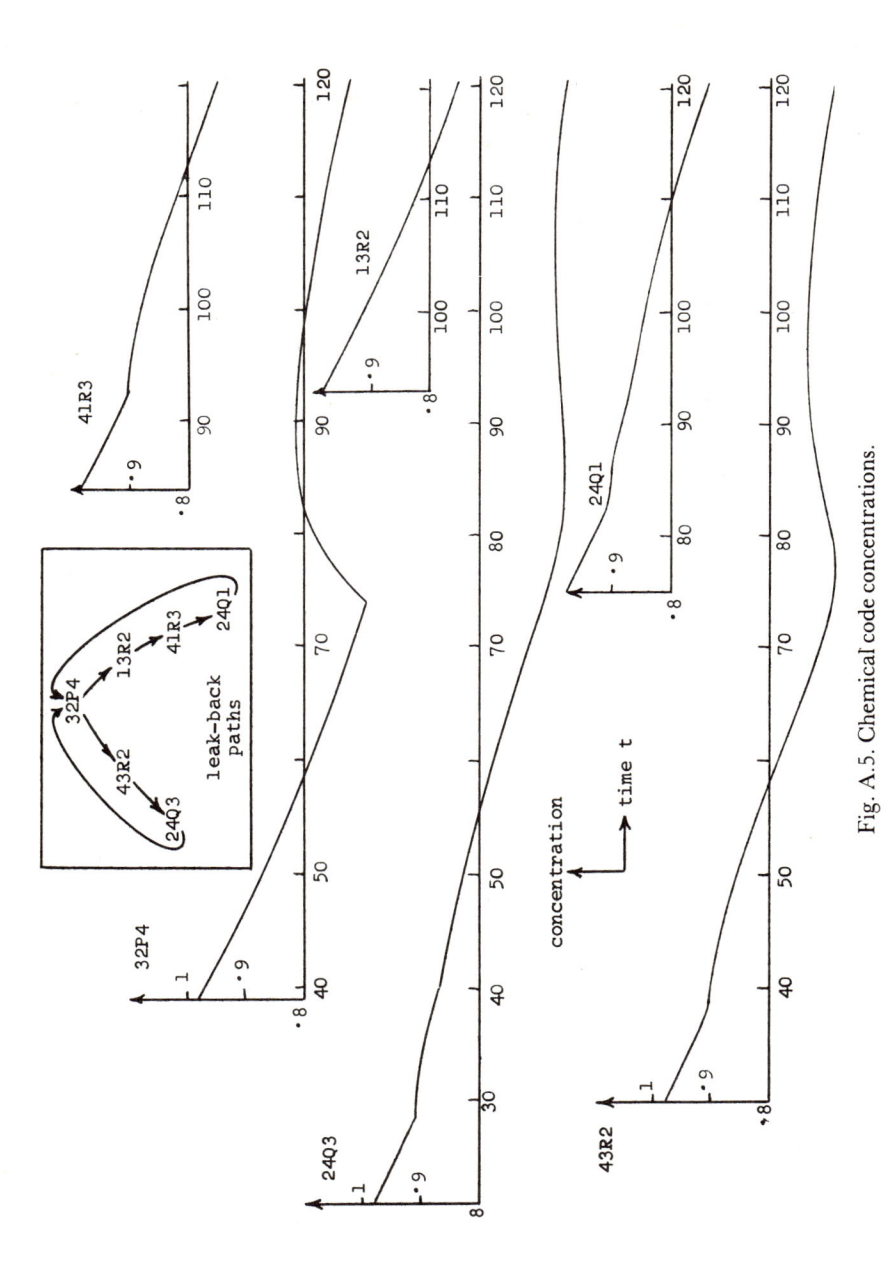

Fig. A.5. Chemical code concentrations.

156   THINKING WITH THE TEACHABLE MACHINE

Notice how the dying away of MOL-24Q3 is interrupted by the appearance and leak-back of MOL-43R2 in cycle t=30. The leak-back paths are indicated by the inset diagram of Fig. A.5.

It was explained above why neuron 3 fired thirteen times from t=19 to t=31. Between t=46 and t=58, there are also thirteen cycles but neuron 3 does not fire during t=57. This is because the strength of the connection from neuron 33 to neuron 39 is now below the firing threshold of neuron 39. However, neuron 39 is an integrating neuron with an initial count (see section A.2.2) of 1, so it accepts two firings from neuron 33 to fire once in cycle t=58. In this way the strength of the connections from context neurons to prediction neurons is reflected in the rate of firing of the latter.

The integrating neurons of the top three layers have an initial count of 9 and thereby produce a delay of nine cycles. The prediction neurons, which also integrate but have an initial count of 1, produce a proportional firing rate. The sequential nature of contexts is produced by the integrating neurons of the top three layers. The varying strength of prediction is effected by the prediction neurons, also using an integration mechanism.

By t=27 all three MOLs produced by the repeated input sequence A2+AP, A4+AQ, A3+AR, . . have decreased in concentration to about 0.7. But with t=73 the input changes to A1+AR and the new context MOL-24Q1 appears. The effect of leak-back to MOL-32P4 is particularly strong, as can be seen in Fig. A.5. The last two MOLs appear in cycles t=84 and t=93. Then the input returns to the first pattern with A3+AR, A2+AP, A4+AQ from t=82 to t=108. Notice neuron 39 predicting input A3 on cycles t=76, 78 and 80, while neuron 44 conveys this prediction to the output on t=77, 79 and 81.

```
Firing potential of integrating neurons is decreased by 0·1
                                                each cycle.
Firing threshold is 0·91.
Initial count for integrating neurons is 9.
Initial count for prediction neurons is 1.
Strengths of connections:-
 Input to prediction neuron                    0·96
 Input to input neuron                         0·96
 Input neuron to context neuron                0·1
 Input neuron to integrating neuron            0·2
 Integrating neuron to integrating neuron      0·2
 Integrating neuron to context neuron          0·32
 Context neuron to prediction neuron           0
Chemical leak-back:-
 Increase concentration of MOL by 10% of difference between
 it and higher concentration of a MOL from which leak-back
 path exists.
 Decrease concentration of every MOL by 1% each cycle.
```

Table A.1. Data used for computer simulation of Fig. A.2.

Finally, input ceases from cycle t=109 and the network predicts the expected input A3 by neurons 39 and 44, and it predicts the alternative input A1 by neurons 40 and 42. (In the past sequence, the context 2,4+Q was followed both by 1 giving MOL-24Q1 and by 3 giving MOL-24Q3, so the prediction of both A1 and A3 is quite reasonable. Because of the higher concentration of MOL-24Q1, the prediction of input A1 will be slightly stronger — it is nearer novelty).

If the firing threshold of the neurons were lowered, the predictions of the network would enable it to carry on actively for much longer than shown, but activity would still stop when the MOL concentrations had dropped low enough.

The neurochemical network of Fig. A.2 is seen to be predictive and stable. Its behaviour is almost as well defined as the behaviour of a PUSS in Chapter 2.

A.5 Mew-Brain as a Complete System

This section is highly speculative so it will be kept brief. First I offer a rough calculation to show that known facts about the human brain are not inconsistent with a large mew-Brain.[6] This is followed by the description of a general scheme for a complete mew-Brain.

A.5.1 A Very Rough Calculation

A rough calculation shows that the kind of system we are talking about is *possible*. None of the figures used in the calculation is sufficiently reliable to make the results of the calculation *likely*.

We start by assuming that the brain (the neocortex, to be specific) receives input at the rate of 2 events per second. This is slower than rates attributed to the senses, but allows for pre-processing between sensors and neocortex. Estimates of the overall information rate of the brain have been as high as 40 bits per second, i.e. a million alternatives per half-second.[7] Let us assume, therefore, that we have a system which can accept any one of a million different possible inputs per half-second. If each of the three inputs to a context neuron in Fig. A.2 has a million different possible identities, there will be a trillion $(10)^{18}$ different possible contexts. (I am using the British trillion which is a million million million). However, since a lifetime contains only about four thousand million half-seconds and there is likely to be a considerable amount of duplication of input sequences, we assume that only a thousand million contexts actually occur. In other words, about a quarter of the new inputs in a lifetime introduce a new context.

The number of neurons in the brain is estimated to be five thousand million or more.[8] If a thousand million of these are context neurons for the thousand million contexts that can occur in a lifetime, three thousand million

158   THINKING WITH THE TEACHABLE MACHINE

can correspond to integrating neurons in the upper, middle and lower layers of mew-Brain. Another thousand million neurons can be input, output and prediction neurons.

It has been estimated that a neuron in the brain can be within range of the connections (axons and dendrites) of up to five thousand other neurons. Suppose that each context neuron is within range of a thousand neurons in each of the layers of integrating neurons. This means that each context neuron has a million million million (i.e. a trillion) possible contexts, only one of which becomes coded in it. Assuming that inputs are randomly (or pseudorandomly) distributed throughout the neocortex, the thousand million context neurons, each with its thousand million possible contexts, present a total potential of a trillion (thousand million times thousand million) possible contexts. But a trillion, being a million million million, is the number of possible contexts that can be produced by a million different inputs taken three at a time.

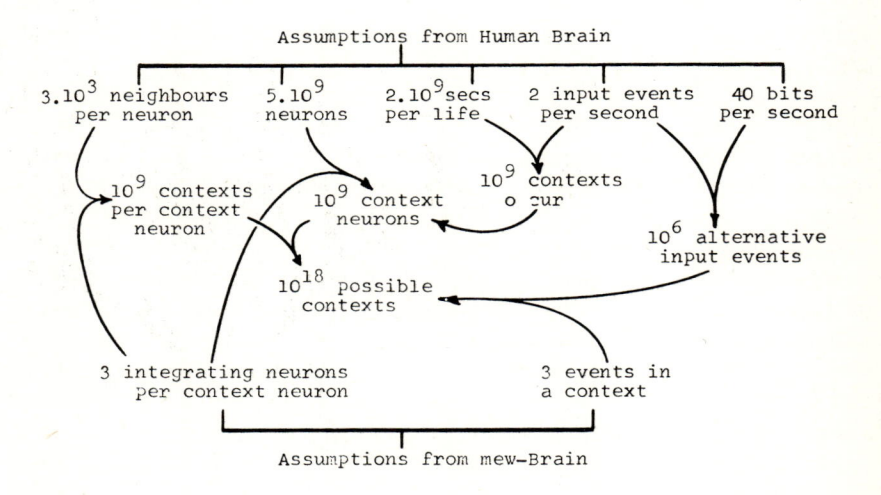

Fig. A.6. Summary of the rough calculation.

This rough calculation is summarised in Fig. A.6. The deduced figures of a thousand million (10^9) context neurons and a trillion (10^{18}) possible contexts are each derived in two independent ways. The calculation may be considered interesting as a means of suggesting rough orders of magnitude, but not more. The way the information rate of 40 bits per second is used is particularly suspect.[9]

A.5.2 The General Scheme for a Mew-Brain

We hope that mew-Brain will develop into a useful model of the brain, so gross errors have been avoided. Thus, mew-Brain is envisaged as a large convoluted sheet (mew-cortex) with the structure of neurons and connections shown in cross-section in Fig. A.2. The layers of neurons in mew-Brain have been arranged with the human cortex in mind, but without any attempt to achieve a close correspondence between neuron types.

The organization of inputs to and outputs from different areas of the mew-cortex demands some way of referring to particular areas, even when the boundaries of those areas are quite fuzzy. An area of mew-cortex characterized by a specific arrangement of inputs and outputs will be called a cortical–PUSS and will be represented in diagrams by the symbol of Fig. A.7. The additional outputs "C" from the context neurons were not shown in Fig. A.2.

A most significant and desirable property of the cortical–PUSS is that its one structure can perform a variety of functions. The "tidying-up" function has been illustrated by the computer simulation of Figs A.4 and A.5. If input impulses are missing or the bursts of input vary in length, then the predictive nature of the cortical-PUSS will ensure that gaps are filled in and that bursts are kept to a standard length.

A second function is "context-synthesis" or "chunking of information". Using the outputs, C, from the context neurons as inputs for other cortical–PUSSes, more elaborate contexts can be built up. Each context of the first PUSS becomes an event in the context of another PUSS, the latter operating with a context of contexts.[10] Sounds combine to form words, words to form phrases, and so on.

A third function provides "novelty-detection". In Fig. A.8, both network and symbolic descriptions of the function are shown. When an input occurs without its prediction, then novelty is detected.[11]

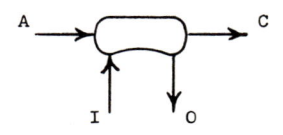

```
A: Auxiliary inputs (AP,AQ,AR in Figure A-2).
I: Inputs (A1,A2,A3,A4 in Figure A-2).
O: Outputs (E1,E2,E3,E4 in Figure A-2).
C: Context events (outputs from context neurons,
                  not shown in Figure A-2).
```

Fig. A.7. Symbol for Cortical–PUSS.

160 THINKING WITH THE TEACHABLE MACHINE

A primary function of any brain is the choice of action, or the taking of decisions. This can be achieved by passing the outputs of a cortical–PUSS through neurons connected for mutual inhibition, as illustrated in Fig. A.9. Mutual inhibition causes each neuron to hinder its neighbours from firing when it is firing so that the strongest firer stops the firing of the others and, at the same time, removes the inhibition that they were imposing on it. Now, the outputs, O, from a cortical–PUSS are strongest when they are driven by inputs, I, or when they are predicted by context neurons with large concentrations of MOLs i.e. they have a strong hypothesis path to novelty. Therefore, the mutual inhibition network will choose outputs according to the rate of firing of the prediction neurons and this will correspond to the desirability of the outputs.

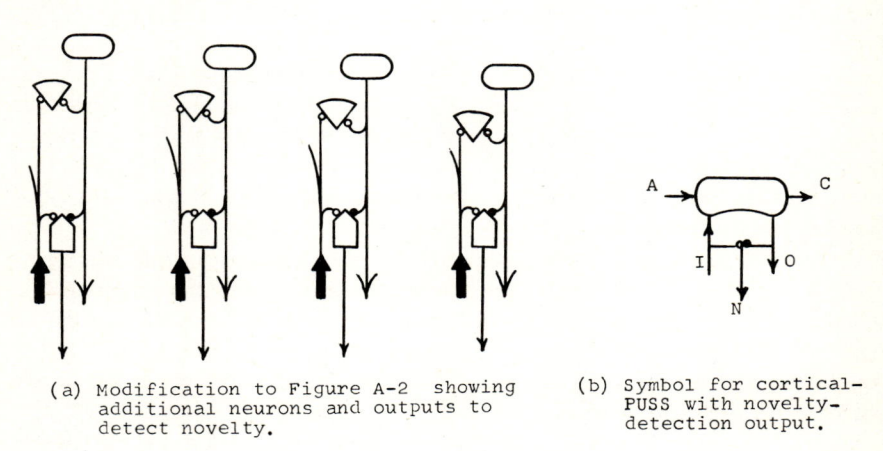

(a) Modification to Figure A-2 showing additional neurons and outputs to detect novelty.

(b) Symbol for cortical-PUSS with novelty-detection output.

Fig. A.8. Network and symbol for novelty-detection.

Having defined four primary functions of tidying-up, context-synthesis, novelty-detection and decision-taking, it is simple to combine them in a minimal mew-Brain, as shown in Fig. A.10. By dividing the sensory input into different modes (sight, sound, touch, etc.) and allowing many kinds of association in the context-synthesis, we could draw diagrams of much more complicated mew-Brains, but these would have little value unless supported by computer simulation and neuropsychological evidence.

A.6 The Clay of Man's Mind

Mew-Brain is the last example of *thinking with PURR–PUSS*.[12] By attempting to design a neurochemical version of PURR–PUSS, we have found some-

APPENDIX 161

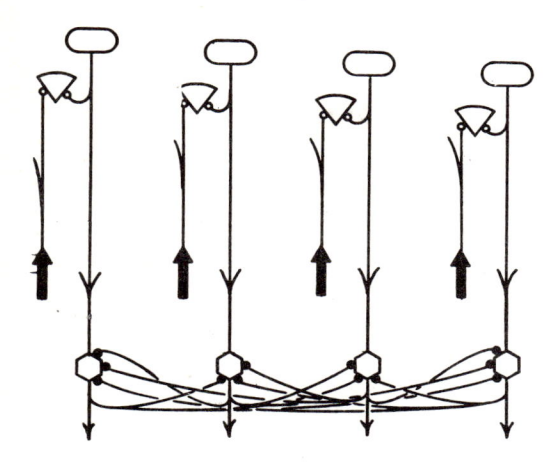

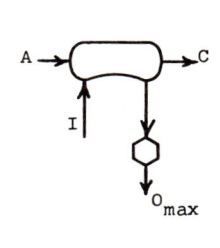

(a) Modification to Figure A-2 showing additional mutual inhibition network. Each "hexagonal" neuron has an inhibitory connection to each other hexagonal neuron.

(b) Symbol for cortical-PUSS with mutual inhibition output for choosing strongest output.

Fig. A.9. Network and symbol for decision-taking

thing which promises to be more powerful than PURR–PUSS, something which suggests modifications to the design of PURR–PUSS, and something which takes us into the area of modelling the brain.[13]

Arbib (1972, page 3) has complained that "too many psychologists and biochemists are *not* model builders". The opposite criticism, of lacking a practical experience of psychology and biochemistry, can be levelled against me. For this reason, I have not forced similarities between mew-Brain and the real brain. For example, the neurons in mew-Brain could have been arranged in a manner closer to neurophysiological proposals that I have

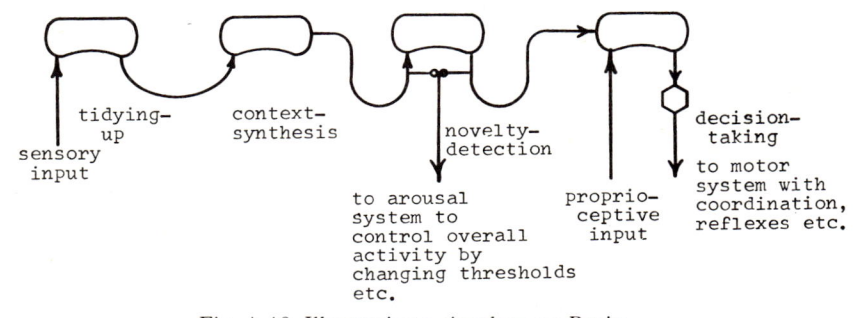

Fig. A.10. Illustrating a simple mew-Brain.

read about. However, there seems to be a lack of general agreement on the physiological organization of neurons in the cortex, and the amateur like me finds no authoritative source to quote. My model is, therefore, a mechanistic model, not a physiological model. If neurophysiologists and neurochemists find the model compelling, they will be able to turn my model into acceptable neurochemical form. It is better that they do this than that I attempt it on the basis of their writings and my poverty of experience.

This Appendix has been speculative. My students and I are busy exploring the consequences of PURR–PUSS and mew-Brain. We are encouraged by the pleasantness of the journey. No dreadful threats of science fiction loom ahead of us. If the brain *is* like PURR–PUSS and mew-Brain, then we shall be able to talk about how the brain works without spoiling the mystery of its nature. We are discovering the clay, not analysing the sculptures. The brain will continue to be an infinite mystery evolving in each life from body, world and experience.

>The clay of man's mind, grey matter and white,
>Is a network of neurons and chemical codes.
>The clay of man's mind is plastic, yet firm:
>It allows him to choose and helps her to learn.
>   It grows!
>   The clay of each man's mind
>   Is shaped by hands divine
>   And, leaving the Child behind,
>   Is set by the life it finds.
>Mysterious clay of all mankind——
>   It knows!

Notes on the Appendix

1. See, for example, Shepherd (1974) and Thompson (1976).

2. PUSS net versions of PURR–PUSS were described in UC–DSE/6 and in Andreae and Cleary (1976).

3. There are good reaons for developing a dual model of the brain. A model of the brain requires a "psychological" aspect which demonstrates behaviour comparable with human behaviour and a "physiological" aspect which shows how it could be constructed from "neurochemical hardware". Psychologically, to be convincing the model must be sufficiently large, complex and fast to interact with humans in real time. Physiologically, a full size model would be a system of billions of components

APPENDIX 163

acting together and it could not be simulated in real time on a digital computer. Therefore, we need a large psychological model designed for real time operation on a serial digital computer *plus* a small parallel physiological model. Development of the dual model would involve psychological testing and improvement of the serial model (PURR–PUSS), physiological testing and improvement of the parallel model (mew–Brain), together with mutual testing and convergence of the two models.

4. The neurons referred to here are "artificial" or "simulated". There have been many attempts to simulate networks of artificial neurons. See, for example, Arbib (1972).

5. The context 41R in MOL–41R3 is a minimal sequential-spatial context with the events "4" and "1" occurring sequentially and the events "1" and "R" occurring spatially (i.e. concurrently or in parallel). A simple context of this form seems to offer great possibilities for context synthesis (see Section A.5.2). One context can combine other contexts either in sequence or in parallel or both together. For example, the individual contexts 12P, 23Q and PQX could be combined into the single context (12P) (23Q) (PQX).

6. There are other interesting relationships between the human brain and mew–Brain which take one far into the depths of speculation. Thus, we may speculate that evolution had two major problems to solve for the animals that would roam the earth. The first problem was the central control of peripheral muscles and it produced that remarkable arrangement, the reflex arc. The special feature of the reflex arc is the way an outward neuron is associated with an inward neuron so that they link with each other at both ends (see, for instance, Shepherd, 1974, Fig. 1). I presume that the information that determines this specific growth pattern is a chemical coding. The growth pattern is not found only in the control of peripheral muscles by spinal control centres but, in mammals, is extended to further links in the lower and higher centres of the brain. That the same trick, developed for central control of peripheral muscles, should be used even in the cognitive centre of the neocortex is particularly likely in view of "the extraordinary rapidity of the evolutionary growth of the human brain — a feat, as we know, unique in evolutionary history" (Koestler, 1967, p. 311). The reflex link between input and output neurons, which is the key to the organization of mew–Brain, is unlikely to raise objections from neurophysiologists.

The second problem faced by evolution was the control of muscles in a sequential pattern for co-ordinated movements (like running). The sequential mechanism proposed for mew–Brain in its layers of integrating neurons may not be the one used by Mother Nature, but we should be safe in saying that whatever trick is used in achieving sequential muscle control is likely to be used again in the higher centres. Mew–Brain may be seen as a working illustration of the thesis that cognitive functions are a natural extension of the neurochemical solutions found by evolution for central control of peripheral muscles. (Mark, 1974).

7. Fitts and Posner (1967), p. 109.

8. Sholl (1956), p. 35.

9. The calculation was carried out as though the whole brain corresponded to a mew–Brain with a single cortical–PUSS (as defined in Section A.5.2). Only an expert could begin to estimate the number and kinds of cortical–PUSSes that would be needed to model the brain, were that possible.

10. A context-synthesising cortical–PUSS would not need prediction and output

neurons, while these are essential to decision-taking. Differences in the populations of particular types of neuron in different parts of the neocortex are quite in keeping with neurophysiological data. For example, "Visual cortex is among the thinnest of the cortical regions. Motor cortex is, by contrast, among the thickest of the cortical regions. There the group of deep pyramidal cells, in layer V, is particularly numerous." (Shepherd, 1974, p. 296.)

The question arises as to which and how many of the context neurons should be connected to where? A partial answer is that extra contexts are needed when predictions are ambiguous or decisions have to be made from several, equal priority alternatives. We have not thought of a satisfactory way of doing this with mew–Brain yet, but Two-level PUSS (UC–DSE/3, p. 26) and John Cleary's Dual FLM (UC–DSE/5, p. 54) illustrate the idea in practical schemes.

11. Novelty-detection could also be achieved chemically.

12. Mew–Brain was first described in UC–DSE/9. Earlier proposals for neurochemical networks appeared in Section A.7 of UC–DSE/3 and in Section A.3 of UC/DSE/7. My neural net modelling of learning systems goes back to Andreae and Joyce (1965).

13. To emphasise the insignificance of mew–Brain as a model of *the* brain, I remind the reader of the paper dart analogy used in the Preface. Beyond the unsolved problems of perception, co-ordinated actions, needs and emotions, we can see dimly such complications as the conflict between old and new brains (Koestler, 1976) and the conflict between left and right hemispheres (Ornstein, 1972; see, also, Eccles, 1973).

References

Note. The development of PURR–PUSS has been described in a series of reports entitled "Man–Machine Studies," Progress Reports UC–DSE/1–11 (1972–7) (ISSN 0110–1188) to the Defence Scientific Establishment of the New Zealand Ministry of Defence, edited by J. H. Andreae and issued from the Department of Electrical Engineering, University of Canterbury, Christchurch, New Zealand. These reports are referred to as UC–DSE/1, UC–DSE/2, etc.

Ambler, A. P., Barrow, H. G., Brown, C. M., Burstall, R. M. and Popplestone, R. J. (1975). A versatile system for computer-controlled assembly. *Artificial Intelligence*, **6**, pp. 129–156.

Anderson, A. R. (1964). "Minds and Machines". Prentice-Hall, Englewood Cliffs, N.J.

Anderson, J. R. and Bower, G. H. (1973). "Human Associative Memory". Wiley, New York.

Andreae, J. H. (1963). STeLLA: A scheme for a learning machine. *In* Proc. 2nd IFAC Congress, Basle, pp. 497–502. Butterworths, London.

Andreae, J. H. (1969). Learning machines: a unified view. *In "Encyclopaedia of Linguistics, Information and Control" (Ed. A. R. Meetham), pp. 261–270.* Pergamon, Oxford.

Andreae, J. H. and Cashin, P. M. (1969). A learning machine with monologue. *Int. J. Man–Machine Studies*, **1**, pp. 1–20.

Andreae, J. H. and Cleary, J. G. (1976). A new mechanism for a brain. *Int. J. Man–Machine Studies*, **8**, 89–119.

Andreae, J. H. and Joyce, P. L. (1965). "Learning Machine". British Patents 1,011,685–7.

Arbib, M. A. (1972). "The Metaphorical Brain". Wiley, New York.

Ashby, W. R. (1952). "Design for a Brain". Chapman and Hall, London.

Austin, J. L. (1962). "How to do things with Words". Oxford University Press, London.

Bakker, D. H. (1976): "Developments with the Learning Program PURR–PUSS". M.E. Report, University of Canterbury, Christchurch, New Zealand.

Berlyne, D. E. (1960). "Conflict, Arousal and Curiosity". McGraw Hill, New York.

Blackwood, A. (1913): "A Prisoner in Fairyland". Macmillan, London.

Broadbent, D. E. (1961). "Behaviour". Eyre and Spottiswoode, London.

Campbell, H. J. (1973). "The Pleasure Areas". Eyre Methuen, London.

Carroll, L. (1865). "Alice's Adventures in Wonderland" and "Through the Looking Glass". Collins, London (1954 edition).

Chomsky, N. (1959). Review of "Verbal Behaviour" by B. F. Skinner. *Language*, **35** (1), 26–58.

Chomsky, N. (1972). "Language and Mind". Harcourt Brace Jovanovich, New York.
Coward, N. (1933). "Private Lives" in "Play Parade". Doubleday, Doran and Co., Garden City, N.Y.
Craik, K. J. W. (1943). "The Nature of Explanation". Cambridge University Press. (Paperback edition, 1967).
Cunningham, M. A. (1972). "Intelligence: Its Organiziation and Development". Academic Press, New York.
Cunningham, M. A. and Gray, H. J. (1974). Design and test of a cognitive model. *Int. J, Man–Machine Studies*, **6**, 49–104.
Dalenoort, G. J. (1976). Simulation of neural networks. *Simula Newsletter*, **4** (2), 5–8.
Deutsch, J. A. (1960). "The Structural Basis of Behaviour". Cambridge University Press, London.
Didday, R. L. and Arbib, M. A. (1975). Eye movements and visual perception: A two visual system model. *Int. J. Man–Machine Studies*, **7**, 547–569.
Dreyfus, H. L. (1972). "What Computers Can't Do". Harper and Row, New York.
Eccles, J. C. (1973). "The Understanding of the Brain". McGraw-Hill, New York.
Eliot, T. S. (1940). "Old Possum's Book of Practical Cats". Faber and Faber, London.
Elithorn, A. and Jones, D. (1973). "Artificial and Human Thinking". Elsevier, Amsterdam.
Estes. W. K. (1970). "Learning Theory and Mental Development". Academic Press, New York.
Feigenbaum, E. A. and Feldman, J. (1963). "Computers and Thought". McGraw-Hill, New York.
Fitts, P. M. and Posner, M. I. (1967). "Human Performance". Prentice-Hall, London (1973 edition).
Freud, S. (1891). On Aphasia: A Critical Study. Excerpt in "Brain and Behaviour 4". (Ed. K. H. Pribram). Harmondsworth: Penguin (1969). pp. 13–57.
Furth, H. G. (1966). "Thinking Without Language". Macmillan, New York.
Gaines, B. R. (1976a). On the complexity of causal models. *I.E.E.E. Trans.* **SMC–6** (1), 56–59.
Gaines, B. R. (1976b). Behaviour/Structure transformations under uncertainty. *Int. J. Man–Machine Studies*, **8**, 337–365.
Gaines, B. R. (1976c). "Foundations of Fuzzy Reasoning". Report No. EES–MMS–FREAS–76, Dept of Electrical Engineering Science, University of Essex, Colchester.
Gaines, B. R. and Andreae, J. H. (1966). A learning machine in the context of the general control problem. *In* Proc. 3rd IFAC Congress. (Paper 14B). Institute of Mechanical Engineers, London.
Gregory, R. L. (1971). Social implications of intelligent machines. *In* "Machine Intelligence 6". (Eds B. Meltzer and D. Michie). pp. 3–13. Edinburgh University Press.
Grossman, S. P. (1973). "Essentials of Physiological Psychology". Wiley, New York.
Guillaume, P. (1926). "Imitation in Children". University of Chicago Press (1971).
Halwes, T. and Jenkins, J. J. (1971). Problem of serial order in behaviour is not resolved by context-sensitive associative memory models. *Psychological Review*, **78** (2), 122–9.
Heads, W. R. (1975). "A Simulated Blindman Task for a Learning Machine". M.E. Report, University of Canterbury, Christchurch, New Zealand. (There are extracts from this Report in UC–DSE/6.)

REFERENCES

Hebb, D. O. (1949). "The Organization of Behaviour". Wiley, New York.
Hedrick, C. L. (1976). Learning production systems from examples. *Artificial Intelligence*, **7**, 21–49.
Hydén, H. (1970). The question of a molecular basis for the memory trace. *In* "Biology of Memory". (Eds. K. H. Pribram and D. E. Broadbent). Academic Press, New York.
Kenny, A. J. P., Longuet-Higgins, H. C., Lucas, J. R. and Waddington, C. H. (1972): "The Nature of Mind". Edinburgh University Press.
Kipling, R. (1908): "The Cat that Walked by Himself". *In* "Just So Stories". Macmillan, London (1962 Edn).
Knuth, D. E. (1973): "The Art of Computer Programming" Vol. 3. Addison-Wesley, Reading, Mass.
Koestler, A. (1967): "The Ghost in the Machine". Pan Books, London.
Lashley, K. S. (1951): The Problem of serial order in behaviour. *In* "Brain and Behaviour 2", (Ed. K. H. Pribram). pp. 515—540. Harmondsworth: Penguin (1969).
Lenneberg, E. H. (1964): Speech as a motor skill with special reference to non-aphasic disorders. *In* "Brain and Behaviour 4", (Ed. K. H. Pribram). pp. 77–102. Harmondsworth: Penguin (1969).
Lighthill, J. (1973): "Artificial Intelligence: A General Survey". In "Artificial Intelligence: A Paper Symposium". pp. 1–21. Science Research Council, London.
Lucas, J. R. (1961): Minds, Machines and Gödel. *In* Anderson (1964). pp. 43–59.
Luria, A. R. (1973); "The Working Brain". Harmondsworth: Penguin.
Magoun, H. W. (1963): "The Waking Brain". Charles C. Thomas, Springfield, Illinois (2nd Edn).
Manna, Z. (1974): "Mathematical Theory of Computation". McGraw-Hill, New York.
Mark, R. (1974): "Memory and nerve cell connections." Oxford University Press.
McGuigan, F. J. and Lumsden, D. B. (1973): "Contemporary Approaches to Conditioning and Learning". Winston, Washington.
Millar, S. (1968): "The Psychology of Play". Harmondsworth: Penguin.
Miller, G. A. (1974): Needed: A better theory of cognitive organization. *I.E.E.E. Trans.***SMC–4**(1), 95–7.
Miller, G. A., Galanter, E. and Pribram, K. H. (1960): "Plans and the Structure of Behaviour". Holt, Rinehart and Winston.
Minsky, M. L. (1967). "Computation: Finite and Infinite Machines". Prentice-Hall, Englewood Cliffs, N.J..
Minksy, M. L. (1974). "A Framework for Representing Knowledge". Memo 306. Artificial Intelligence Laboratory, M.I.T., Cambridge, Mass.
Montessori, M. (1949). "The Absorbent Mind". Kalakshetra, Madras (1973 edition).
Mooers, C. N. (1966). TRAC, a procedure-describing language for the reactive typewriter. *Comm.ACM,* **9** (3), 215–9.
Narasimhan, R. (1969). Computer simulation of natural language behaviour. *In* "Picture Language Manchines", (Ed. S. Kaneff). pp. 257–90. Academic Press, London.
Neisser, U. (1967). "Cognitive Psychology". Appleton-Century-Crofts, New York.
Newell, A. and Simon, H. A. (1972). "Human Problem Solving". Prentice-Hall, Englewood Cliffs, N.J.

Norman, D. A. (1973). Memory, knowledge and the answering of questions. *In* "Contemporary Issues in Cognitive Psychology", (Ed. R. L. Solso), pp. 135–165. Winston, Washington, D.C.

Norman, D. A. and Rumelhart, D. E. (1975). "Explorations in Cognition". Freeman, San Francisco.

Noton, D. and Stark, L. (1971). "Eye movements and visual perception". *Scientific American* **224** June 34–43.

Ornstein, R. E. (1972). "The Psychology of Consciousness". Freeman, San Francisco. (Pelican edn 1975).

Penfield, W. and Roberts, L. (1959). "Speech and Brain-Mechanisms". Princeton University Press.

Piaget, J. (1951). "Play, Dreams and Imitation in Childhood". Routledge and Kegan Paul, London.

Piaget, J. (1964). "Six Psychological Studies". University of London Press.

Piaget, J. (1972). "The Child and Reality". Frederick Muller, London (1974).

Piaget, J. and Inhelder, B. (1966). "The Psychology of the Child". Routledge and Kegan Paul, London.

Pribram, K. H. (1969a). The neurophysiology of remembering. *Scientific American*, **220**, January, pp. 73–86.

Pribram, K. H. (1969b), "On the Biology of Learning". Harper and Row, New York.

Pribram, K. H. (1971). "Languages of the Brain". Prentice-Hall, Englewood Cliffs, N.J.

Ryle, G. (1949). "The Concept of Mind". Harmondsworth: Penguin.

Samuel, A. L. (1959). Some Studies in machine learning using the game of checkers, *IBM J.* **3**, pp. 211–99.

Shepherd, G. M. (1974). "The Synaptic Organization of the Brain". Oxford University Press, New York.

Sholl, D. A. (1956): "The Organization of the Cerebral Cortex". Methuen, London.

Simon, H. A. (1968). "The Sciences of the Artificial". M.I.T. Press, Cambridge, Mass.

Simon, H. A. and Chase, W. G. (1973). Skill in chess. *American Scientist*, **61**, July/August, pp. 394–403.

Thompson, R. F. (1976). The Search for the Engram. *American Psychologist*, **31**, March, pp. 209–227.

Uhr, L. (1973). "Pattern Recognition, Learning and Thought". Prentice-Hall, Englewood Cliffs, N.J.

Van Heerden, P. J. (1963): Theory of Optical Information Storage in Solids. *J. Applied Optics* **2** (4), pp. 393–400.

Watanabe, S. (1974). Paradigmatic Symbol — A comparative study of human and artificial intelligence. *I.E.E.E. Trans.* **SMC-4** (1), pp. 100–103.

Waterman, D. (1970). Generalization learning techniques for automating the learning of heuristics. *Artificial Intelligence*, **1**, pp. 121–170.

Waterman, N. (1966): Tame animals I have known. *In* "Oh. What Nonsense!" compiled by W. Cole. Methuen, London.

Wickelgren, W. A. (1969): Context-sensitive coding, Associative memory and serial order in (speech) behaviour. *Psychological Review*, **10**, pp. 1–14.

Wildmann, M. (1975): Terabit memory systems: A design history. *Proc. I.E.E.E.* **63** (8), pp. 1160-5.

Willshaw, D. J., Buneman, O.P. and Longuet-Higgins, H. C. (1969): Non-holographic associative memory. *Nature*, **222**, pp. 960–2,

Winograd, T. (1972): "Understanding Natural Language". Edinburgh University Press.
Winston, P. H. (1975): "The Psychology of Computer Vision". McGraw-Hill, New York.
Wolff, J. G. (1973): "Language, Brain and Hearing". Methuen, London.
Young, J. Z. (1964): "A Model of the Brain". Oxford University Press, London.

Author Index

Numbers in italics refer to pages where references are listed.

A

Ambler, A. P., 144, *165*
Anderson, A. R., 13, *165*
Anderson, J. R., 15, 60, *165*
Andreae, J. H., 13, 15, 43, 45, 60, 83, 100, 145, 162, 164, *165*, *166*
Arbib, M. A., 13, 43, 144, 161, 163, *165*, *166*
Ashby, W. R., 12, *165*
Austin, J. L., 143, *165*

B

Bakker, D. H., 13, 61, *165*
Barrow, H. G., 144, *165*
Berlyne, D. E., vi, 13, 81, *165*
Blackwood, A., 47, *165*
Bower, G. H., 15, 60, *165*
Broadbent, D. E., 13, *165*
Brown, C. M., 144, *165*
Buneman, O. P., 43, *169*
Burstall, R. M., 144, *165*

C

Campbell, H. J., 14, *165*
Carroll, L., 62, 120, *165*
Cashin, P. M., 13, 83, *165*
Chase, W. G., 99, *168*
Chomsky, N., 81, *165*, *166*
Cleary, J. G., 12, 15, 43, 45, 60, 100, 145, 162, 164, *165*
Coward, N., 147, *166*
Craik, K. J. W., 103, *166*
Cunningham, M. A., 12, *166*

D

Dalenoort, G. J., 61, *166*
Deutsch, J. A., 13, *166*

Didday, R. L., 144, *166*
Dreyfus, H. L., 13, 15, 103, *166*

E

Eccles, J. C., 164, *166*
Eliot, T. S., 146, *166*
Elithorn, A., 13, *166*
Estes, W. K., 81, *166*

F

Feigenbaum, E. A., 13, *166*
Feldman, J., 13, *166*
Fitts, P. M., 163, *166*
Freud, S., 84, *166*
Furth, H. G., 102, *166*

G

Gaines, B. R., 45, 83, 100, 118, *166*
Galanter, E., 44, *167*
Gray, H. J., 12, *166*
Gregory, R. L., 13, *166*
Grossman, S. P., 14, *166*
Guillaume, P., 84, *166*

H

Halwes, T., 60, *166*
Heads, W. R., 12, 13, *166*
Hebb, D. O., v, 13, *167*
Hedrick, C. L., 45, *167*
Hydén, H., 44, *167*

I

Inhelder, B., 115, *168*

171

AUTHOR INDEX

J

Jenkins, J. J., 60, *166*
Jones, D., 13, *166*
Joyce, P. L., 83, 164, *165*

K

Kenny, A. J. P., 13, 102, 104, 144, *167*
Kipling, R., 16, *167*
Knuth, D. E., 43, *167*
Koestler, A., 163, 164, *167*

L

Lashley, K. S., 60, *167*
Lenneberg, E. H., 84, *167*
Lighthill, J., vi, *167*
Longuet-Higgins, H. C., 13, 43, 102, 144, *167, 169*
Lucas, J. R., 6, 13, 15, 102, 115, 144, *167*
Lumsden, D. B., vi, *167*
Luria, A. R., v, 82, 101, *167*

M

McGuigan, F. J., vi, *167*
Magoun, H. W., 14, *167*
Manna, Z., 15, 45, 61, *167*
Mark, R., 163, *167*
Millar, S., 82, 84, *167*
Miller, G. A., v, 44, *167*
Minsky, M. L., 15, 61, 145, *167*
Montessori, M., 84, 102, *167*
Mooers, C. N., 81, *167*

N

Narasimhan, R., 15, 144, *167*
Neisser, U., 1, *167*
Newell, A., v, 14, 44, 99, 118, *167*
Norman, D. A., 101, 144, *168*
Noton, D., 144, *168*

O

Ornstein, R. E., 103, 164, *168*

P

Penfield, W., 84, *168*
Piaget, J., vi, 84, 101, 115, *168*
Popplestone, R. J., 144, *165*
Posner, M. I., 163, *166*
Pribram, K. H., 43, 44, 81, 101, *167, 168*

R

Roberts, L., 84, *168*
Rumelhart, D. E., 101, 144, *168*
Ryle, G., 144, *168*

S

Samuel, A. L., v, *168*
Shepherd, G. M., vi, 162, 163, 164, *168*
Sholl, D. A., 163, *168*
Simon, H. A., v, 14, 44, 99, 118, 145, *168*
Stark, L., 144, *168*

T

Thompson, R. F., 162, *168*

U

Uhr, L., 143, 144, *168*

V

Van Heerden, P. J., 43, *168*

W

Waddington, C. H., iii, 13, 102, 144, *167*
Watanabe, S., 144, *168*
Waterman, D., 45, *168*
Waterman, N., 85, *168*
Wickelgren, W. A., 60, *168*
Wildmann, M., 43, *168*
Willshaw, D. J., 43, *169*
Winograd, T., v, 144, *169*
Winston, P. H., 144, 145, *169*
Wolff, J. G., 84, *169*

Y

Young, J. Z., 12, *169*

Subject Index

A

ABACUS, 8, 70, 81, 95, *96*, 102, 108, 112
Action
    as a response, 81
    as part of an event, 86
    choice of, viii, ix, 34, 63, *67*, 68, *92*, 160
    directing attention, 102
    in real time, 82
    types of, 7, 36, 75, 95
Action match, ix, 10, 68, 71, 75, 92
Action–pattern (a-p), 68, 70, 75, 101, 148
Action–PUSS, ix, 10, 68, *71*, 72, 76
    given speech action, 77
    in face-scanning, 126
    net, 80
    window, 82, 85, 86
Artificial intelligence, v, viii, xv, 5, 6, 15, 100, 144, 145
Attention, 12, 102
Automata, 12, 45

B

Baby, vi, 14, 84
Biology, 1, 5, 23, 44
Bit, 38, 46, 103
Blindman, 12
Body
    robot, vi, xv, *2*, 5, 70, 85, *94*, 128
    importance of, *6*, 14, 15, 67, 102, 103, 120, 145, 162
Body–coding, 101
Brain
    model of, v, 1, 2, 11, 12, 145, *161–163*
    characteristics of, ix, 5, 43, 147, 158, 162–164

C

CAESAR, 3, 13, 98, 100, 128
Cake, viii, ix, 139

Chain, 54, 60, 73
Chemical code, 100, 149, *150*, 163
Circular reaction, 101
Coin-tossing machine, 12, 31
Console typewriter, 62, 78
Context, see also Multiple context, Parallel context, Spatial context
    importance of, xv, *3*, 10, 36, 53, 104, 111, 114
    neuron, 150, 157–159
    of events, 16, 19, 47, 59, 73, 87
    of PUSSes, 11, 71, 78, 118
    prediction from, 16, 18, 23, 91
    storage of, 38, 43, 52
    synthesis, 159, 163
Conversation, 9, 13, 121, 126, 143, 144
Cortical–PUSS, 148, 159
Counting, vi, xv, 9, 12, *104*, 106, 115
    beads, 8, 108, 111
    objects with fingers, 7, 95, 107, 109
    problem, 34, 45
    with speech, 37, 56
Creativity, viii
Cumulative learning, vi, 4, 104, 114

D

Dense event, 51–55, 60, 104, 107
Determinism, 12, 38, 43
Design strategy, 5, 13, 100
Disapproval
    effect of, 5, 34, 87, 90–92, 129
    in use, 8, 111–114, 116, 118, 135
Drawing, vi, 12, 55, 61, 99
Dual model, 12, 162
Dump, 127

E

Echo–speech
    mechanism of, 36, *75*, 77, 83, 95, 101

174 SUBJECT INDEX

use of, 7, 15, 45, 105
Education, vi, 1, 5, 14, 101, 145
Emotion, 5, 12, 81, 83, 90, 164
Endless repetition, 91, 93, 94
English, 9
ESAW, 3, 13, 98, 99, 128
Event, see also Dense event, Head event, Sparse event
  coding of, 19, 43
  in context, 3, *16*, 47, 54, 118, 163
  in net, 25, 33, 49
  sequences, 10, 17, 25, 40, 47–49, 59
  storage of, 39–42, 45, 53
  types of, 26, 29, 35, 73, *86*
Evolution, ix, 5, 44, 163
Experience
  effect of, xv, 5, 30, 104, 145, 146, 162
  made accessible, 92, 100
  source of, vi, 2, 101
Exploration, 13, 100
EYE, 98, 121, 122

F

Finite state machine, 14, 15, 45
Finger-raising, 7, 8, 55, 95, *106*, 111–114
Flag, 40, 45, 46
Forgetting, 12, 28, 44
Formal system, *6*, 14, 15, 103, 115, 145
Free-will, viii, 2

G

Goal
  novelty and reward, viii, 12, 100, 102, 147
  setting, xv, 5, 99, 121, 139, 143, 144
Gödel's theorem, 6, 15, 115

H

HAND, 7, 70, 81, 95, *96*, 102, 104, 109
Happening, viii, 59
Hashing, *18*, 19, 23, 43–45.
Head event, 27, 39, 49
HELLO task, 9, 120, *121*, 144
Hierarchy, 99
Holographic memory, 23, 43, 44, 61
Hunger, 100
Hurry, 82

Hypothesis
  effect of, 9, 65, 83, 101, 102, 135
  formation of, ix, 10, 13, 68, 69, 82, *87–91*, 117, 147
  on nature of mind, ix, 103, 145
Hypothesis match, ix, 10, 67–69, *92*

I

Imitation, 77, 84
Instinct, 5, 84, 100
Intelligence, see also Artificial intelligence
  conditions for, ix, 6, 13, 100, 102, 145
  nature of, viii, 1, 144
Interaction
  description of, 6–9, 63–77, 104, 109, 111–114, 131–139
  need for, viii, 30, 127
Interaction listings
  counting, 110, 112, 114
  HELLO task, 124, 125
  illustrative, 66, 74
  ROOMS task, 132, 134, 136–138, 140–142
Interleave, 54, 72

K

Kit set, 31, 33
KORSHN, 92–*94*, 101, 126, 129

L

Language
  teaching with, vi, xv, 14
  nature of, 15, 84, 99, 102, 119, 144
Leak-back, 100, 147, 152
Learning, see also Cumulative learning, Paradigmatic learning, Thicket learning
  ability, v, 1, 92, 114
  in PUSSes, 26, 28, 50, 53
  speed of, 53, 83, 118
  theory, v, 81
  to be Turing machine, 45
  transfer of, 8, 104, 111, 143
Loops, 92, 93, 101

M

Machine, see also Automata, Coin-tossing machine, Turing machine
  as a formal system, 14, 15, 115

equivalent to program, 12
  nature of, viii, 6, 11, 13, 121, *143*, 145
Main–PUSS
  contexts, ix, 10, 68, 72, 76
  predictions, 64, 117
  window, 82, 85, 86
Maze, 12, 95
MEDEATOR
  the auxiliary program, 3, 4, 14, 81, 86
  functions of, 62, 63, 70, 73, 75, *88*, 95, 98, 133
Memory, *see also* Holographic memory, Loops, Mew-gram, Short term memory
  additive, 28, 50
  associative, 15, 55, 60
  in body and world, 95, 101
  of PUSSes, 18–26, 38–45, 87
  size of, vi, 5, *23*, 43, 53, 143
  something not in, 61
  wandering through, 29, 30
Mew–gram (or mew)
  as associative memory, 55
  compared with mew–Brain, 147
  compared with net, 24–26, 38, 60, 100
  is holographic, 43
  probabilistic, 44
  storage requirements, 42–44, 46, 52, 81
Mew–Brain, 12, 44, 100, *147*, 158–164
Mimic–speech
  as body feature, 14, 95, 101
  mechanism of, 77
  need for, 83, 84
MOL, *see* Chemical code
Monologue, 83, 144
Multiple context
  analogies for, 4, 79
  illustrations of, ix, 10, 54–58, 68
  importance of, vi, viii, 13, 34, 93, 104, 143
  in mew-Brain, 148
  mechanism of, 47–49, 60
  theory of, 53, 99
Muscles, 83, 84, 102, 163
Music, 60

N

Needs, 13, 90, 100, 164

Net, *see also* Neural network
  from schedule, 50
  from sequence, 24
  old version, 12, 42, 43, 100, 147, 162
  representation, 25–30, 33, 34, 38, 49, 60
Neural network, 43, 44, 100, 147, 164
Neurons
  artificial, 148–154, 161, 163
  firing of, 148, 152
  of brain, 12, 44, 157, 158, 164
  prediction by, 156, 157
Neurophysiology, vi, 5, 147, 148, 161, 163
Never-seen-before object, 8, 69, 104, 109, 114
Node, 24, 25, 28, 39, 40
Non-determinism, 12, 43, 119
Novelty
  for consolidation, 92, 100
  for exploration, 13
  goal, viii, 4, 5, 100, 102, 139
  hypothesis to, ix, 10, 11, 68, 69, 88–91, 99
  injection of, 25, 128, 131, 139
  in mew–Brain, 147, 152, 157, 159–161, 164
  in psychology, vi, xv, 81, 82, 84
  marker, 69, 85, 87
  measured by KORSHN, 94
  removal, 65, 67, 70, 93
Null, patterns and actions, *see also* Pauses, 73, 82, 89, 92, 95, 105
  action replaced by speech, 75, 77, 84, 88, 126
Number, 106, 114, 115
Nursery rhyme, vi, 74

O

ONE–PUSS, 34, 45, 78
Open system, 14, 15, 115
Originality, vii, 114

P

Pain, 5, 14
Paradigmatic learning, viii, 9, 15, 103, 115, 144, 145
Parallel contexts, 53, 54, 163

SUBJECT INDEX

Parallel processes, 12, 100, 163
Patterns
   affect Tempo, 83
   equivalent to stimuli, 7, 81
   in events, 86
   given by Teacher, 7, 62, 78, 98
   given by MEDEATOR, 75, 95–97, 103
   on hypothesis, 90–92, 99
   stream of, 68
Pattern–action (p-a), 64, 68, 86, 148
Pattern match, ix, 10, 67, 68, *92*
Pattern–PUSS
   context, ix, 10, 68, 72, 76
   for hypothesis, 69, 88, 99
   net, 79
   window length, 82, 86
Pause, *see also* Null patterns and actions, Thinking focus
   7, 14, 67, 73, 79, 101
Philosophy, viii, 1, 81
Physical–PUSS
   context, ix, 10, 68, 72
   for physical events, 70
   in HELLO task, 127
   window length, 82, 86
Physiology, 5, 12, 13, 162
Pipes, xv, 145
Plan, 44, 99
Prediction, *see also* Recall
   for hypothesis, 88–91, 102
   for resolving ambiguity, 47, 53, 113
   in mew–Brain, 157, 159
   in psychology, xv, 44, 61, 82
   mechanism of, 16, 23, 59, 87
   of main–PUSS, 64, 117
   of PUSSes, ix, 10, 68
   past dense event, 54, 55, 109
   storage of, 18, 38
Prime, 19–24, 23, 43, 44, 87
Priority
   and KORSHN, 94, 101
   assignment of, 67, 116
   of decision, ix, 10, 70, *92*
   sacrificed for speed, 83
Probability, 44, 94, 100, 118, 119
Problem-solving, v, 1, 5, 45, 118
Productions, 44, 45, 118
Program
   equivalent to machine, 12

MEDEATOR, 3, 14, 62
PURR–PUSS, viii, 11, 55, 81, 84, *98*, 103
   that learns, v, 1, 144
Psychology
   implications of, 1, 115, 161
   of attention, 102
   of body, 102, 103
   of brain, v, 5, 12, 81, 148, 162
   of conversation, 9, 143, 144
   of memory, 15, 45, 60, 101
   of novelty, xv, 13, 84
   of prediction, xv, 44
Punishment, 4
PURR
   decision strategy, ix, 10, 63, 68, *92*, 143
   limited by time, 83
   origin of, 12
   role of, 3, 86, 89–94, 99
PURR–PUSS
   as brain model, v, 12, 148, 161, 162
   compared with ONE–PUSS, 78
   education of, 14, 101
   features of, 1–6, 81, 103, 114, 115
   implementation of, 81, 84, 98, 99
   needs body and world, 3, 94, 102
   operation of, 86–88
   origin of, 12
   structure of, ix, 10, 68, 86, 98
PUSS, *see also* Action–PUSS, Cortical–PUSS, Main–PUSS, ONE–PUSS, Pattern–PUSS, Physical–PUSS, Speech–PUSS, Threading PUSS.
   mechanism of, 3, 16, 59, *87*
   net, *see* Net
   on its own, 34, 45, 47
   origin of, 12, 43
   production, *see* Productions
   structures, 38–42

R

Randomness
   coped with, 33
   in choosing action, 34, 92
   in hypothesis, *88*, 100, 139, 148
   of infant's movements, 101
   of storage, 23

Reachableness, 92, 93, 101
Recall, 23, 28, 44
Recursion, xv, 58, 61
Reflex
   built-in, 14, 100, 163
   conditioned, vi, 115, 145
Remainder, 19, 43, 44, 87
Remember, vi, 17, 23, 95, 126
Response, 7, 44, 81, 118
Reverberant-sound-images, 101
Reward, 4, 5, 12–14, 100
River, xv, 145
RNA, 44, 150
Robot, *see also* CAESAR, ESAW
   body and world, vi, 3, 98, 128
   intelligent, 145
   with needs, 90, 100
   with Tempo, 83
ROOMS task, 9, 98, 120, *127*, 143

S

Schedule
   of events, 49, 50, 78
   for counting tasks, 105–108
   for HELLO task, 123
   for ROOMS task, 130
Scratch, vi, xv, 14, 145, 146
Search, vi, 23, 25, 41, 44, 61, 82
Short form description, 104, 131
Short term memory, 102, 115, 118
Sounds, 84, 159
Space bar, 62, 73
Sparse event, 51, 52, 60, 126
Spatial context, 54, 60, 148, 163
Speech, *see also* Echo–speech, Mimic–speech
   as body feature, 14, 67, 73–77, 95, 101
   as temporal organization, 60
   for context control, 55–58
   for counting, 36, 37, 45, 56
   for introducing novelty, 128, 139
   for talking to herself, 105
   in conversation, 121
   threads, 113
Speech–PUSS
   context, ix, 10, 68, 76, 84
   for speech events, 75, 88
   in HELLO task, 127
   predictions, 113
   window length, 82, 86

Speed
   of backward processing, 43
   of learning, 53, 83
   of storage, 23, 42, 44, 143
SQUARES, 70, 81, 95, *97*, 98, 102, 103
STeLLA, 13, 83, 100
Stimulus, vi, 7, 81, 84, 118
Storage, *see also* Speed of storage
   of events, 17–23, 85–87
   other methods of, 33, 38–44
   requirements, 45, 46, 51, 52
Stream, 53, 54, 60, 68
Substitution, xv, 121
Survival, 5, 90, 101
Synapse, 12, 44, 148

T

Teachableness, vii, viii, 14, 34, *91*, 145
Teacher
   as part of the world, 3, 6, 14, 86
   can introduce novelty, 94, 100, 128
   can make mistakes, 91
   helped by MEDEATOR, 3, 75, 133
   provides patterns and actions, 7, 34, 63, 82, 98
   time does not wait for, 73
Teaching, *see also* Interaction listings
   ONE–PUSS, 34, 45
   PURR–PUSS, 6–9, 62–78, 104–115, 120–143
   with disapproval, 114
   with novelty, 13, 128
   with reward, 4, 13
   with schedules, 108, 127, 131
   with words, 84
Tempo, 83
Terabit, 43
Thicket learning, 118
Thinking with PURR–PUSS, 1, 9, 83, 143, 160
Thinking focus, 82, 131, 133
Thread, 47, 48, 53, 60, 111, 113
Threading PUSS, *see also* Physical–PUSS, Speech–PUSS, 60, 82, 92, 99, 101, 126, 133
Thread match, ix, 10, 68, 75, 92
Time, 12, 73, 82, 83, 95, 101
Time-sharing, 100

178 SUBJECT INDEX

TRAC, 81
Trace, 38–42, 45, 46, 118
Transition, 39, 46, 50
Tree, 41, 42, 45, 46
Turing machine, 15, 45

U

Underlining, 7, 35, 40, 50, 72, 105

V

Vision, 101, 121–127

W

Wanting, 9, 129

Window
  early versions of, 12, 43
  effect of length of, 17, 34, 47, 52, 82
  of PUSSes, ix, 4, 10, 68, *86*
Words
  as events, 29
  English, 9, 84
  into her mouth, 77, 135
  use of, 99, 143, 159
World
  as memory, 101, 103
  as part of the environment, 2, 14, 67, 70, 86, *94–99*, 143
  for novelty, 81
  interaction with real, xv, 3, 6, 115, 162
  knowledge of, 5